CANOVA IDEAL HEADS

WILLELMO . HAMILTONIO
VIRO . INLVSTRI . ET . AMICO
ANTONIVS . CANOVA
OB . SINGVLAREM . ERGA . SE
BENEVOLENTIAM . AC . PATROCINIVM
IN . RECVPERANDIS . A . GALLIA
MONVMENTIS . ARTIVM
L . F .

ANTONIO CANOVA MADE THIS
GLADLY FOR WILLIAM HAMILTON
A MAN OF DISTINCTION AND A FRIEND
IN ACKNOWLEDGEMENT OF HIS
EXCEPTIONAL GOODWILL TO HIMSELF
AND OF HIS PATRONAGE IN THE RECOVERY
OF ARTISTIC MONUMENTS FROM FRANCE

ARTVRO . WELLESLEYO
DVCI . WELLINGTONIO
ANTONIVS . CANOVA
DE . ARTE . SVA . DDD

ANTONIO CANOVA PRESENTED
THIS AS A GIFT
A PRODUCT OF HIS OWN SKILL
TO ARTHUR WELLESLEY
DUKE OF WELLINGTON

CAROLO . LONGIO
V . CL .
ANTONIVS . CANOVA
LIBENS . F .

ANTONIO CANOVA
MADE THIS GLADLY
FOR THE MOST DISTINGUISHED
CHARLES LONG

VICECOMITI . CASTELREGHIO
VIRO . PRESTANTISSIMO
ANTONIVS . CANOVA
FECIT . AC . D . D

ANTONIO CANOVA
MADE AND PRESENTED
THIS AS A GIFT TO THE
MOST EMINENT
VISCOUNT CASTLEREAGH

CANOVA

IDEAL HEADS

First published by the Ashmolean Museum, Oxford to coincide with the exhibition of the *Ideal Heads* in the Chambers Hall Gallery, Ashmolean Museum 11 July – 14 September 1997

Text and illustrations
© copyright the University of Oxford:
Ashmolean Museum, Oxford, 1997
All rights reserved

British Library Cataloguing in Publication Data

A catalogue record for this book is available from the British Library

ISBN 1 85444 083 7

AmericanAirlines

Edited by Katharine Eustace

Catalogue designed by Ted Harrison
Typeset in 10$^{1/2}$ on 14pt Walbaum by Mark White at Rayfount, Coventry

Photograph Credits:
Bassano del Grappa, Museo Civico, Figs. 3, 4, 12; Cambridge, Trinity College, Fig. 1;
London, National Portrait Gallery, Figs. 13, 14, 15, 16; Rome, Musei Vaticani, Fig. 2;
James Hamilton, Figs. 5, 18; Oxford, Ashmolean Museum, the rest.

Printed and bound in Great Britain by
Saunders and Williams Printers Ltd, Belmont, Sutton, Surrey, 1997

Contents

Acknowledgements

Besides adding my thanks to those of the Director for the generosity of the lenders and benefactors, there are a great many people who helped make this all come about, and in record time. I would like to thank my fellow contributors, who were given little notice and all of whom came up trumps. I would also like to thank Renata Del Sal and Carla De Martini and the staff of the Biblioteca and Museo Civico at Bassano for their help, and to Giampetro Mondin at the Gipsoteca Canoviana at Possagno; Nicholas Savage and Colin Penman at the Royal Academy Library; Georgina Stonor, Archivist to the Duke of Wellington; Alison Sproston and her colleagues at Trinity College Library, Cambridge; and my own colleagues in the Libraries in Oxford, in particular Eunice Martin, Linda Whiteley, John Taylor, and Colin Harris. My thanks too to Museum colleagues: to Nick Mayhew and Cathy King in the Coin Room; Mark Norman and Daniel Bone in Antiquities Conservation who never let on that my demands were the last straw in an already overpacked programme; Robert Taylor and Ray Anstey in the Workshop, whose middle names should be Perfectionism; Jonathan Moffet who redeemed lost copy from backup files I did not know existed; to Michael Dudley, whose photographs of the *Heads* are his swansong; and Anne Holly, Jane Inskipp and Nick Pollard. In my own Department all my colleagues were forbearing and generous in their support, but particular thanks are due to Anne Steinberg, whose melifluous Italian was so persuasive on the telephone; Vera Magyar, who is always more than a Registrar; Wendy Hepple, Ananda Rutherford and Polly Holbrook who found themselves to be volunteers in the project; Roger Hobby suspended disbelief for the duration and made things happen. Beyond the Museum Hugh Honour, R. B. Rutherford, Giuseppe Pavanello, Giorgio Marini and Paolo Liverani all helped with enquiries, and Timothy Stevens was supportive of the project throughout. Stewart Meese was, as always, the soul of conservation integrity and professionalism, Ted Harrison is the mastercraftsman that had made *Art and Language* into art works; Richard Feroze of Hayles and Howe knew exactly what a neoclassical plinth in *Giallo di Verona* should look like; my husband James Hamilton kept my courage up and took over when my technological skills failed me, and last but not least I would like to thank the descendants of William Richard Hamilton who have inherited his generosity of spirit and his *joie de vivre*.

Katharine Eustace

The authors would like to thank the following organisations for permission to quote from manuscript material in their possession: Biblioteca and Museo Civico, Bassano; Trinity College, Cambridge; Natural History Museum, London; Royal Academy of Arts, London; Royal Institution, London.

Foreword

The riches of the sculpture collections in the Ashmolean Museum have largely been acquired through gifts, from John Selden's *Lapidarium*, the Pomfret bequest of the Arundel Marbles and Sir Roger Newdigate's Piranesian Candlelabra in the seventeenth and eighteenth centuries. C. D. E. Fortnum's outstanding gift of Renaissance bronzes came to us at the end of the nineteenth century and the Rev. J. W. R. Brocklebank Bequest of bronzes by Leighton, Gilbert and others, in the first quarter of the twentieth. All of them draw their inspiration from the Classical World and are housed in C. R. Cockerell's finest Greek Revival building.

It is rare, however, that the Museum makes a purchase in this medium and quite exceptional that it should do so to the tune of three quarters of a million pounds, as it has in the case of Canova's *Ideal Head*. That it was able to do so, in the short space of time allowed by an Export Ban, was thanks to one man, Brian Murgatroyd. He read James Fenton's eloquent piece in *The Times* of 11 July 1996, and found us the necessary shortfall that enabled us to go forward with bids to the National Lottery Heritage Fund and the government funds administered by the Museums and Galleries Commission, both of whom responded most generously. He did so in memory of his wife Angela King, daughter and granddaughter of Oxford City Fathers, whom he had met in the Ashmolean Library as a demobbed undergraduate after the War. To him and all those other generous individuals who contributed to our appeal, our thanks are due as they are too for the splendid support of the National Art Collections Fund, the Pilgrim Trust, a donor who wishes to remain anonymous, the Society of Dilettanti and Browns Restaurant.

Brian Murgatroyd also made it possible for the eighteenth century gallery, known as Chambers Hall, to receive the *Ideal Head*. This gave us the opportunity to be yet more ambitious and bring together all four of the *Ideal Heads* which marked Canova's gratitude to the Britons who had made his mission to the Peace Conference, at Paris in the Autumn of 1815, so successful. The corporate sponsorship of American Airlines, the financial support of the Henry Moore Foundation and the generosity of Ralph and Jane Bernstein through the Parnassus Foundation have made this exhibition possible and we are grateful to them all. Our thanks are due to the lenders to the exhibition too, all of whom responded with encouraging enthusiasm, despite the logistical and other problems associated with such loans.

This is an exhibition which has called on the expertise and co-operation of almost all the Deparments in the Museum, and as such is a fitting tribute to an acquisition which embodies so much of the Museum's collecting traditions.

Christopher White
Director

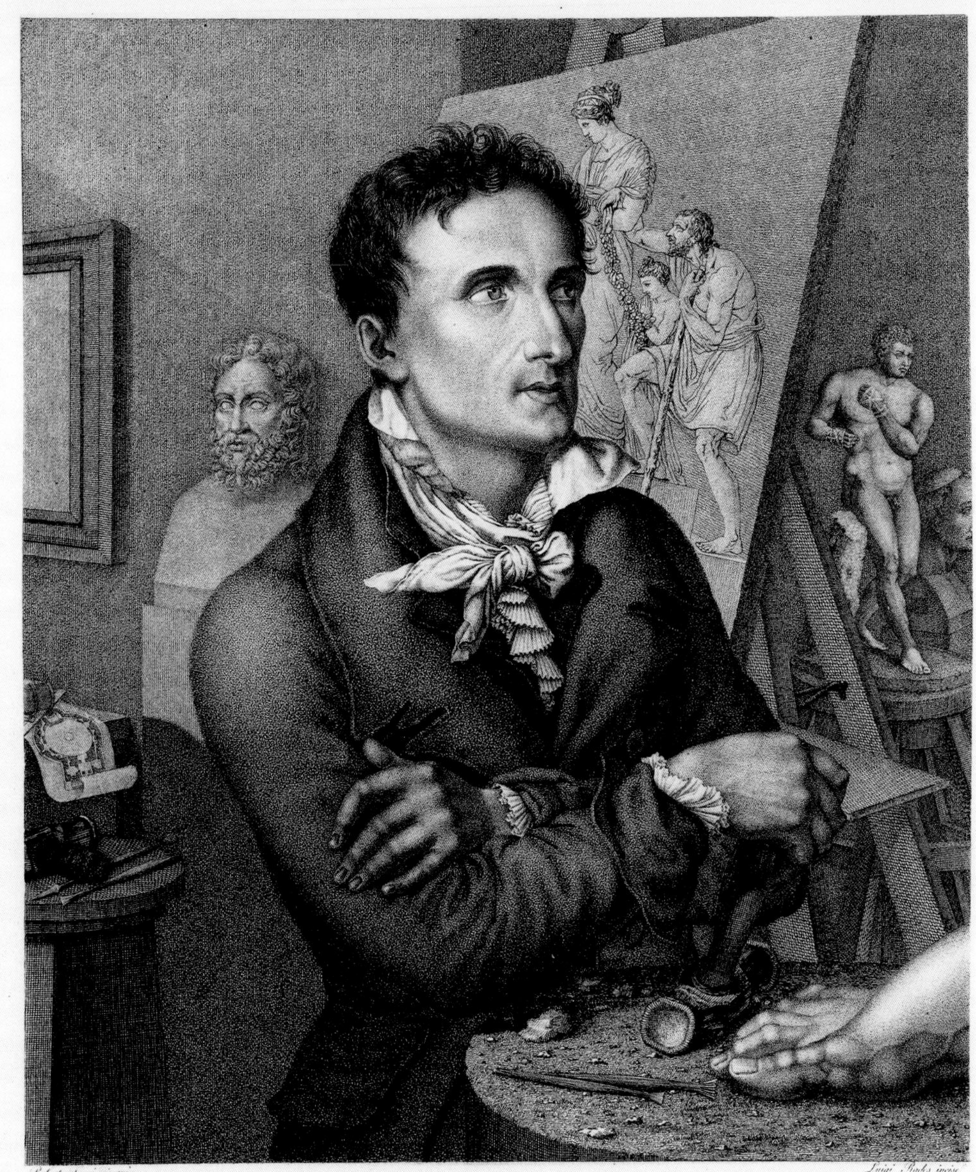

Cat. No.9

viii

'Questa Scabrosa Missione'

Canova in Paris and London in 1815

Katharine Eustace

The year 1815 is one of those resounding dates, like 1066, 1789 or 1945, that are bench-marks for every book of European history. For Britain it marked a watershed between the old order and the new, as the sixty year reign of George III came slowly to an end, and the nation emerged as the leader of Europe and of an Empire which counted one in five of the world's population.[1] For the French it marked a halt in the passage of change which had begun so dramatically twenty five years earlier. It brought the Russian Empire onto the European stage for the first time, and consolidated Prussian ambitions for Germany. For the Italians it fuelled a liberation movement which led eventually to the dismantling of the Austro-Hungarian Empire. For the first time – and this is surely Napoleon's farthest reaching legacy – an awareness of being European is expressed, a consciousness of Europeanism which found political expression under Lord Castlereagh's initiative in the 'Concert of Europe'.[2]

The swift drama of Napoleon's 100 Days, and the sudden and surprising reversal and rout of his Armies at Waterloo on 18th June 1815, excited the public imagination and became a source of inspiration to literature and the arts for decades to come. Royal Academy exhibitions in the ten years after Waterloo were increasingly filled with subject paintings which people flocked to see – David Wilkie's *Chelsea Pensioners Reading the Waterloo Despatch* (Wellington Museum, Apsley House) had to be protected from the crowds by a barrier in 1822.[3] Poets, notably Byron,[4] and the novelists of the next two generations, from Thackeray to Kipling, responded to the dramatic events and wove them into their plots. Even architecture responded in commemorative fashion in the Waterloo Chamber at Windsor, with its great series of portraits of the protagonists by Sir Thomas Lawrence, and Benjamin Dean Wyatt's Gallery for the Duke of Wellington at Apsley House (1828-29).

For one man the Battle of Waterloo and its aftermath proved particularly momentous. Antonio Canova (1757-1822), the greatest sculptor of the day, was sent as the representative of Pope Pius VII to the Paris Peace Conference to make a claim for 'la restituzione de'capi d'opera dell'arte antica e dei quadri' that had been removed from Italy to Paris by Napoleon's forces.[5] As the representative of the Holy See and the City State of Rome, under the direction of Cardinal Consalvi, Secretary of State, his role was central to the deliberations of the Conference, yet the standard histories of the period fail to mention him. Not only did he write a full account of his sojourn in Paris,[6] but he kept copies of every letter, every document relating to the proceedings from rough drafts and fair copies to entire newspapers. He had access to British diplomatic papers, and made copies, and across several months it is possible to chart almost every move he made.[7]

On the 12th August 1815 the Roman Senate, in the person of Giovanni Patrizi, formally appointed Canova 'emulatore del Greco Scalpello, e Principe perpetuo della Romana Accademia delle Belle Arti'[8] to approach His Most Christian Majesty Louis XVIII for the restitution of the works of art that were Rome's chief splendour.

The historical context of the negotiation for the return of the works of art revolved around an interpretation of two treaties. The first was the Treaty of Tolentino of 1797 in which Pope Pius VI had, in an attempt to preserve the integrity of the Catholic Church and the Papal States, ceded to the Revolutionary Armies of France under Napoleon the great works of art, ancient and modern, which adorned the museums of the Vatican and the Capitol. The debate over their restitution centred on the legality of a treaty made under duress, annulled, it was argued, by the French invasion of the Papal States two years later, the dethronement of the Pope, his exile and subsequent death. The other treaty was that which marked Napoleon's abdication in May 1814, the first Treaty of Paris. Purposefully benign, it had carefully avoided all occasions of wounding French pride, in an attempt to re-establish the Bourbon monarchy under Louis XVIII. The great galleries of the Musée Napoléon, immediately renamed the Musée Royale, at the Louvre, remained intact, being one of the wonders of the world, a powerful symbol of national pride.

Napoleon's success after his return from Elba had taken Europe by surprise. The magnanimity of the previous year evaporated, though its spirit still informed the successful *Realpolitik* conducted by Castlereagh and Wellington over the next few months.[9] In the Military Convention that preceded the occupation of Paris by the Allied Forces in the first week of July, cultural property, over which the French and the Prussians had taken uncompromising positions, was, at Wellington's insistence, excluded from the final agreement.[10] It was on the interpretation of these three agreements that Canova had to argue the Papal cause, which he did with great persistence, and no doubt his success led to a modern commentator describing him as 'the greediest' of claimants.[11] He later reported to Consalvi that he had been informed that until he came to Paris the restitution of works of art had not been seriously discussed.[12]

Tourists hurried in great numbers to the battlefields of Waterloo, 'this place of skulls',[13] and went on to Paris to catch sight of the greatest exhibition of European works of art ever assembled in one place. Guide books had been rushed out or reprinted, and Louis Trouchet's *Picture of Paris; Being a Complete Guide . . .* was reviewed in the *Gentlemen's Magazine* of August 1815.[14] Andrew Robertson (1777-

1845), the Scottish miniaturist, whose visit to Paris coincided exactly with Canova's, had on his first morning rushed to the Gallery of the Louvre where he saw

> 'the first and greatest productions of human genius, and then the bare walls and frames where a number of the pictures had been taken away by the allies and the original proprietors.'[15]

These will have been the works of art taken by Blücher's troops on the grounds that Louis XVIII had failed to keep his promise of the previous year. Robertson gives a graphic description of Paris, its visitors civil and military and its entertainments. He is surprised by the vivacity of Parisian night-life, the cafés, the music, dancing and the well-dressed people. He lists some of the many other British tourists he met, fellow painters and sculptors among them:

> 'I met besides Boville, Lane, Jones, Beechey, Dr McCleod, Davis, Garrard, Daw – afterwards came Stothard, Chantrey, Westmacott, Lawrence, Hayter, D. Robertson, Shaw, Salt, Cooke, Harrison, Reinagle, Phillips, Hilton, Perigal, Saunders – private individuals without number.'[16]

The masterpieces that the tourists could see in the Louvre included Michelangelo's *Madonna and Child* from Notre Dame at Bruges, Titian's *Transfiguration*, Raphael's *Madonna della Sedia*, and the great icons of antiquity, the *Apollo Belvedere* and the *Venus de' Mecidi* from the Vatican and the Uffizi.

Another early tourist was Walter Scott, who hurried out *Paul's Letters to his Kinsfolk* which, as a purely commercial speculation, provided an eye-witness account of the Low Countries and France in the wake of the momentous days in June.[17] Scott's account is as tendentious as Robertson's is lively. In Letters XII and XIII 'to his sister' Scott gives an account of the grandeur of Paris even under occupation, its architecture and gardens, the watch-fires of the English camped in the Champs Elysées for the first time since 1436, he notes with characteristic historical accuracy.

Canova himself was no stranger to Paris. He had been there twice already, once in 1803 and again in 1811, on both occasions to work to commission for Napoleon. He was, however, under no illusions. Antonio d'Este recorded that he returned from the Quirinale pallid and in a bad mood.[18] He noted the dangers and difficulties of the expedition and the uncertainty of its success,[19] and the day following his acceptance he made his will.[20] He set out with his half-brother the Abate Giovanni Battista Sartori Canova (1755-1858) who since 1800 had been his secretary and constant companion. Armed with letters for the Allied Sovereigns from Pope Pius VII he arrived on the morning of Monday 28th August, and, having settled at 'Mᵈ. R', number 23 Rue Basse du Remparts,[21] set out at once to deliver a letter to Baron Humboldt, the Prussian Minister of State.[22] Consalvi must have advised Canova to start with the Prussians, as they were known to be adamant that the works of art should be returned, and they had already used force to achieve this, as Robertson had observed. Canova was informed that his mission was likely to prove impossible: the

Treaty of Tolentino was the stumbling block, coupled with English and Russian anxiety not to wound French *amour propre*.[23] On the 30th August he delivered a letter to the British Foreign Secretary, Lord Castlereagh, making a case for the annulment of Tolentino.[24] This added a further argument by appealing on behalf of Rome as the Repository of Art, Antiquity and History, and the training ground of artists. The educative point stressed here may well have emerged from discussions with the man who was to prove the most useful in Canova's cause, William Richard Hamilton, Under-Secretary of State in Castlereagh's Ministry. Hamilton had been an active propagandist for the educative importance of the Elgin Marbles, and was later to support Thomas Lawrence and others in their efforts to establish a British School in Rome.[25] In 1815 Hamilton, as Under-Secretary of State for Foreign Affairs, was an active participant in the diplomatic negotiations at the Conference in Paris.

Canova's meeting with Hamilton was fortuitous and decisive. Though the circumstances surrounding it are obscure, it appears to have happened on his second day in Paris.[26] The meeting was effected by an Italian expatriate, who may have been Luigi Angeloni, a literary figure of some note, or Dr Granville, a distinguished physician of Italian extraction. Angeloni almost certainly helped in the drafting of the Papal case, and Canova, never mean in giving credit where it was due, acknowledged his debt to him,[27] while Granville, who was a friend both of Hamilton and Thomas Lawrence, was Canova's constant companion later in London. Farington later suggested that Canova and Hamilton already knew each other in Rome, which is entirely possible.[28] At any rate their confidence in each other must have been immediate, for Canova obtained copies of British diplomatic documents, or had the opportunity to copy them out.[29] A briefing document, probably for Castlereagh from Hamilton, is headed 'Project of a letter intended to be addressed to the King of France', and annotated 'Mr Hamilton / Upon the Fine Arts in the Louvre'.[30] A copy of Talleyrand's reply to Castlereagh, in which the French invoked the first Treaty of Paris of May 1814, can only be among the Canova Papers through the agency of Hamilton.[31]

The documents give the impression that over the subsequent few weeks a group of Canova's supporters established the equivalent of a campaign office to prepare and present the Papal case. There is evidence of defining and refining the arguments, writing and rewriting drafts in the task of persuading the various elements among the Allied powers. Many of the documents have revisions in several hands, and others are annotated in yet different hands.[32] Some were not in the end presented, but ideas were incorporated into other documents and became statements of policy.[33] One long and detailed document, of which there are no less than eight copies in various stages from rough to fair, sets out the historic background to Tolentino and its immediate violation by the French.[34]

On Sunday 10th September Canova was received by Louis XVIII, who paid him the compliment of speaking Italian and commanded him to make his portrait.[35] This, after almost two weeks in Paris, must be regarded as the diplomatic breakthrough. Canova may have been wearing the diplomatic coat in black wool with a ribbed cream silk waistcoat, both suitably bordered in green and gold embroidered olive leaves and fruit, which survives at the Museo Canova at Possagno. On the following day, Canova put a formal address before the Ministers Plenipotentiary of the Allied Sovereigns.[36] It asked for the restitution of statues, paintings, manuscripts, medals, cameos and engravings, and called into question the validity of the Treaty of Tolentino. Less emotive than Hamilton's original document[37] – gone are phrases such as 'sacrilegious hands still warm with the blood of Royal Martyrs' – it admitted that Pius VI had provoked the anger of the French Republic by offering asylum to many (including the aunts of Louis XVIII), and stressed that Pius VII was not asking for financial indemnification for the ravages of the countryside, only for the objects to be returned both for the people of Rome and for 'l'utilité et l'avantage de toutes les nations civilisées de l'Europe.'

On the same day Canova reported to Consalvi[38] that matters were more hopeful and appeared to be moving towards a restitution on just grounds, thanks to the English minister – Hamilton – who had been of the greatest service. The Duke of Wellington had declared in favour of the Holy Father and of Art, and was prepared to use all means to the desired end; Castlereagh had been vigorous in his support, and Canova believed everything had turned on that. Only the Russians remained inimical. So optimistic and confident was he that Canova asked for lists to be prepared of the paintings ceded under Tolentino, and for letters to be sent to the Prince Regent and Wellington, and for Alessandro d'Este to be sent to help him. This optimism comes over even more forcefully in a second letter to Consalvi, written by Canova immediately after speaking to Hamilton, which repeats in greater depth what he had already said about Hamilton's zeal and lively interest, and the need for someone to help him with the business of packing up the sculpture and paintings.[39]

Canova's assessment of Castlereagh's crucial support was right. The Foreign Minister's memorandum to the Ministers of the Allied Powers was decisive,[40] and the text was later published in full on several occasions.[41] Castlereagh, in a consummate piece of statesmanship, took the moral high ground on behalf of the Prince Regent, never descending into detail or individual cases, though inferences are clear. It trod a knife edge between reminding the French of their obligations and the weakness of their actual position, while not affecting their dignity. In a series of rhetorical questions Castlereagh put the onus on the Allied powers to see justice done. In so doing, he invested 'these Trophies' with enormous symbolic power. The 'Principle of property', a principle of 'virtue, conciliation and peace', was the 'surest and only guide to Justice' which would 'settle the public mind of Europe'.

Nevertheless, Canova had to endure another six arduous weeks in which further arguments were raised against the works being returned to Rome, and further accommodations and compromises reached. Some of these amounted to no more than rumour, incensing the French as Robertson discovered when he called on the painter Baron Gros.[42] One rumour, that the Pope only wanted the works returned so that he could sell them to the English,[43] was robustly scotched by Castlereagh in his memorandum when he declared that far from seeking to take personal advantage from the situation, the Prince Regent intended to pay the cost of the transport of the works back to their 'Temples and Galleries'.[44] A further rumour that the *Apollo Belvedere* had been promised to the Prince Regent as a present was reported in *La Quotidienne* of 9th October from the *Courier* of 4th October.[45] It was pointed out that one thousand Apollos would be poor compensation for the loss of the high moral character acquired by the English in avoiding accusations of plundering the defeated. The English were scrupulous. Later they paid the French government £35,000 for Canova's *Napoleon as Mars*, decidedly not an emblem the new regime would wish to retain, before presenting it to the Duke of Wellington. Wellington 'might have had the statues of Canova for £2,500, but missed them', Robertson reported:[46] in the event the Tsar Alexander I of Russia purchased them from the Beauharnais family at Malmaison.

More seriously, Canova still had to persuade the other members of the Allied powers. The Prussians and the Austrians had themselves a close interest in the restitution of the works of art, but the Russians remained implacable. On 14th September Canova asked Prince Metternich for an audience to present letters from Pius VII,[47] and in a similar vein wrote to Count Nesselrode, Minister to Tsar Alexander.[48] The rough draft of the letter to Nesselrode is heavily scored as though expressive of Canova's frustration, and some days later Canova followed it up with a letter to Alexander I himself in which he appealed in the names of Alexander of Macedon and the Pope, whose unhappy treatment at the hands of the French must touch the Tsar's sense of justice.[49]

Minor obstacles were put forward. One, the question of accessibility, has a very modern ring to it. Canova responded to the accusation that scholars would not be able to study the five hundred manuscripts if they were returned to the Vatican Library with the words 'è sempre aperta al pubblico'.[50] In letters to Prince Metternich, Castlereagh and the Emperor Francis I of Austria he emphasised the public nature of the Vatican and Capitoline Museums.[51] Perhaps as a result of his own optimism and evident success, Canova now became the recipient of numerous requests from Italian local officials asking for his assistance. He was approached by Perugia,[52] from Bologna,[53] from Carlo Albani demanding the return of a colossal head of Pallas Athene to the Villa Albani,[54] and in a different but no less irritating vein from Abate Marini Custodian of the Vatican Library stereotypically unco-operative over a request for information.[55]

At this point the restitution process moved from words to action. The Duke of

Wellington, as General-in-Chief of the Army of the Netherlands, forced the issue by announcing that, if the non-cooperation of Talleyrand and 'Monsieur DeNon' the Director of the Louvre were to continue, the paintings belonging to the King of the Netherlands would be removed under armed escort at 12 noon on 20th September. Wellington wrote a memorandum to Castlereagh in defence of his action,[56] which was widely published verbatim.[57] For the pragmatic Wellington, the Prussians, who patrolled the galleries, had already set a precedent by removing their pictures, as had the French by agreeing to it. For Canova, Wellington's action was both a precedent and a surety. He had his own copy of Wellington's memorandum,[58] which may well have been put together with Hamilton's help, and which contained a full-scale casuistical demolition of French claims under the Military Convention of June 1815. It is likely that Canova made his next move in the knowledge that Wellington was on the point of defending a similar earlier action.

On the evening of 23rd September he and the Commissioners for Tuscany and Austria had invoked the mediation of the Emperor Francis I to ensure that the Louvre was shut in the mornings until 2 pm for several days, and then entry to be by ticket only. As Canova pointed out in a letter thanking the Duke of Wellington for his support, the work of removing the sculpture and paintings could then proceed without the murmurs and confusion of curious people.[59] In the event, perhaps both Wellington and Canova were too sanguine in their accounts of what happened. Walter Scott had remarked in July that the

> '[French] attachment to these paintings and statues, or rather to the national glory which they conceive them to illustrate, is as excessive as if the Apollo and Venus were still objects of actual adoration.'[60]

Andrew Robertson gives a vivid day-to-day description of the dismantling of the Louvre from 20th September to 12th October.[61] On the 19th September he had met Stothard (probably the sculptor Alfred Joseph Stothard, 1793-1864) and Francis Chantrey in Alexander Lenoir's salvaged Museum of French Monuments, who told him that the Louvre was shut 'as they were taking away the Dutch pictures.' There seems to have been a conflict of authority between Wellington and Baron Müffling, the Prussian Governor of Paris. Müffling had insisted on the Museum being opened and a British regiment, the 71st, stationed all along the gallery. Robertson reported 'a terrible scene of confusion . . . one division of the room almost entirely naked – the large works of Rubens being taken down made a dreadful blank on the wall,' and 'the people in a rage.'[62]

Robertson was concerned at the careless manner in which paintings on panel, chiefly by Rubens, and of immense size, were being handled. The French would not allow them the use of so much as a hammer, and the paintings had to be removed to a place of safety a mile and a half away on the Rue Mont Blanc. The confusion continued. Robertson met Thomas Lawrence who said that

'every artist must lament the breaking up of a collection in a place so centrical
to Europe where everything was laid open to the public with a degree of liberality
unknown elsewhere.'[63]

Robertson concluded the entry for the day:

'Paris is in a ferment about these pictures and the review tomorrow of the whole
army under Lord Wellington is a very prudent measure.'

The review was held on the 22nd September, a timely reminder of the Allies'
strength.

On Saturday 24th Robertson found 'the Italian pictures going fast, the same degree
of confusion, the guards trebled.' These were the paintings belonging to Tuscany.[64]
Of the reaction to this event by Baron Gros, Robertson reported 'I have never seen a
volcano – but after this interview I can conceive an eruption of Vesuvius.'[65] On the
25th when the *Venus de' Medici* was removed the Museum was shut and a guard
under arms posted round the clock. In the confusion, artists continued to copy,
Robertson himself making a coloured sketch after Correggio's *Holy Family*. When
the bronze horses from St Mark's, Venice were removed from the triumphal arch on
the 30th, all the avenues to the Tuileries were shut by Austrian dragoons.[66]

Formal recognition of the Papal claim to restitution did not come until 30th
September when it was confirmed that the works belonging to the Roman state
should be returned by France.[67] The following day Canova received a note from
Hamilton, the only time the latter wrote to Canova in his official capacity, advising
him on Castlereagh's behalf that Prince Metternich would, at last, receive him and
give him instructions on removing the works from the galleries.[68] This was the least
of their worries, as Canova and Hamilton were both uniquely experienced in the
moving of large-scale sculpture in adverse circumstances, and they had the assistance of British military engineers.

On 2nd October Robertson noted 'there is now no bounds to the rage of the
French,' and on the 5th the Director of the Louvre, Vivant Denon, faced with the
inexorable dismantling of all he had set up, resigned. On the 12th October,
Robertson wrote:

'The Louvre is truely doleful to look at now, all the best statues are gone, and
half the rest, the place full of dust, ropes, triangles, and pulleys, with boards,
rollers etc.'[69]

Canova, having gained the principal object of his mission, 'i capi d'opera dell'arte
antica e dei quadri,' found that there were still concessions and accommodations to
be made. First came a deputation from the University of Heidelberg which, address-
ing 'l'artiste le plus distingué de nôtre siècle,'[70] proceeded to make a prior claim to
thirty-nine Greek and Latin manuscripts that had been given by the Elector
Maximilian of Bavaria to Pope Gregory xv in 1622 at the height of the fury of the
Thirty Years War.[71] Canova, exhausted by the negotiations of the past month, and

apparently acting on his own initiative, was prepared to concede these thirty-nine from the five hundred due to be returned to the Vatican.[72] Authorisation came *post factum*.[73] Some of the paintings from the Vatican had been hanging in the Royal Apartments and some in Nôtre Dame, the 'Parish Church' where Louis XVIII went daily to hear Mass.[74] On Humboldt and Hamilton's advice it was considered wise to leave them as a reconciliatory gesture.[75] Some Etruscan vases from Bologna were difficult to identify,[76] and a number of works had been dispersed to the Departments, or Regions, under Jean Antoine Chaptal's cultural policies of 1800.[77] Though Perugia singled out a Perugino at Lyons, most of these were not reclaimed.

Once the Council of Ministers had formally acknowledged Papal claims, Canova's standing markedly improved. The powerful Prince Schwarzenberg expressed delight at having a *rapport* with a man so celebrated 'dont l'Europe oppose le nom aux grandes maîtres du siècle des Medicis.'[78] And a couple of reasoned and reasonable articles in *La Quotidienne* for Monday 9th and Wednesday 18th October signed 'MB' which Canova marked in the margin and kept,[79] must in their resigned and accepting tone have reassured Canova that not all Frenchmen vilified him.[80]

It is quite clear from Canova's letters to Consalvi, which are far from diplomatic and often charged with personal emotion, that the process of negotiations had taken its toll. On 24th September a letter full of weariness speaks of that process as full of 'tenebre, incertezze e disparesi continui,' and stresses the 'vigilie, cure, e fatiche che io duro ogni di per trovare se posso la fine di questa scabrosa missione.' Canova revealed that his task had preyed on him, for he had to steel himself 'dalla diffidenza e dal timore,' and had no idea how desperate things were going to be in the face of the 'malcontento universale di un popolo che vede con ira e sdegno ritogliersi questi monumenti delle sue conquiste.'[81] A hurried note from Consalvi in response to this begs that Canova 'conservi la sua preziosa salute.'[82]

Hamilton too was clearly concerned about Canova's health suffering 'dalla fatica della settimana passata – mà ahora potrà dormire tranquillamente.'[83] At this point there is indeed a gap of about ten days in the documentary evidence, the only extant document being *La Quotidienne* for Wednesday 18th October. Perhaps Canova found time to see Mme Catalani in *La Semiramide* at the Théâtre Royal Italien, reviewed in that day's edition of the journal. Canova enjoyed the opera, and was to recommend the Duchess of Bedford to hear Mme Violante Camporese at the King's Theatre Haymarket when she visited London in 1817.[84] Andrew Robertson, who saw Catalani on 7th and 13th October, wrote of her:

'her beauty is almost perfect – her head and arms are like the Antique – her
hands superior, quite ideal – no painting or sculpture has equalled them.'[85]
Quatremère de Quincy, clearly embarrassed by the contrast in reception between Canova's earlier visits and the present one, recalled, however, that he spent his evenings with a coterie of close friends working on a volume of his engravings.[86]

The last weeks of Canova's Paris sojourn were taken up with finalising details of the convoys. There were to be two, the first of which was to go over land, the second by sea in a British naval ship. The first, under Captain Mayern, included all the sculpture for Rome, and the works for Bologna, Perugia and Cento.[87] His letters are marked by a characteristic generosity of spirit, repeatedly stressing his debt to others,[88] to the English and 'il favore immenso che questa generosa nazione donò alle arti e a Roma in questa causa già del tutto disperata'[89] to the Prince Regent, Castlereagh and Wellington, but most particularly to Hamilton 'un uomo appassionato per le Arti Belle . . . grande Amico mio,' without whom, as Baron Humboldt had told Canova, the affair would not have come to such a successful conclusion. He repeatedly asks for letters of thanks to be sent to all of these, and to Captain Mayern, Baron Humboldt, Prince Hardenberg, Signor Angeloni and even Abate Marini of the Vatican Library who had in the event proved himself.

Canova had mixed motives for travelling to London after his triumph in Paris. Some were official, some purely personal, and his feelings were mixed too.[90] The generally accepted motive is that he was invited to give his opinion on the Elgin Marbles, of which the British government was currently deliberating the purchase, although he had already seen them, in Lord Elgin's presence, in Rome in 1803.[91] *The Times* made it clear that Canova was 'not to be employed on public works,' a point echoed by Farington.[92] Hamilton, who had been so closely involved in the acquisition and transport of the Elgin Marbles, and in the ensuing aesthetic and political debate about their future, must surely have talked about them with Canova in their six weeks together in Paris, and would have encouraged him to come and see them, if encouragement were needed. Certainly, Canova's opinions were subsequently invoked by those in favour of acquiring them for the nation.

In his last letter to Consalvi before leaving for London, Canova suggested there was a financial motive, the need to raise yet more money in Britain to pay for the transport of the works of art from Paris to the Vatican.[93] A further motive, suggested by *The Times* as 'simply one of curiosity' was disingenuous but understandable. London had become one of the great capitals of the world, to which, post-Napoleon, post-Waterloo, the magnetism of power and patronage was already shifting. James Mudie was almost immediately able to attract a team of French medallists to London [Cat. Nos 21 and 22] while the papers were full of notices advertising the advent of everyone and everything French, from *modistes* and milliners to Hydropneumatic French Lamps.[94]

Canova had many English friends whose acquaintance he might renew: the Duke and Duchess of Bedford, whom he had met earlier in the year in Rome, Sir Humphry and Lady Davy, Lord Cawdor his earliest English patron, the Misses Berry whom he had known since 1784, and many more. And how much warmer could an invitation be than Hamilton's, sent from London on 20th October?[95] Written in the euphoria of the knowledge that 'oggi, se non mi sbaglio dovevan partire da Parigi, l'Apollo, il Laocoonte, la Trasfigurazione, etcera,' it is a paean of romantic fervour in which Hamilton apostrophises those deities whose images are on the move. He called on Minerva, Mercury and Jove to lead, make straight the route and provide good weather and clear skies; Hercules to assist the carts crossing Mont Cenis and the Apennines; Apollo to provide good speed; flowers for Venus to maintain peace and harmony; and Bacchus to preside over the festivals which will proclaim to the Italians the blessed returns of their joys, while the Laocoon and his sons represented Italy and the loss she has suffered. Canova and his brother, the letter declares, will be welcomed with open arms.

The two months that Canova and his brother had spent in Paris had been exhausting, worse 'scabrosa', an 'inferno', and there can be no doubt from the letters that Canova took personally the hostility of the French populace at large. 'La pena, la angustia, e i fastidi da me sofferti, e vi voleva... solo tutto il mio amore per le arti, e per servire S.S. onde sottopormi a un peso troppo incompatibile col mio carattere, e con la delicatezza de' miei sentimenti.'[96] Cold-shouldering from fellow artists like Baron Gros or Houdon must have been extremely hurtful. The painter Richard Reinagle provided a fascinating account of visiting the Halle d'Etudes at the Academy where Houdon refused to speak to him, and he and others were pelted with bread pellets by the students.[97] The 'timore' he wrote of in letters to Consalvi was no exaggeration. It was a fear which no doubt encouraged the delay to his return to Paris, for as he told Thomas Phillips RA (1770-1845) he feared for his life and

> 'he was often afraid to go to his lodging there for fear of being murdered and
> that one day one of the French *artists* said in his hearing that he should like to
> stick a dagger in him.'[98]

Encouragement in the form of friendly letters of congratulation at his success in Paris must have been further inducement to come to London.[99]

The warmth of Canova's reception, the hospitality he received, the comfortable way of life of those who received him, was in sharp contrast to occupied Paris, where Andrew Robertson had marvelled at the domestic discomfort verging on the squalid.[100] Certainly his visit was to take on in restrospect the quality of an idyll, confirming his gratitude and esteem for the English. He and his brother travelled with the intention of staying ten days, which eventually stretched to more than a month. They set out from Paris on Sunday 29th October, the day that Andrew Robertson was almost drowned in Channel storms.[101] It is not clear when they arrived in London. 1st November, the date often given,[102] is probably too soon, and Thomas Phillips reported that it was a Friday, which would make it 3rd November. [103] They put up at Brunet's Hotel in Leicester Square, where rooms had been reserved for them by Hamilton,[104] and while Talleyrand may have mocked 'Monsieur l'emballeur',[105] in England he was received with all the dignity and esteem due to an Ambassador, and with a cordiality that will have soothed his frayed nerves. The Duke of Bedford was among the first to welcome him, in a note addressed to Brunet's Hotel on Friday 3rd November.[106] He offered his services, suggested that if Canova were to call at 1 o'clock at 2 Hamilton Place, Bedford's town house, they might visit Richard Westmacott's studio, and then they might look at the sights and dine together.

We do not know what the Canova brothers did on their first Saturday; on Sunday, tourists in London, they looked at the monuments in Westminster Abbey, but, being without a guide, could make little of them.[107] They went to St Paul's Cathedral where many of the monuments were modern and by sculptors known to Canova. He will have seen work by the Bacons, father and son – John the elder (1740-99) and John the younger (1777-1859) – notably the elder's romanising monuments to *John Howard* (1796) and to *Samuel Johnson* (1796) and the monument to *General Sir John Moore* by John Bacon the younger which had just been completed.[108] Canova will also have seen the monument by Thomas Banks (1735-1805) to *Captain Richard Burgess* (1802), with its direct reference to antique Roman sculpture,[109] and John Flaxman's to *Lord Howe* (1803-11). *Horatio, Lord Nelson* (1808-18) by Flaxman (1775-1826) was not yet complete, but in both his St Paul's monuments the lion motif perhaps pays homage to the lions that Canova incorporated in his *Monument to Clement* XIII (St Peter's, Rome.) Canova had befriended Flaxman when the latter was in Rome in 1787-94. Now Professor of Sculpture at the Royal Academy, he was the leading British sculptor of the day, and he and Canova were often set on a par by contemporaries.[110] Canova will have been interested in the work of his former pupil, now highly successful, Richard Westmacott (1775-1856). His ambitious *General Sir Ralph Abercromby* (1802-5)[111] was, as yet, his only completed work in St Paul's. He will also have seen work by John Charles Rossi (1762-1839) who had been in Rome from 1785 to 1788 on a Royal Academy travelling scholarship, and the relief to General Bowes (c.1811) by the much younger, but rising star, Francis Chantrey (1781-1841)[112]

On his first Monday in London, Canova called on John Bacon at 17 Newman Street, where Bacon insisted on drawing his portrait as they discussed the monuments in St Paul's.[113] The following day Canova went to the Foreign Office in Downing Street to deliver a personal letter of thanks to the Prime Minister, Lord Liverpool, on behalf of Pope Pius VII and the people of Rome, conveying their gratitude to the Prince Regent.[114] This happy duty done, Canova went, almost certainly with a group of connoisseurs, to the British Museum, then still accommodated in Montagu House and the recently completed Towneley Gallery.

While he was in London, Canova wrote a series of brief notes, in which he strictly confined himself to the collections he visited and their contents. An *aide-memoire* but presumably chronological, it conveys nothing of the hectic social round that we know from other sources that Canova enjoyed, nor observations of the people he met.[115] It begins with a description of some of the antique sculpture Canova saw in the British Museum. His comments are informed by a sculptor's educated eye, noting the restorations and comparing with other works known to him, and distinguished by the sensuality of his observations, his interest in 'la carnosità' or fleshiness. It reflects a sculptor's thoughtful reaction to the objects, often in comparison with his own work.

On Thursday 9th November Canova and his brother were invited by Sir Humphry Davy to the Royal Society in Somerset House to hear him give his paper 'On the Fire Damp and an Account of lighting mines so as to prevent explosion.' Michael Faraday and Charles Babbage were also present that evening.[116] Davy was a charismatic lecturer, whose regular public lectures at the Royal Institution in Albemarle Street had made him a popular figure. He and his wife, the heiress Jane Apreece, were old acquaintances of Canova's in Rome, and Davy, a prolific amateur poet, had written some unfinished lines of praise to the sculptor:

> Thou wert a sight of brightness in an age
> When Italy was in the night of art
> She was thy country, but the world thy stage
> On which thou acted thy creative part.
> Blameless thy life Thy manners playful, mild,
> Master in Art yet Nature's simplest child.
>
> Phideas of Rome like him thou stand'st sublime
> And after artists shall essay to climb
> To that high temple where thou dwell'st alone,
> Generous to all . . .[117]

A letter, written in Italian from Holland House on Sunday 12th November to Canova's brother,[118] infers that there had been an earlier communication, and is evidence of how firmly Canova was held in the sights and conversation of London society. Lord and Lady Holland were Whigs in opposition. The 3rd Lord Holland (1773-1840) was the nephew of Charles James Fox, the radical politician, and like him espoused liberal causes. Lady Holland (1770-1845) was a political hostess and held salons at Holland House in Kensington. Hearing that the two Canovas were to lunch with Mr Hamilton at Stanley Grove, would they on their return dine at Holland House as they would pass close by? Lord and Lady Holland were most desirous that the two brothers should spend the end of Sunday and the night. Lady Davy, who was also lunching with Mr Hamilton, would ensure that the Canovas left Mr Hamilton's in good time. The slightly bossy tone was typical of Lady Holland's salon style. It seems that the Marquis of Lansdowne had come in haste to London to meet the Canovas, and Lord Holland would be very sad if Lord Lansdowne's journey was in vain. A further proposition: tomorrow morning (Monday 13th November) the Marquis was going to Lansdowne House, Berkeley Square, and invited the Signori Canova to breakfast with him, to see 'una bella collezione di <quadri e di – *erased*> statue' after which the Marquis would return to the country. A reply was required and a note of their likely arrival. Lord Holland would put his carriage at their disposal.

Lord Lansdowne – Henry Petty Fitzmaurice (1780-1863) 3rd Marquis of Lansdowne, married to Louisa Fox Strangways – showed Canova over his collection after breakfast on Monday 13th November. The antique sculpture had been collected through the agency of the painter and archaeologist-dealer Gavin Hamilton (1723-98), Canova's mentor and friend. Canova remarked on, among other things, an 'Amore e Psyche' excavated by Hamilton at Hadrian's Villa, and compared it to his own standing version.[119]

On returning to their hotel the Canova brothers would have found a number of letters waiting for them. One, from Earl Bathurst, a Principal Secretary of State at the Foreign Office, acknowledged Canova's to Lord Liverpool.[120] 'The return of the works of art was an occasion so truly interesting to the cause of justice in general & to the future encouragement of the Fine Arts' – can one not hear once again the voice of William Richard Hamilton? – Canova, it is hoped, will prolong his stay until the return of the Prince Regent to London, in which case His Royal Highness would no doubt be desirous to grant to Cavalier Canova a personal Audience.

Another from the Duke of Bedford hoped that, despite the time of year, Canova and his half-brother might pay a visit to Woburn where they were awaited with great impatience.[121] A further invitation came from George Bullock of 4 Tenterden St, Hanover Square.[122] Bullock (1782-1818) was a sculptor-turned-cabinet maker entrepreneur from Liverpool, the brother of William Bullock, owner of the Egyptian Hall in Piccadilly and promoter of spectacular exhibitions from Mexican raingods to live Laplanders and their moose. Bullock himself had been President of the Liverpool Academy before moving to London, where he lived in style, as a patron of the arts. In 1816 he received the commission from the Paymaster General's Office to furnish Longwood House, on St Helena, for Napoleon.[123] Canova was invited 'to meet a few of the select Artists,' and he was asked to bring his half-brother and anyone else to dinner 'on Friday next', the 17th November. Evidence of the eagerness of Londoners to meet him is implied in the postscript that offered Saturday or Monday equally if Friday was not convenient for Canova. He annotated the invitation 'Granville'.

Canova's notes are undated, but after his visit to Lansdowne House, sometime during that week, he took up an invitation to breakfast with Thomas Hope and to tour his collection in the company of John Flaxman.[124] Hope (1769-1831), a Dutch banker of Scottish descent, was an amateur designer of furniture and fittings. He was a Governing Director of the British Institution, set up in 1806 to encourage British art, and a member of the seven-strong Committee for the Superintendence of Models of Public Monuments, of which Charles Long was the President. Hope had been acquainted with Canova since his first visit to Rome in 1802.[125] He lived at 1 Mansfield St, in an Adam house known as Duchess Street, demolished in 1851. It was described by Passavant as a heavy, gloomy building, almost entirely devoid of windows, blackened with accumulations of soot, and to all outward appearences conveying rather the idea of a large brewery, than of an opulent banker's town residence.[126] Canova noted that it was one of the finest private collections in London, remarking on the 'Bellissimi vasi etruschi,' paintings by Paolo Veronese and antique sculpture. He saw Flaxman's *Aurora Visiting Cephalus on Mount Ida* (1789-90), which he described as 'di grandezza quasi al naturale.'[127]

During that same week, if the chronology of his notes is to be followed, Canova was received by Queen Charlotte and the Royal Princesses at Windsor Castle, 'con molta benegnita.' He was shown over the Castle by the Governor, General Taylor, and saw Van Dycks, Zuccarellis and armour, and admired the gothic architecture of St George's Chapel.

The only surviving letter to Consalvi from London is written by Canova when, having received Bathurst's note, he must have decided to await the Prince Regent's return from the country to present himself and offer him 'l'omaggio della nostra riconoscenza.'[128] Consalvi is informed that Alessandro d'Este had advised that the second convoy had set out for Antwerp the previous week, and he remarks that he looked forward to returning to his studio 'che abbandonai per tanto tempo e che mi aspetta!' and needs to return to his occupation. Nevertheless Canova had clearly been seduced by London: 'io dovrei far qui una vita beata, festeggiato, onorato universalmente,' people have all received him with the utmost courtesy which is impossible to resist, and if the season were not winter it would be tempting to make a much longer sojourn 'in una capitale si magnifica, e piena di cose mirabili.'

On 16th November Canova received an invitation from Sir Simon Houghton Clarke, who had commissioned *Terpsichore*[129] the year before, and who now hoped to see him on the following Sunday 19th November at his house, Oak Hill, East Barnet.[130] There he made a note about the type of pedestal the *Terpsichore* would need and recorded that he had seen the *Colonna Venus* by Veronese, and engravings by Pietro Vitalli.

Sir Joseph Banks (1744-1820), President of the Royal Society, took Canova to call on Richard Payne Knight on Monday 20th November to view his collection. The following morning he set out with his brother in the company of the architect Jeffry Wyatt, later Sir Jeffry Wyatville (1766-1840), and Richard Westmacott for Woburn, the Duke of Bedford's country seat in Bedfordshire. Canova recorded with careful accuracy seeing nearly twenty Van Dycks and more than twenty Canalettos. In recording his visit to Woburn Canova allows himself a personal comment on the Duke's 'palazzo e delizia,' where he found 'tutti i comodi e delizie reali.'[151] Though he does not mention the Sculpture Gallery and its Temple of Liberty,[152] he must have seen it and discussed its development with the Duke, Wyatt and Westmacott, with the Duke's commission of *The Three Graces* in mind. The following year Jeffry Wyatt designed the Temple of the Graces, adorned with bas reliefs by Westmacott.[153] The visit was clearly a success, and the Duchess's note of 26th November was warm in her affectionate farewell.[154]

Canova had been in London for some time before Joseph Farington (1747-1821), the watercolourist and diarist, first made a note of his presence.[155] This must have been because Farington had been out of circulation with a cold, and Robert Smirke brought Farington up to date on the 21st November on Canova and his opinions. Canova's view of the Elgin Marbles was that he 'never before saw sculpture at such a height of perfection.' Farington repeats the newspaper assertions that it was not intended to consult or employ him on any of the proposed British government monuments, and records the gratitude that Canova showed to Hamilton. Second hand, Farington confirms our understanding of Canova's desperation: 'He had in vain applied to the French Ministry to restore them [the art treasures]. His time was consumed in vain attendance upon them.' Farington then adds that Canova had known Hamilton in Rome. We learn that Canova had visited Charles Long at Bromley Hill, and been taken on a ride and shown London from the heights about Sydenham: 'Canova was in raptures at the prospect.' Farington further records that Canova had been to Hampton Court, and was full of admiration for the Raphael Cartoons;[156] and confirms his having gone to the Duke of Bedford's at Woburn. On Monday 27th November we hear that Canova was expected to attend Carlisle's lecture'[157] at the Royal Academy in the company of the President, Benjamin West.

Reinagle later reported that Canova did attend the lecture, as he was introduced to the assembled Academicians by West.[158] After the lecture Canova dined at Hamilton's, 'a delightful evening,' as the artist and diarist Benjamin Robert Haydon noted.[159] The following day Haydon accompanied Canova to see the Duke of Devonshire's collection, to meet J. M. W. Turner at his gallery in Queen Anne Street, and on to James Northcote the portrait painter. Then on 29th November Canova went again to see the Elgin Marbles, where Haydon met him.

There was a wish among Academicians to honour Canova with a dinner, which took place on Friday 1st December at 5 o'clock. The guests assembled in the Academy Library in Somerset House, where twenty five Academicians received Canova and his brother, William Richard Hamilton, Dr Granville 'and another Italian',[140] undoubtedly Antonio d'Este. The four leading British sculptors, Nollekens, Flaxman, Rossi and Westmacott, were present at the party, for which Farington provided a seating plan. Canova, as the honoured guest, sat between the President and Henry Fuseli (1741-1825), Keeper of the Royal Academy and Professor of Painting. While Dr Burney and Dr Granville were put side by side, Hamilton next to Abate Canova and Turner at the far end. The President proposed the toasts – to Canova and Hamilton – and the visitors departed before ten o'clock. Fuseli spoke approvingly of Canova to Farington, 'thinking highly of his modesty and his talents.'

Undoubtedly the Royal Academy wanted to honour this most celebrated of European artists, but they also had a more serious motive. For more than a decade the Academy had suffered divisions and factions, and the added rivalry of the British Institution.[141] There was an active desire to see a development of the encouragement of art among artists and patrons, which was heightened by observations in Paris of French liberality towards the arts in the late summer and autumn of 1815.[142] As the *Courier* put it on Tuesday 5th December, the dinner for Canova 'presented a most pleasing example of the harmony and cordiality which should subsist in the community of the Fine Arts.'

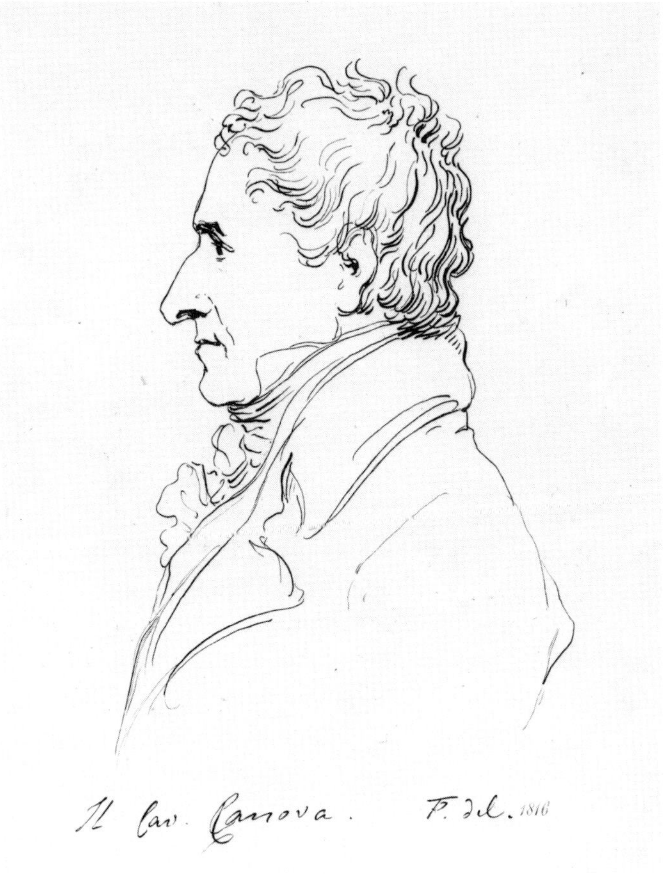

Fig. 1

During his month in London, Canova had made a great impression on the friendly English artists whom he met. The contrary and volatile Haydon was enchanted by him. 'He has a fine Italian head, & when he smiles the feeling sent forth is so exquisite that one fancied music would follow the motions of his lips.'[143] And 'on better acquaintance he is a facetious, unaffected, delightful man.'[144] Through Farington, Lawrence described his '*manners . . .* a pattern for an Artist, that he had modest but manly deportment.' Smirke recorded that his English was 'remarkably pure and consistent', people were delighted with him and he with them. Canova's likeness was taken at least five times during his stay. The accomplished amateur artist Mary Turner, wife of the Yarmouth banker and collector Dawson Turner, included Canova's portrait in her *One Hundred Etchings* (Fig.1).[145] This she etched after a pencil drawing by Thomas Phillips. John Bacon the younger also took Canova's likeness, which Hamilton annotated 'Very Like',[146] as did Flaxman when he called on him for breakfast on 2nd December.[147] Richard Reinagle drew a profile after seeing Canova at Carlisle's lecture, and promptly circulated it.[148] All reports of Canova's good nature concur. Richard Cook, a correspondent of Dawson Turner, wrote: 'Since my return to London I have been introduced to Cano[va]. He appears naturally cheerful & good natured, qualities which I must conff his countenance, while in Paris, did not indicate. He was highly gratified with this country, and the hospitable reception he received. Independently of anything else, to see the Elgin Marbles, he said, was alone worth the journey from Rome.'[149]

Canova had extended his stay and waited to be presented by Castlereagh to the Prince Regent at a Levée at Carlton House. The Prince Regent gave him a jewelled gold snuffbox containing 'un magnifico dono' of £500,[150] and another for Cardinal Consalvi,[151] which was left behind and subsequently lost.[152] Canova kept the *Courier* of 5th December, his last day. This edition of the pro-government newspaper reported, perhaps by sheer coincidence, Castlereagh's memorandum on British policy to the Allied Ministers of 11th September and Wellington's account of the restitution.[153] It also recorded the dinner given for Canova by the Royal Academy, and announced that he had the day before been 'most graciously received' by the Prince Regent.

On the 6th January 1816 the *Diario di Roma* reported that two days earlier: 'diversi Carri contenenti vari dei migliori nostri Capi d'opera in Pittura, e Scultura . . . eccitato il più grande entusiasmo nel Popolo Romano. Tutti gli Artisti, e un gran numero di amatori delle Arti andarono ad incontrare . . . e ne festeggiarono l'arrivo.'[154] Canova was received in Rome the following day by Pope Pius VII, and during almost an hour's audience was presented with a letter announcing that his name was to be written into the 'Libro d'oro del Campidoglio,' and the title Marchese d'Ischia conferred upon him with an annual pension of three million *scudi*. Canova's mission had been completed. He had achieved the impossible. And moreover he had succeeded in persuading someone else to pay for it.

Despite popular hostility to the cost of peace, Canova secured much more than the original 100,000 *franchi* promised towards cost of transport by the British government. On his last morning in London, he had been to the Foreign Office to receive a note for Cardinal Consalvi, signed by William Hamilton, for the sum of 250,000 *franchi*.[155] 200,000 of this was to recover costs involved in the restitution of the works of art and their transport from Paris to Rome, while the balance was the Prince Regent's contribution to the monument that Canova was to make in St Peter's, Rome, to Cardinal York. So, despite native reservations about his employment in Britain, Canova succeeded also in terms of his own career as a sculptor, with what amounted to a semi-public commission for that extraordinary historical statement the *Monument to the House of Stuart*, to 'Jacopo iii' and his sons Charles Edward and Henry, Cardinal York installed in St Peter's.[156] Indeed it might be said that Canova's career at the age of fifty-eight took on a renewed energy as his English patrons plied him with commissions, replacing the Napoleonic dynasty as his main source of employment, and fulfilling Farington's prophesy.[157] It is significant that the notes Canova made in England had concentrated largely on the collections of those who would be his chief patrons in the last seven years of his life – Hope, Lansdowne, Clarke, Bedford and the Prince Regent, whose patronage was conducted through Charles Long and William Hamilton.

Long and Hamilton also obtained the agreement of the Prince Regent and the Royal Academy respectively for the exhibition of Canova's work, in effect using the Academy exhibitions as showcases as the sculpture came into England. Minutes of the Royal Academy Council for 15th April 1817 accepted Hamilton's offer of two marble statues by Canova. These were Lord Cawdor's *Hebe* and Sir Simon Clarke's *Terpsichore*, which Hamilton and Canova were anxious should be seen publicly before being despatched to their destinations in the country.[158] The following year Charles Long wrote to Canova to say that the Prince Regent's permission had been given to show the *Nymph* at the Royal Academy or British Institution.[159] This would appear to lend credence to the characteristically jaundiced report by Benjamin Robert Haydon that Canova had come to London looking for work.

However the effects of the visit were far from being one-sided. Four days after Canova's departure John Flaxman moved a motion in the Royal Academy General Assembly and Council for the procurement of a new collection of casts from the Antique, as the existing ones were 'so discoloured and injured' in the course of nearly half a century of use 'that they no longer afford the students sufficient means of improvement.'[160] It is likely that this intervention was the direct result of Canova's being shown round the Academy Schools. Historically, taking casts from the antique had been a matter of diplomatic negotiation, the Papacy in particular having always been jealous of its copyright.[161] Now the Council agreed to present an address to the Prince Regent requesting his assistance in obtaining 'new & perfect casts' from

Rome, Florence and Naples, and allowing them free conveyance to London 'in some of His Majesty's vessels'. This last request could possibly have been made on Hamilton's advice, perhaps in discussion over dinner when the Academy entertained Canova. It would scarcely be an exaggeration to suggest that in the next few years casts became a currency of diplomacy, and once it was known that the Prince Regent desired casts they came in on every side.[162] Much of Charles Long's correspondence with Canova and business with the Academy (which mirrors the correspondence) is taken up with the matter of casts, and on 2nd August 1816 the Council Minutes record that Long had given the President a list of twenty six casts from marbles 'in the Pope's Museum' which the Prince Regent would present to the Royal Academy, and would 'use his influence' to obtain others. There followed the list, in Italian, of twenty six 'Jessi' which suggests that its ultimate source was Canova himself, as Long did not speak Italian and conducted his correspondence with Canova in French.

This traffic in casts was not one way, for Pius VII was sent the so-called Hercules from the Parthenon pediment, 'un gesso intiero',[163] and later a set of casts from the Parthenon frieze and metopes taken by Richard Westmacott.[164] That these exchanges were a matter of official diplomatic policy is clear from the *Notizie del Giorno* for 24th September 1818,[165] which announced that casts of the most beautiful statues in His Holiness's collection had been sent to England for the Prince Regent, who would present them to the Royal Academy 'per uso degli studenti.'

At a personal level Canova was generous to a fault. He was anxious throughout the crisis months in Paris that due acknowledgement should be made to the efforts of individuals who were by no means forgotten. It is sometimes thought that the Papacy failed to acknowledge this debt of gratitude. This is not so, as we have seen in the matter of casts, and in all this individuals were remembered in various ways too. Luigi Angeloni received a 'Scatola d'oro, ornata di cammeo, e d'una catena per orivolo d'onici orientali antiche' from Cardinal Consalvi.[166] Angeloni pursued the matter of the Perugino at Lyons with the help of Quatremère de Quincy.[167]

While William Richard Hamilton was presented by the Pope with a pair of obelisks in *rosso antico*, probably referred in a letter of 9th September 1816 'per ornar la mia casa, ed annoblir il mio Museo,'[168] Canova's own thanks took a variety of forms. As he was *principe perpetuo* of the Accademia di San Luca, it is not perhaps surprising that Benjamin West, Fuseli, John Flaxman and Thomas Lawrence should be made members of the Academy in Rome.[169] What is more remarkable is that Hamilton was also made a member, a singular distinction for someone who had no claims to being an artist. Equally remarkable was the inclusion of a *trompe l'oeil* portrait bust of him in the fresco depicting the return of the works of art to Rome, painted in celebration, under Canova's supervision, by Francesco Hayez (1791-1882) in the series of allegorical lunettes of *The Life of Pius* VII in the Chiaramonti Gallery in the Vatican.[170] (Fig.2)

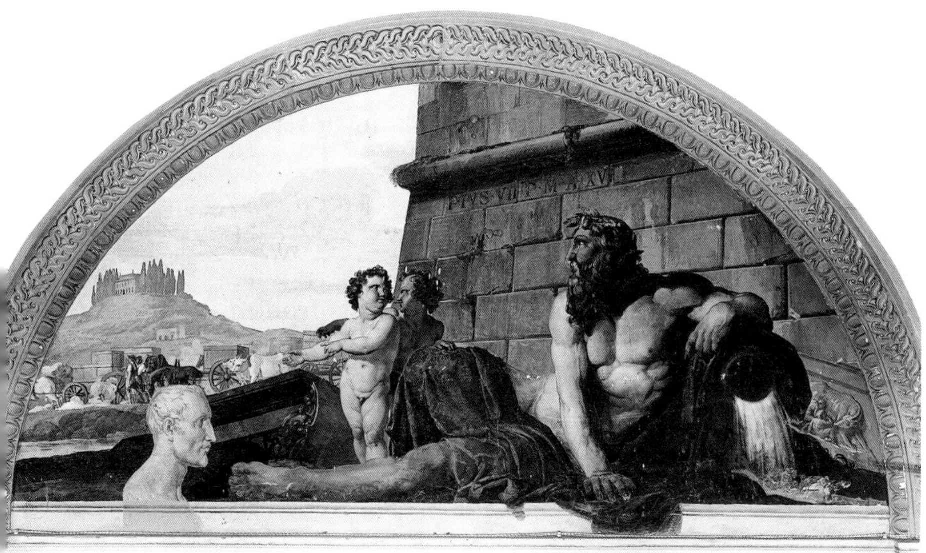

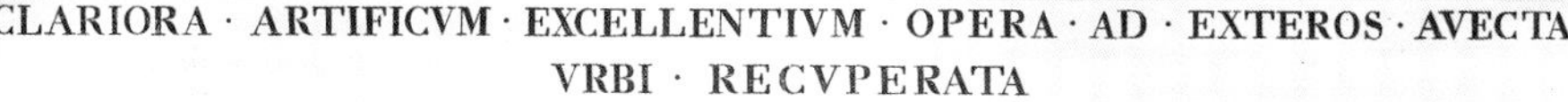

g. 2

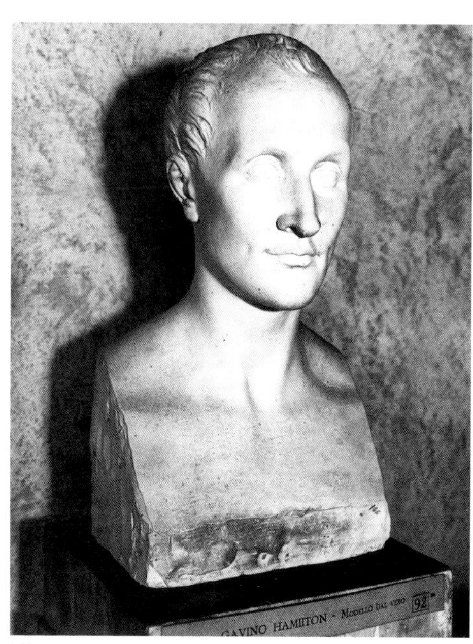

Fig. 3

It has been identified in the past as a portrait of the painter, archaeologist and dealer Gavin Hamilton (1723-98), Canova's first friend among the expatriate colony of Britons in Rome, and a link has been made between it and the plaster cast of a young man, now in the Gipsoteca at Possagno, also identified as Gavin Hamilton.[171] (Fig.3) While the plaster is of a very young man and the *trompe l'oeil* is clearly older and wiser, the likeness between the two is close, the same most distinctive mouth, cherubic or pursed with pronounced dimples in the corners under a long, Hamilton nose. Forty years later Baugniet's likeness of Hamilton [Cat. No.11] does not emphasise the mouth in this way, but another engraving after Thomas Phillips's portrait of William Richard Hamilton does (Fig.17). There is, however, one piece of contemporary documentary evidence associating the plaster and the *trompe l'oeil* with William Richard. His lifelong friend, confidant and studio manager Antonio d'Este, who had accompanied Canova to Paris and London, recorded 'la testa monocromatica ... e il ritratto del Cav. Guglielmo Hamilton.'[172] D'Este knew Hamilton well and was often remembered in the latter's letters to Canova.[173] It is incontrovertible that the singular honour of being included in the *Allegory of the Life of Pius* VII in the Pope's eponymous gallery, built and displayed under Canova's supervision, was given to the man most responsible for the return of its contents.[174]

Small presents passed back and forth between Canova and his friends in London. Canova sent a 'libro delle stampe' to the Longs very soon after leaving London, and Hamilton asked for 'una copia dei *Marmi di Phygelia* pubblicati di Wagner in Roma.'[175] These were reciprocated – Hamilton sent Canova a sculpting instrument made by Rossi by way of 'una piccola memorietta,'[176] and Long sent him a snuff box.[177] After Canova had been especially hospitable to Hamilton's sisters visiting Rome in 1817, Hamilton sent a service 'per l'ornamento della tavola.'[178] How nicely appropriate would have been Spode's blue and white transfer print of the 'Greek', 'Rome' or Italian' pattern. Larger exchanges included casts from the Elgin marbles which Hamilton wanted to present to Canova, who asked for the River Ilissus figure, while Canova was to send him a Colossal Head, a self portrait in plaster so that Hamilton could have 'un Canova in casa.'[179] In September 1816 Canova sent Hamilton a painting by Titian, said to be a portrait of Cardinal Cornaro.[180]

The grandest material expression of Canova's thanks to his friends in England was, however, his presentation of four *Ideal Heads* to the chief protagonists in the drama of what Hamilton described as 'il felice anno di 1815, che ha stabilito la pace di Europa, e restituito alla bella Italia i suoi capi d'opera.'[181] Canova's first letter to Hamilton suggesting this gift does not survive, but it is clear from the latter's reply that originally there were to be three heads, for the Prince Regent, Wellington and Castlereagh, and Canova's response confirms this: 'ai tre busti, ai quali vado pensando seriamente per eseguirli.'[182] There is no mention of Charles Long, and if Hamilton was to have one clearly it was to be a highly personal afterthought. A year later, Canova writing to Hamilton on 27th May[183] about the shipment of casts for the Prince Regent, added that the marble 'busti ideali' would go in the same shipment 'e quell' ancora destinato da me a voi' in testimony of Canova's affection and gratitude which he will never be able fully to recompense. In fact they took more than a year to reach London, and there are further references to their despatch in correspondence.[184] On the arrival of 'La bellissima Testa, che mi viene regalata da mio buon Amico, Antonio Canova,' Hamilton wrote to Canova: 'Mi fate troppo onore, e non so come rispondere a tanti e tanti atti di generosità ed amicizia.'[185] His enthusiasm and deep gratitude was repeated when writing again to Canova on 9th November[186] and in the following January: 'onore e buona fortuna di possedere una si bella prova della stima di Canova.'[187]

Canova's visit to London had some surprising and hitherto unassessed effects on the nascent British school of sculpture, and upon architectural designs for its display. Canova was himself a self-taught architect, the remarkable mausoleum at Possagno, inspired by the Roman Pantheon, being the consummation of this aspect of his genius. He had for many years been adviser to successive Popes on the housing and display of their collections of sculpture, antique and modern. It cannot be coincidence that three private galleries, and those in Smirke's new building for the British Museum, were undertaken in the years immediately following his visit. As we have seen, Jeffry Wyatt and Richard Westmacott were of the party that went to Woburn, and the following year the greenhouse-cum-orangery was altered by Wyatt to make a sculpture gallery. In 1816 Lord Lansdowne began the building of a sculpture

gallery at Lansdowne House under the supervision of Hamilton's friend Smirke.[188]
Passavant, who saw it little more than a decade after its completion described its
'princely splendour', and commented on the apsidal lighting which 'leaves the
centre in a fairy kind of half-light. The effect produced by this reflection is as novel
as it is charming.' The antique sculpture was arranged in niches within these apses,
'which, standing in the full blaze of light, and relieved by the drapery of the crimson
hangings behind them, have a most striking appearence.'[189]

On a lesser scale, William Richard Hamilton added a library, twenty feet by fifteen,
to Stanley Grove, his country house in Chelsea, completed in 1817.[190] Round the walls
run casts of the Parthenon frieze, and in addition there are three metopes of the
Battle of the Lapiths and the Centaurs probably taken by Haydon or Westmacott.
Hamilton sent Canova a drawing of the black marble chimneypiece,[191] showing one
of the metope casts flanked by a pair of obelisks given to Hamilton by the Pope (Fig.4).
The chimneypiece survives, but the obelisks have long since gone (Fig.5). It is conjec-
tural that Hamilton and Canova discussed what the former described as 'mio museo',

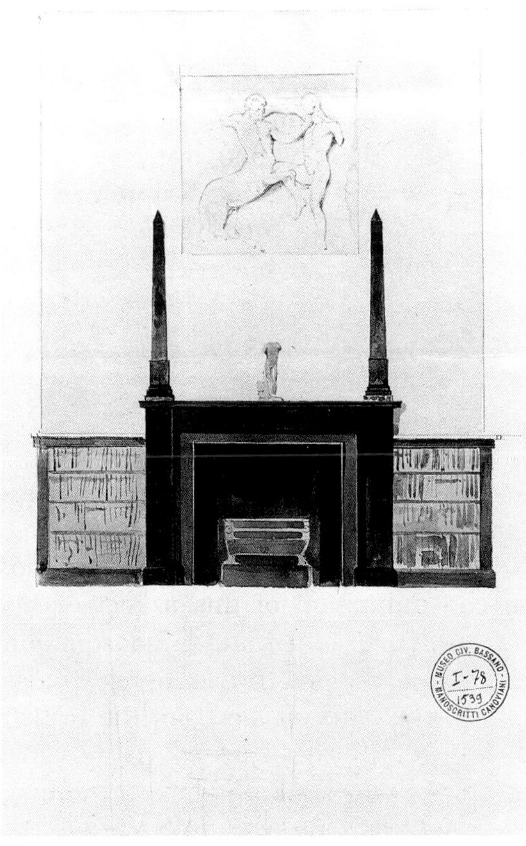

Fig. 4

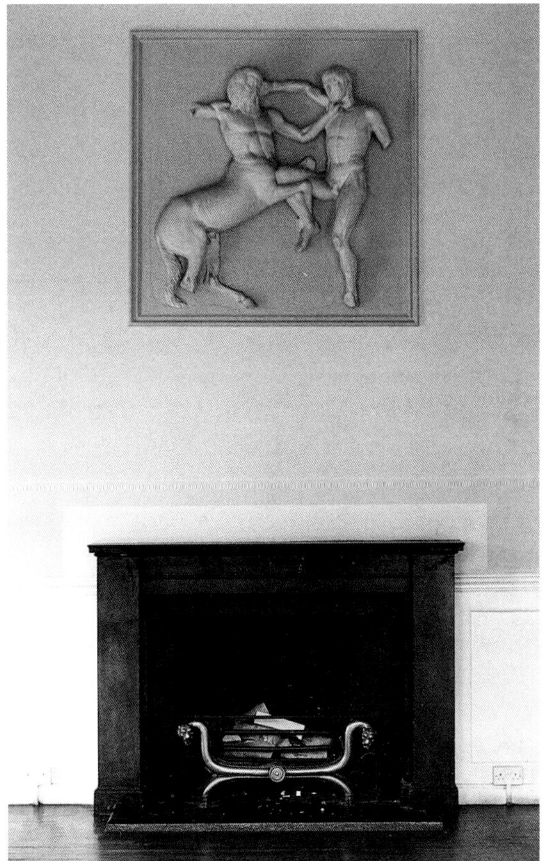

Fig. 5

but all the circumstantial evidence suggests they did, and the papal present must have been chosen with this scheme in mind. In this room Hamilton will have displayed the plaster cast of Canova's colossal self-portrait, and the *Ideal Head*.

Far from diminishing the status of British sculptors or reducing their employment, Canova's visit undoubtedly gave them a boost. Westmacott's eighteen feet high bronze *Achilles*, completed in June 1822 and dedicated to the Duke of Wellington by his fellow countrywomen, is an adaptation of the so-called *Horsetamers*, or *Alexander and Bucephalus* on the Quirinale, which both Canova and Flaxman considered to be the work of Phidias, and comparable to the Parthenon frieze.Flaxman's pupil, Edward Hodges Baily, who was a student at the Royal Academy Schools at the time of Canova's visit, took the Canovian precepts of truth to nature and ideal beauty a stage further. With works like *Eve at the Fountain* (Bristol City Museum and Art Gallery) and *Eve Listening to the Voice* (Victoria and Albert Museum, and Royal Academy), Baily was to develop the potential for poetic sensibility in sculpture allied to a technical virtuosity and attention to surface finish that were the hallmarks of Canova's style. It was an ideal of beauty that had far reaching effects, emerging in the work of both sculptors and painters as late as the American sculptor William Waldo Story's *The Fallen Angel* of 1887, and the painter Philip Burne-Jones in his *Pygmalion* and *Perseus* series as late as 1885 (Birmingham and Southampton City Art Galleries).

The legacy of the eighteenth century Grand Tour, in which Britons had acquainted themselves with the Antique and fallen in love with Italy, provided the intellectual sympathy and energy behind the support for Canova's cause, and the economic motivation to the restitution of such important tourist attractions as the sequestered works of art. The return of the treasures amounted to the last expression of the Grand Tour, for meanwhile the impact of the Elgin Marbles had contributed to a shift of focus in taste to Greece, where tourists now made a 'pelegrinaggio di Atene.'[192]

[1] L. Colley: *Britons: Forging the Nation 1707-1837*; London, 1992, pp.321.

[2] G. Rudé: *Revolutionary Europe 1783-1815*; 1964, p.285.

[3] Commisioned by the Duke of Wellington in 1816, Charles Long [*qv*] had a hand in the content and composition; C. M. Kauffmann: *Catalogue of the Paintings in the Wellington Museum*; London, 1982, no. 194. Studies for it are in the Print Room of the Ashmolean Museum.

[4] *Childe Harold*, canto III, stanzas xvii–xliii.

[5] B. E-1/5587.

[6] B. H-6/6089.

[7] Presented to the Canova Archive in the Museo, Archivio e Biblioteca di Bassano by Canova's brother the Abate Giovanni-Battista Sartori Canova in 1853, they amount to more than 80 groups of papers. They became the basis of the official report, written in the third person probably for Consalvi, the draft of which survives, annotated in Canova's hand. B. E-77/5663.

[8] B. E-2/5588.

9   P. Schroeder: *The Transformation of European Politics 1763-1848*; Oxford, 1996, pp.555-59.

10 Wellington to Castlereagh B. E 22/5608, later Paris 25 September 1815.

11 Bazin, p.186.

12 Canova to Consalvi, 24 Sept; B. E 26/5612.

13 *Childe Harold*, canto III, stanza xviii.

14 *Gentleman's Magazine*, vol. 85, no. 2 (1815) p.137.

15 Robertson, p.230.

16 *Ibid.*

17 E. Johnson: *Sir Walter Scott; The Great Unknown*; London, 1970, vol I, pp. 494-5. *Paul's Letters to his Kinsfolk* was published anonymously, Edinburgh, Jan 1816.

18 d'Este, p.199.

19 B. E 1/5587.

20 11 Aug 1815. reproduced in H. Honour (1994), pp.375-378.

21 B. E 20/5606; 25(bis)/5611; and 37/5623. Rue Basse du Remparts was just to the north of the Champs Elysées, running north from the Madeleine. It has since been incorporated into the Rue des Cappucines.

22 Canova to Consalvi, 29 August 1815. B. E 3/5589.

23 *Ibid.*

24 *Ibid.*

25 As Minister at Naples in 1822 he sent £100 to the nascent organisation in Rome. Joseph Severn to Thomas Lawrence; Lawrence Correspondence, Law/4/69. Royal Academy Archive.

26 'Il secondo giorno'; the relevant passage in both Canova's own account and the rough draft of the official report are heavily scored at this point in the narrative; B. H 6/6089 and 77/5663.

27 B. E 59/5645 and 74/5660.

28 *Farington Diaries*, 21st Nov 1815.

29 B. E 10/5596 and 22/5608.

30 1 Sept; B. E 6/5592. This was later privately printed in England (National Art Library, V&A Museum, 34 B 189); and in Milan in an Italian translation in 1816 under the title *Riflessioni sul Restituirsi dalla Francia I Monumenti delle Arti* ... B. E 33[?illeg]/5671[?].

31 No date; B. E 23/5609. As must the copy of a letter from G. A. Fagel, Minister to the King of the Netherlands to the Council of Ministers making a claim for the Cities, Churches and Communities of the 'Provinces Meridionales' and for the Stadtholder [2 Sept; B. E7/5593] and later Nesselrode's memorandum to the Council of Ministers which set out the Russian reasons for abiding by the Treaty of Paris of May 1814 [no date (Sept)] B. E 24/5610.

32 B. E 79/8665; B. E 87/5673-92/5678; B. E 78/5664 and bis.

33 B. E 78/5664 bis annotated: 'Cette protestation n'à été pas accepté, ni présenté.' See also B. E 9/5595 and 10/5596.

34 B. E 5/5591; 86/5762; 87/5673-92/5678.

35 Canova to Consalvi, 12 Sept; B. E 11/5597.

36 11 Sept. B. E 9/5595.

37 B. E 6/5592.

38 11 Sept; B. E 8/5594.

39 12 Sept; B. E 11/5597.

40 Sept, B. E 10/5596.

41 *Courier*, 5 Dec 1815; *Annual Register* 1815, p.601-4.

42 Robertson, p.241.

43 Canova to Consalvi, 11 Sept; B. E-8/5594.

44 B. E. 10/5596.

45 B. E 95/5681.

46 Robertson, p.270-71.

47 B. E 13/5599.

48 B. E 14/5600 and 14bis/5600.

49 Possibly 16th or 17th Sept, suggestive of procrastination; B. E 15/5601 and 15bis/5601.

50 B. E 27/5613 and 28/5614. The rough draft is written in one column in Italian in Canova's hand and beside it in another hand in French.

51 28 Sept; B. E 19/5605,18/5604 and 29/5615

52 14 Sept; B. E 12/5598, claiming the work of the 'immortal Pietro Perugino.'

53 From Consalvi on behalf of the Bolognese Museum of Antiquities, B. E 17/5603 and 25/5611.

54 21 Sept; B. E 21/5607.

55 19 Sept; B. E 20/5606.

56 25 Sept, B. E 22/5608.

57 *Journal des Debâts: Politiques et Litteraires*, 13 Oct, where it filled the front page; B. 96/568a; *The Courier*, 5 Dec 1815; *The Gentlemen's Magazine*, Vol 85, no. 2 (1815), pp.620-22.

58 B. E 22/5608.

59 24 Sept; B. E 25bis/5611.

60 Walter Scott: *Paul's Letters to his Kinsfolk*; Edinburgh, 1816, p.329.

61 Robertson, pp.242-65.

62 *Ibid*, p.242.

63 *Ibid*, p.244.

64 B. E 26/5612.

65 Robertson, p.251.

66 *Ibid*, p.255.

67 B. E 41/5227.

68 B. E 31/5617.

69 Robertson, p.265.

70 1 and 3 Oct; B. E 32/5618 and 33/5619; B. 34/5620.

71 List; B. E 34bis/5620.

72 3 Oct; B. E 35/5621; 37/5623 and 41/5227.

73 Consalvi to Canova, 26 Oct; B. E 56/5642. Heidelberg's success is communicated in detail in the *Gentleman's Magazine*, vol. 85, no. 2 (1815), p.614.

74 Robertson, p.260.

75 Canova to Lavallée, Dir. Gen. of the Musée Royal, Oct 22, B. E 53/5639; Canova to and from Consalvi 25 Oct, B. E 55/5641; 6 Nov, B. E 62/5648; 9 Nov, B. E 64/5650; 15 Nov, B. E 71/5657; Canova to Pradel, 29 Oct, B. E 61/5647.

76 B. E 50/5636

77 Bazin, p. 180.

78 3 Oct; B. E 36/5622. The saved envelope and its formal direction 'A Monsieur/Monsieur le Chevalier Canova/Commissaire de la Cour de Rome/à Paris' is indicative.

79 Nos. 282 and 291. B. E 95/5681.

80 The first piece concluded: 'La France doît trouver la protection de sa juste et véritable gloire dans le principe de l'égalité des nations européenes.' (B. E 95/5681) and the second

(no inventory number) referred its readers to the polemic written in 1797. It was attributed to M. Quatremére de Quincy, and heavily scored in the margin by Canova: 'Lettre sur la préjudice qu'occasionnerait aux arts et à la science le déplacement des monuments de l'art de l'Italie, le démembrement de ses Ecoles et la spoliation de ses collections, galeries et musées.'

81 B. E 26/5612.

82 6 Oct; B. E 39/5625.

83 7 Oct; B. E 40/5626.

84 H. Honour and A. Weston-Lewis (eds.), *The Three Graces - Antonio Canova*, National Galleries of Scotland, 1996. [Hereafter cited as *The Three Graces*] Appendix 10, p.103.

85 Robertson, p.261.

86 Q. de Quincy, *Canova et ses Ouvrages*, p.283.

87 Canova to Consalvi, 8 Oct; B. E 50/5636.

88 B. E 26/5612.

89 B. E 41/5227.

90 Canova to Consalvi, 28 Oct B. E 59/5645.

91 Canova's first responses to the marbles in Rome are described by WRH in *Memorandum on the subject of the Earl of Elgin's Pursuits in Greece*, London, 1815 (2nd ed.), p.39 ff. *The Times*, 31 Oct, gave sight of the Elgin Marbles as Canova's principal reason for coming to London.

92 *Farington's Diary*, 21st Nov 1815.

93 Canova had spent, on Hamilton's word, most of the 100,000 *franchi* contributed by the British government on packing, casing and ensuring the security of the first convoy as far as Bologna. Canova to Consalvi, 8 and 28 Oct, B. E 50/5636 and 59/5645.

94 *The Courier* 5 Dec: 'Two of the most celebrated *FRENCH MILLINERS* and *DRESS INVEN-TRESSES* . . . positively the most unique things ever introduced into this country.'

95 B. E 52/5638.

96 Canova to Consalvi, 10 Oct; B. E 42/5628.

97 R. Reinagle to Dawson Turner, 23 Nov 1815; Dawson Turner Papers, Trinity College, Cambridge.

98 Thomas Phillips to Dawson Turner, 10 Nov 1815; Dawson Turner Papers, Trinity College, Cambridge.

99 Ellis Cornelia Knight to Canova, 18 Oct; B. E 49/5635.

100 Robertson, p.231 and passim.

101 Robertson to John Ewen, 6 Nov; Robertson, pp.278-9.

102 T. Clifford, 'Canova in Context,' in *The Three Graces*, p.9.

103 Thomas Phillips letter *cit*. In a letter to Quatremère de Quincy dated 13 Nov 1815 Canova said he had been in London ten days 'in continuo movimento'; Q. de Quincy, p.392.

104 B. E 52/5638.

105 Bazin, p.186.

106 B. 2113; *The Three Graces*, Appendix 5, p.101.

107 Bacon notebook; private collection. Quoted T. Clifford in *The Three Graces*, p.14.

108 Whinney, pls 164b and 162b.

109 *Ibid*, pls 140 and 142.

110 Irwin (1979), p.65.

111 Whinney., pl.158.

112 *Ibid*, pl.163a.

113 Clifford, *op. cit.*, fig. 10, p.14.

114 B. E 63/5649.

115 B. H 4/6082. Transcribed in Honour (1994), pp.389-90.

116 Royal Society Journal Book, 1812-20.

117 'Canova' by Sir Humphry Davy. Transcribed from Davy notebook 14e, p.53, Royal Institution, London.

118 B. E 66/5652.

119 B. H 4/6082.

120 B. E 67/5653.

121 12 Nov; *The Three Graces*, Appendix 6, p.101.

122 B. E 68/5654.

123 Gunnis; C. Wainwright in *London - World City*, 1800-40; ex. cat, [ed C. Fox]; Essen, 1992 p.115-7.

124 Watkin, p.239 and n131.

125 *Ibid*, p.9.

126 Passavant, vol I, p.224.

127 B. H 4.6082. Honour (1994), p. 390. Now Lady Lever Art Gallery, Port Sunlight.

128 14 Nov; B. E 69/5653.

129 Cleveland Museum of Art, Ohio.

130 H. Honour, (1994), p.394.

131 E. H 4/6082,

132 Designed by Henry Howard (1745-1806) as a greenhouse, the addition of a Temple of Liberty to house busts of the Whig radical Charles James Fox and six friends and associates recalls Lord Cobham's political buildings of the 1730s at Stowe, Bucks.

133 J. Kenworthy-Browne: 'The Sculpture Gallery'; *The Three Graces*, p.65.

134 B 2144; quoted in full *ibid*, Appendix 7, p.102.

135 *Farington's Diary*, 21 Nov 1815.

136 H.M. the Queen; Victoria and Albert Museum.

137 Sir Anthony Carlisle (1768-1840), Professor of Anatomy at the Royal Academy.

138 R. Reinagle to Dawson Turner, 2 Dec 1815. Dawson Turner Papers, Trinity College, Cambridge.

139 Haydon, Vol I, p.484.

140 *Farington's Diary*, 1 Dec 1815; Minutes of the Royal Academy Council, Vol 5, 28 Nov 1815.

141 See P. Funnell: 'The London Art World and its Institutions;' *London – World City 1800-1840*; p.155-166.

142 Robertson, pp.274-6.

143 Haydon, Vol I, p.481.

144 *Ibid*, p.485.

145 Copy in Trinity College Library, Cambridge, among the Dawson Turner Papers; uncatalogued.

146 *The Three Graces*; fig. 10.

147 Fitzwilliam Museum, Cambridge. Gauci to Dawson Turner, 26.1.1835; Dawson Turner Papers, Trinity College, Cambridge. Irwin (1979), Fig. 259. A rather poor likeness drawn and etched by T. Perletti was published by B. N., 201 Piccadilly, on 20th Nov 1815 under the heading ANTH' CANVVA. National Portrait Gallery Archive.

148 R. Reinagle to Dawson Turner, 2 Dec 1815. Dawson Turner Papers, Trinity College, Cambridge.

149 Richard Cook to Dawson Turner, 22 Dec 1815. *Loc. cit.*

150 *Diario di Roma*, 6 Jan 1816; B. E 97/5683; The note of hand was for £500. T. Clifford, 'Canova in Context,' *The Three Graces*, p.14.

151 'una scatola'; WRH to Canova, 5 Dec 1815; B. I 78/1506.

152 WRH to Canova 22 Dec 1815; B. I 78/1507.

153 25 Sept, misdated 23 Sept. B. E 94/5680.

154 B. E 97/5683.

155 B. I 78/1505.

156 *The Three Graces*, Fig.11.

157 *Farington's Diary*, 9th August 1815.

158 WRH to Canova, 18 Oct 1816; B. I 78/1514; 6 Jan 1817, B. I 78/1517; 1 May 1817, B. I 78/1519.

159 23 Oct 1818; B. 4-XCVI-3/1164.

160 Royal Academy Council Minutes, 14 Dec 1815.

161 K. Eustace in *Thomas Howard Earl of Arundel*; Oxford, 1985, p.66.

162 30 Dec 1816, B. 4 XCVI-2/1153; 9 Sept 1817[?], B. 4-XCII-23/1184.

163 B. I 78/1508bis; B. 78/1509.

164 Long to Canova, 23 Oct 1818, B. 4-XCVI-3/1164; WHR to Canova 26 Nov 1819, B. I-78/1534; Elizabeth Duchess of Devonshire to Lawrence 20 April 1820, Law 3/111, Royal Academy.

165 Num. 38; B. E 98/5684.

166 Angeloni to Canova, 27 Feb 1816; B. E-74/5660.

167 B. E-76/5662.

168 B. I-78/1513.

169 WRH to Canova 4 May 1816, B. I-78/1509. Later that year Hamilton was made an honorary member of the Roman Academy of Archaeology – WRH to Canova, 9 Sept 1816; and Canova to WRH 23 Sept 1816; Private Collection.

170 Castellaneta, no. 25D. W. R. Hamilton is identified in U. Hiesinger, pp. 655-665. I am grateful to Paolo Liverani for arranging scaffolding from which I could view the lunette.

171 Pavanello, no. 55. E. Bassi suggested a date of 1797, the year before Gavin Hamilton died, but doubted Canova's authorship. E. Bassi (1957), p.112, No. 92.

172 d'Este, p.254.

173 WRH to Canova 22 Dec 1815, B. I-78/1507; WRH to Canova, 26 Nov 1819, B. I-78/1534.

174 I am grateful to Hugh Honour for sharing his views on this matter with me.

175 B. I-78/1517.

176 WRH to Canova 26 March 1816, B. I-78/1508bis.

177 23 July 1819, B. 4-XCII-13.1164.

178 WRH to Canova, 10 Feb 1817; B. I-78/1518.

179 Canova to WRH 7 June 1816; Private Collection. WRH to Canova 8 April ; B. I-78/1508 & 4 May 1816, B. I-78/1509.

180 d'Este, p. 245. Dr Granville was also given an untraced Titian. Canova to WRH 4 Sept 1816, Private Collection; and B. I-78/1513.

181 WRH to Canova, 4 May 1816; B. I-78/1509.

182 Canova to WRH, 7 June 1816; Private Collection.

183 Private Collection.

184 Canova to WRH 6 & 22 Nov (?) 1817; 16 Feb 1818; Private Collection.

185 13 Sept 1818, B. I-78/1527.

186 B. I-78/1528.

187 25 Jan 1819, B. I-78/1529.
188 Stillman, Fig.15.
189 Passavant, p.196.
190 WRH to Canova; B. I-78/1517. It survives in very good order, having been, until recently, part of King's College, London. At the time of writing it is empty and for sale.
191 B. I-78/1539.
192 Letter of introduction for a Mr Sotheby, WRH to Canova, 12 May 1816; B. I-78/1510.

Ideal Beauty

James Fenton

Zeuxis, Pliny tells us, was so scrupulously careful over one commission for the city of Girgenti that 'he held an inspection of the maidens of the place paraded naked and chose five, for the purpose of reproducing in the picture the most admirable points in the form of each.'[1] Ideal beauty, the story tells us, is a synthesis, an amalgam of the best bits of the most beautiful people. But the selection of the best bits would require, of course, a connoisseur.

Raphael, in his famous letter to Castiglione, says that in order to paint a beautiful woman he would have to see many beautiful women, 'with this condition, that your Grace assists in selecting the best. But being deprived of good judges and of beautiful women I make do with a certain idea (*certa idea*) which comes to my head. Whether this has in it some artistic excellence I know not; I certainly toil to acquire it.'[2] The method of Zeuxis, the parade of the best, is relegated to the realm of courtly compliment. Raphael's method is to consult the internal representation, the *idea* of beauty contained within himself.

Later theorists believed that this method of operation mirrored that of God himself: 'That high and eternal intellect, the creator of nature, in making his marvellous works by reflecting deeply within himself, established the first forms called "ideas" so that each species was derived from that first "idea", and so was formed the admirable web of created things.' For man, for the artist, the way to form the idea was to contemplate nature itself: 'The noble painters and sculptors, imitating that first creator, form in their minds also an example of superior beauty and, reflecting on it, improve upon nature until it is without fault of colour or of line. This "idea", or we might say goddess of painting and sculpture ... unveils herself to us, and descends upon the marbles and canvases. Originating from nature, she rises upon her origin and becomes in herself the original of art; measured by the compass of the intellect, she becomes the measure of the hand; and animated by the imagination, she gives life to the image.'[3]

The author of these lines, Giovanni Pietro Bellori, was so convinced that art involved improving on nature that he argued that the Trojan War must have been precipitated not by an imperfect woman, but by a representation – not by Helen, but by a plundered statue of Helen.

And Winckelmann, who suspected that the bodies of the ancient Greeks were probably more beautiful than those of his contemporaries – 'framed with more unity of system, a nobler harmony of parts, and a completeness of the whole, above our lean tensions and hollow wrinkles' – nevertheless thought that, from having so much occasion to observe the nude, the Greeks began 'to form certain general ideas of beauty, with regard to the proportions of the inferior parts, as well as of the whole frame: these they raised above the reach of mortality, according to the superior model of some ideal nature.'[4]

In what reads like an attack on Bernini, Winckelmann says that 'in most of the modern figures, if the skin happens to be any where pressed, you see there several little smart wrinkles: when, on the contrary, the same parts, pressed in the same manner on Greek statues, by their soft undulations, form at last but one noble pressure. These masterpieces never show us the skin forcibly stretched, but softly embracing the firm flesh, which fills it up without any tumid expansion, and harmoniously follows its directions ... Modern works are likewise distinguished from the ancient by parts; a crowd of small touches and dimples too sensibly drawn. In ancient works you find these distributed with sparing sagacity ...'[5].

For Winckelmann, art could take one of two routes: the imitation of the single object in all its individuality (and that route led straight to Dutch painting, which he considered a kind of copying) or the route the Greeks chose, leading to 'general beauty and its ideal images'. It is, of course, in the latter spirit that these *Ideal Heads* by Canova were produced.

When, during the nineteenth century, the prestige of the neo-classical aesthetic collapsed, and Canova went into a long eclipse, it became impossible, for a while, to share and appreciate that conception of ideal beauty which had once held Europe and America in its grip. And even as late as Kenneth Clark's *The Nude* (1956) we find a hysterical diatribe against Canova's *Perseus*, in the course of which, however, Clark concedes that the sculptor was a 'brilliant portraitist' – he is allowed, in other words, to imitate the individual object, but not to propose the general thesis about beauty.

And many of us will remember the same kind of allergic reaction among our parents or our teachers or the guides, whoever they were, who first hurried us past some 'hideous' neo-classical monument on our way to some good, nutritive, wholesome Gothic or renaissance fresco or fragment – fragments which sometimes came in the shape of the neo-classical wall monument that had preserved their integrity over the years.

But taste is always on the move, and in time the objects we were hurried past began to lose their supposed power to harm us. We can view these *Ideal Heads*, not as something we have to rebel against (any more than we have to rebel against the byzantine or baroque aesthetic) but as cool proposals of geometry, contour, tone. We are the grandchildren of abstraction, and in our imaginary museum we are more than happy to juxtapose Brancusi, Arp, these *Heads* ... We understand the story of Zeuxis as a parable for abstraction, and we understand the 'ideal', once again, not as some proposed goal that we are being told to follow, but more like that *certa idea* which the artist must grasp and follow, instinctively and without any comforting assurance (however much the popes applaud, or the crowned heads of Europe queue up with their commissions) whether it has any excellence or not.

1 Pliny *Natural History*, Book xxxv, 1964 ed. Loeb.
2 R. Jones and N. Penny, *Raphael*, New Haven and London, 1983, p.97.
3 Cited in *Winckelmann Writings on Art*, selected and edited by D. Irwin, London, 1972, p.35.
4 *Ibid*, 'On the Imitation of the Painting and Sculpture of the Greeks', 1755, p.65.
5 *Ibid*, p.66.

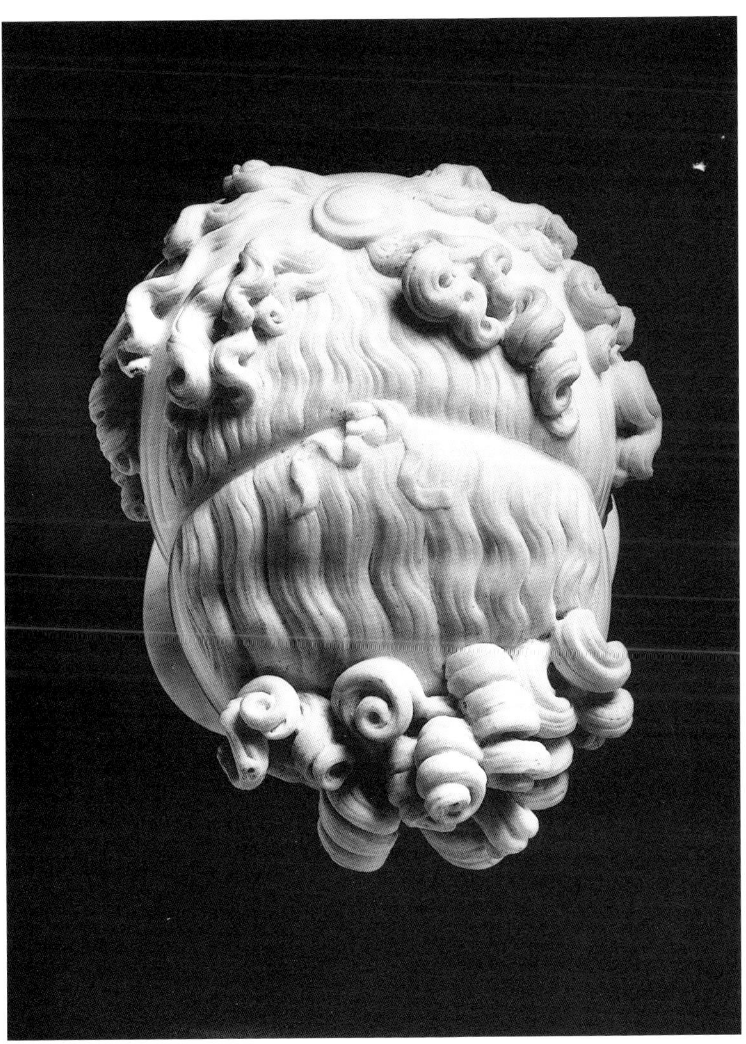

Cat. No.1

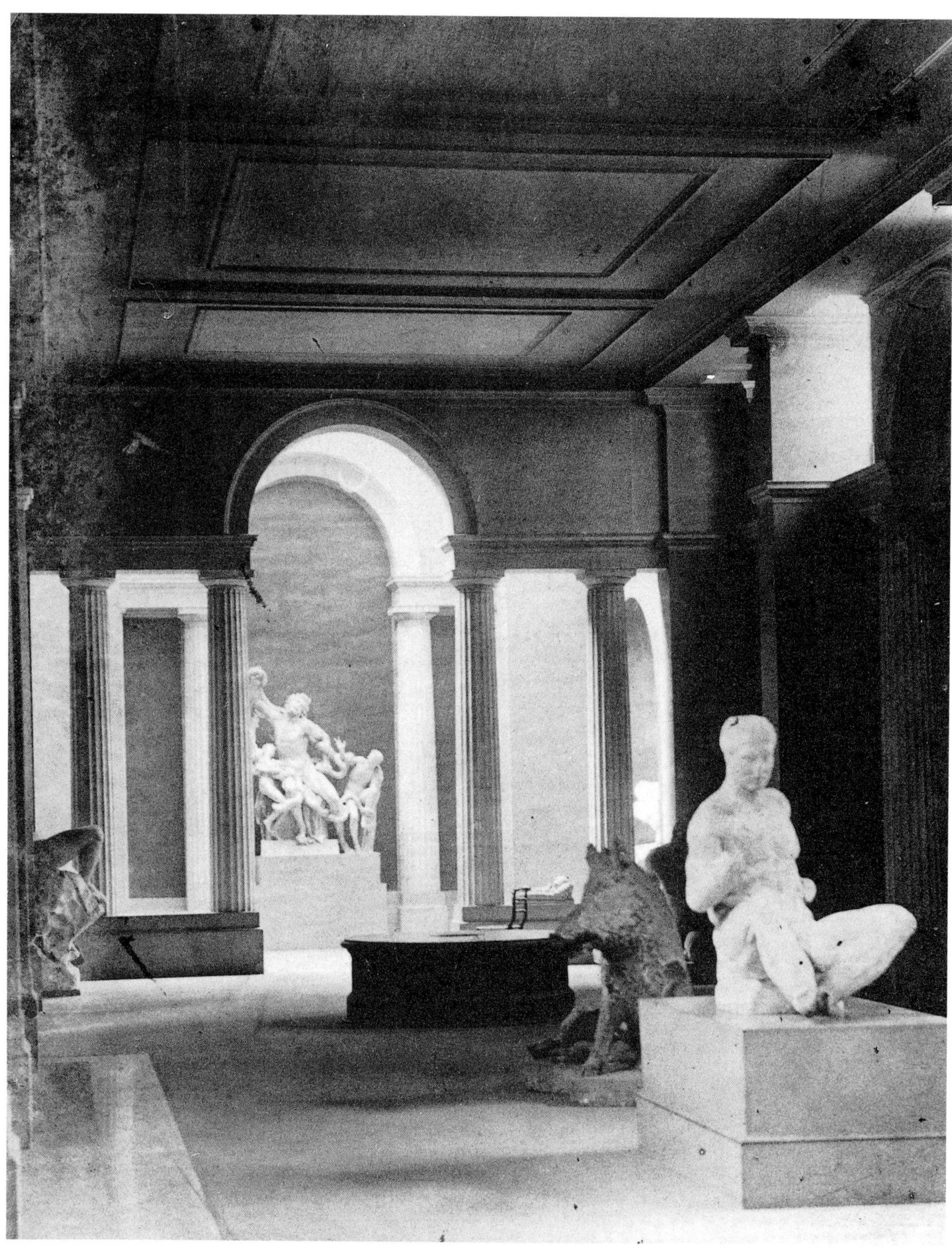

Fig. 6

Chantrey and Cockerell:

The Ashmolean Museum's Early Collection of Casts from the Antique

Donna Kurtz

The acquisition of the *Ideal Head* provides an opportunity to draw attention to the close relationship which has existed between 'modern' sculptors and antique sculpture since the Renaissance, to the importance of plaster casts for the study of sculpture, and to the early development of the Museum's collection of plaster casts from the antique.

Knowledge of antique sculpture in three-dimensional form was gained in the Renaissance, as it is now, from 'originals', themselves often Roman copies of Greek marbles or bronzes, or from exact copies made from moulds and cast in a variety of materials, most often plaster or *gesso*. From the time of the Renaissance casts from the antique were used in art schools and sculptors collected casts, from the antique as well as of their own work. Canova and his English contemporary Francis Chantrey had large collections. After Canova's death casts from his sculpture were placed in the Gipsoteca Canoviana in Possagno which opened in 1836. The following year the Danish Neoclassical sculptor, Bertel Thorvaldsen, who had been in Rome during the 1830s, gave his collection of casts and a considerable part of his personal fortune to the city of Copenhagen for the Thorvaldsens Museum which opened in 1848. These examples probably encouraged Lady Chantrey to offer her husband's collection of casts to the University of Oxford shortly after his death in 1841. Her insistence on a permanent display in the University Galleries, and her detailed knowledge of the exhibition space under construction in Oxford between 1840 and 1845 to a design by Charles Cockerell, suggest that she envisaged a similar memorial for her husband and that she had the support of Cockerell himself.

Chantrey and Cockerell provided some of the earliest casts from the antique preserved in the Museum today. Chantrey's were displayed in the Randolph Gallery; they included traditional favourites, such as the *Torso Belvedere*, and pedimental sculpture from the Parthenon. His busts from the antique were set on pilasters in the Great Niche (destroyed) which Cockerell designed as a special display area for ancient sculpture opposite the porticoed entrance. Following a fashion already well established for the interior decoration of museums, Cockerell chose casts of friezes from the Parthenon and from the Temple of Apollo at Bassae for the walls of the West Gallery and Great Stairs. These architectural casts and a number of Chantrey's, were acquired in London. Although moulds had been taken and casts of the friezes had been available almost from the time of the marbles' arrival in London formal arrangements for supplying casts in quantity were not made until the 1830s.

When the Napoleonic Wars ended, Canova was chosen to supervise the restitution of art looted from Italy; roughly eighty percent was antique sculpture, an indication of the high regard for classical antiquities in the age of the Grand Tour. Canova had worked with scholars, archaeologists, and antiquarian sculptors in Rome to perfect his style. Considered the Phidias of his time, he was asked to carve a substitute for the *Venus de' Medici* when it was removed from display in the Uffizi to avoid capture by the French, and when the *Apollo Belvedere* was taken from the Vatican it was his *Perseus and Medusa* which was placed on the empty pedestal. Canova's avowed aim was to emulate the antique rather than copy it slavishly. The fame he continues to enjoy testifies to the success of his vision of the antique.

When Canova came to London in 1815 he saw original Greek sculpture from the fifth century BC and his perception of the antique ideal was transformed. He preferred the clarity and simplicity of Phidias' sculpture for the Parthenon, which Lord Elgin had brought from Athens less than a decade earlier, to the traditional favourites praised by Winckelmann, such as the *Torso Belvedere* and *Laocoon*. In 1816, when a Select Committee was set up to consider the purchase of the Elgin Marbles for the Nation, the members of the Committee in favour of the purchase welcomed his support. Canova was instrumental in arranging the Pope's gift to the Prince Regent of twenty-nine casts from the most famous antique pieces in the Vatican Museums.

The Grand Tour had been halted by Napoleon's invasion of the Kingdoms of Italy in 1798. When hostilities ceased and the British could again travel to Italy some had a new ideal of classical beauty formed by personal knowledge of the Elgin Marbles which had been in Lord Elgin's house in Park Lane from 1806. When Canova came to London in 1815 he saw the Parthenon sculpture; when Chantrey went to Paris in the same year he saw antique sculpture in the Musée Napoléon before its restitution. Unable to embark on a Grand Tour in the traditional manner, Cockerell left London in 1807 for Greece and the eastern Mediterranean where he participated in major archaeological excavations and studied many of the most famous ancient monuments of the fifth and fourth centuries BC. As soon as peace was declared he sailed for Rome, to see the traditional antique favourites praised by the Grand Tourists. The new antique style, represented principally by the sculpture from the Parthenon, and the old, by traditional favourites such as the *Torso Belvedere*, helped to enhance the importance of contemporary sculpture of which Canova was the acknowledged master. Chantrey, whose own style was less overtly Neo-Classical, also held Canova in the highest esteem. The only fault he said he could find in Canova's *Endymion* was that it was modern not ancient.

In Oxford in 1815 the appreciation of classical art can be said to have been modest. Sir Roger Newdigate, who had been Member of Parliament for the University from 1750 to 1780, had tried to enlighten the University, helping it to acquire the Pomfret Statues and giving it two antique marble candelabra composed by Piranesi of pieces found in the excavations of Hadrian's Villa at Tivoli. Shortly before his death in 1806 Newdigate had offered to transform the Radcliffe Camera into a Temple of the Arts for the Arundel Marbles and Pomfret Statues to a design by John Flaxman, but his offer was rejected. The candelabra remained in the Library for more than a century until they were transferred to the Museum's Randolph Gallery. The cast of the Wild Boar, which Newdigate brought back on his second Grand Tour in the 1770s, is the oldest surviving cast in the Museum, taking the origins of the collection back to the second half of the eighteenth century.

Chantrey is said to have purchased his first plaster casts from the antique in Paris in 1815. When he arrived in Rome he acquired more casts from the antique, some with the assistance of Canova. In London he also acquired casts, from the Parthenon and from sculpture in the British Museum which had been found near Rome towards the end of the eighteenth century. Chantrey's collection, which would be displayed in his studio in London in a special antechamber designed by Sir John Soane in 1830, combined the old and new styles of antique sculpture. For that reason it was especially useful to artists of the Drawing Schools which came to be established in the Museum from the 1860s.

When Chantrey died in 1841 his body was laid out in the cast antechamber, surrounded by the masterpieces of classical sculpture. Another indication of the importance which he and his contemporaries attached to casts from the antique is revealed by the terms of Lady Chantrey's offer to the University. She proposed to give the casts from the antique only if those of her husband's own work were accepted on conditions which she laid down in some detail.

When the University Galleries opened in 1845 the ground floor had Chantrey's casts from his own work in the West Gallery and his casts from the antique in the Long (Randolph) Gallery and Great Niche. Additional casts of his own portrait busts were displayed on the first floor in the Great Gallery. On the ground floor only a few ancient marbles from the Pomfret Benefaction were displayed, despite the fact that Randolph's Benefaction, which enabled the University Galleries to be built, had been intended specifically for them. The mixing of ancient and modern sculpture, marble and plaster casts, was typical of the period although not to everyone's taste. As early as 1846 an Oxonian produced a flysheet denouncing the exhibits in the University Galleries with the statement that a single specimen of modern sculpture was sufficient in such a museum. Undeterred by such criticism, Sir Richard Westmacott offered the University Galleries a selection of casts of his own work in 1851.

During the second half of the nineteenth century the modern casts fell from favour and were eased out of the galleries. Casts from the antique, on the other hand, found favour first with the Drawing Schools from the late 1860s, and later with archaeologists, but their number was not increased. Until 1884 the Museum's casts from the antique were Chantrey's and Cockerell's. Newdigate's Wild Boar was still in Queen's College, whose Boars' Head Festival had attracted the original benefaction. With the creation of the Professorship of Classical Archaeology in the 1880s antique casts assumed great importance, following a practice already established on the continent of creating cast collections as an apparatus of classical scholarship. Initially a subscription was raised to purchase them, then the University made annual grants. Large numbers were acquired before 1913 and displayed in chronological order in six rooms in the centre of the Museum (Fig.6). They remained in these rooms until a Department of Eastern Art was created in the late 1950s and installed in their place. At that time a gallery was built to the north of the Museum specifically for the casts, but not to the full size of the architect's original plan. It is hoped that the University's intention to build a new Cast Gallery, to a design by Robert Adam, will provide adequate space for students, artists and the public to study Classical Art in facsimile. It is also hoped that the new gallery will enable the reception of the Classical Tradition by other arts and periods to be appreciated more fully, especially through collaborative special exhibitions – such as this one in honour of Canova.

Adapted from *Casts from the Antique: An Oxford Collection* (in preparation)
Principal sources: N. Penny, 'Chantrey, Westmacott and casts after the Antique', *Journal of the History of Collections* 3 (1991) 255-264; *Catalogue of European Sculpture in the Ashmolean Museum, 1540 to the Present Day*, Oxford, 1992; Penny and Haskell, *Taste and the Antique* New Haven and London, 1981.

'Just a tiny bit of rouge upon the lips and cheeks':
Canova, Colour, and the Classical Ideal.

Mark Norman and Richard Cook

After Canova's death in 1822 a number of biographies were written by friends and admirers of Canova that paid tribute to his life and work.[1] These sought to review Canova's life, and, in some cases included a catalogue raisonnée of his work and contemporary remarks about particularly well known pieces that had achieved fame, or indeed some notoriety, when first exhibited. Of these biographies, some were based upon first hand recollections of the sculptor whilst others seem more likely to have been based upon anecdotal accounts. This latter category also drew upon, or merely reproduced, essays that are common to more than one author – for example the memoir by Cicognara that occurs in the engraved catalogue of his work published by Henry Moses in London in 1824.[2] One of the last accounts to include first hand memories of working with Canova was written by Antonio d'Este, his studio assistant of many years standing, published in 1864.[3] Canova himself signalled his intention to write about his work in a letter to Cicognara in October 1812, and this is quoted in the latter's own biography of the sculptor published in 1823[4], Moses and Memes *Memoir* published in Edinburgh in 1825.[5] As quoted by Memes, Canova wrote

> '. . . I have not composed a single line on the subject of my art: I have indeed always intended to do so, but the time for carrying forward my resolution has never arrived . . . I am determined . . . to give observations on my own works . . . I could never be so vain as to think of composing a treatise. I shall confine myself solely to the principles of my own labours, nothing more',

This autobiography might have addressed many of the practical points currently under discussion but it was never even begun and, even if it had been written, it might not have included the detail of his working practices that are so fascinating to students of sculptural technique.

Common to all these works are descriptions of Canova's working practices but in every case they are tantalisingly imprecise – possibly because they were written, in the main, by people without practical skill. However, even those authors, like Antonio d'Este, who had first hand knowledge of Canova's studio, felt it unnecessary to enter into any great degree of detail. Similarly, pupils and contemporaries of Canova like Flaxman, Westmacott, and Gibson did not consider it appropriate to mention any but the most general of techniques in any of their writings - presumably in the belief that such practical detail was of no interest to their readers and therefore not worthy of inclusion. There is also the fact that, like many practical people, they might have found any description of what they saw as basic sculptural technique simply unnecessary. Renowned as Canova was for the surface finish of his sculptures as much as for their composition, his posthumous biographers are all adamant that the skills that he employed resided solely in his ability to carve and finish his work using purely mechanical processes. Memes[6] writes

> 'This exquisite purity of surface and of contour have given rise to the idea that this splendour and softness of polish were not produced by the legitimate operations of sculpture, but by some secret wishes or preparations. That such processes were employed by the Greek sculptors is by no means a singular belief; and in the search of these he [Canova] even instituted experiments the results of which were either fruitless or disregarded. It is certain, therefore, that his statues owe their unrivalled softness wholly to the use of the chisel and the file applied by his own hand'

He goes on, however, to concede that

> 'When they had thus received their last finish, they were indeed washed in a mixture of water and pumice stone or emery reduced to a very fine powder, which, by its different action or adhesion on surfaces variously polished, was supposed to anticipate the effects of time, diffusing over the crude brightness of recent labour an agreeable and harmonious coating'

and in Cicognara's brief account of his life in Moses'[7] book he refers to Canova's use of nothing more than *acqua di rota* in the finishing of his work to dull a freshly worked surface. He wrote

> 'The opponents of Canova have also charged him with not having confined himself to the use of the chisel in his marbles, and with having had recourse to factitious means of giving to them an extreme softness and delicacy; which, if it had been the case, would only have been following, in modern times, the example of Nicias, who produced these effects by his washes on the marbles of Praxiteles; but Canova rarely used any other means than that of washing his marbles after they had received their polish with *acqua di rota*; their soft and delicate surface being produced solely by his consummate chisel, and the diligent use of the file'

This belief in the benign action of *acqua di rota* as a temporary patinating agent that merely toned down the brightness of newly carved marble surfaces, until it was replaced naturally as time passed by 'an agreeable and harmonious coating', was widely held but even a brief survey of the literature indicates that this was not necessarily the case and brings into focus the issue of patination and deliberate colouring of sculpture.

The whole question of precisely what *acqua di rota* was, and why, and how, it was applied, remains inadequately answered and the extent to which Canova used this, and other materials, is far from clear. To some, *acqua di rota* was nothing more than the slurry from the water filled trough below a sharpening wheel which, once sieved, was used as an abrasive polish by sculptors and their *lustratori* (or polishers) to impart the final finish to a statue. It was a cheap alternative to a specially formulated polishing compound made from clean and graded sand or pumice and water. In his work on sculpture published in 1802, Francesco Carradori[8] states that *rota* is a gritstone found in the region of Sarzana and goes on to explain how it is used in varying degrees of fineness, followed by fine pumice applied with a wooden lath and wet linen, to achieve a polished surface on marble. Although these polishing agents might have similar abrasive properties, they could equally be subtly, or totally, different in their effect depending upon their source. If, for example, the *acqua di rota* being used contained traces of iron, the long term effect on the marble could be profound and, whereas the sculptor could ensure that this impurity was not present with specially selected abrasive powder, he could not be sure that it would not be included in a polish derived from the trough of the grindstone that he regularly used for sharpening his tools. On the contrary, he would be perfectly well aware of the fact that *acqua di rota* from this source certainly contained iron in solution, and also that one of the main consequences of its use would be the permanent staining of the marble surface to which it was applied.

This *acqua di rota* mentioned by many contemporary authors is cited by Sartori,[9] Canova's secretary and half brother, in a letter of 1811 responding to a question from P. Giordani who had written enquiring about Canova's use of *quella preparazione* to colour statues. This reply is of particular interest for the following year the sculptor Zauner had contacted Canova because he was concerned about the discoloration and staining of the monument to the Archduchess Marina Christina that Canova had completed in 1805 – he was unwilling to attempt to deal with this staining, or *macchie*, until he had heard what had been done to the surface by the sculptor because he had found that the staining originated in the applied surface tinting. The reply to this request for information has not survived but in that to Giordani, Sartori writes, on Canova's behalf, that he had used pure wax (*pura cera*) and water treated by a chemist (*acqua elaborata dallo speziale*) on the surface of his sculptures early in his career but that he had long since given up these practices. In his time he had

> 'found it sufficient to pass the brush dipped in dirty water coming from the wheels sharpening the chisels' ('*si contentava di passare sul nudo solo il penello intinto in acqua sporca della rota a cui s'arruotano i ferri*')

but had stopped doing it because these devices ('*artifizi*')

> 'were of no use even to those who are not able to work well in marble and give the nude the appearance of real flesh' ('*non sapra lavorare il marmo bene, e*

ridurre il nudo a somigliare la vera carne').

Canova himself admitted in a letter to the Earl of Cawdor[10] on 27 March 1817 that
> 'I also want to tell you … that some believe that I use a sort of encaustic paint on
> the marble of my finished sculpture, which was true in my early work, but of
> which crime I can no longer – for many years – be accused of. I challenge you
> to look and examine again the two statues of Hebe and Terpsichore, which
> were not treated with any wash, except that I passed over them a brush soaked
> in sandy water, which can be removed and washed off simply with a sponge'

The sandy, or earthy water, to which Canova refers could be either a simple wash of muddy water or, perhaps, slurry from a sandstone sharpening wheel. In the light of these letters from Zauner and to Cawdor, it is perhaps worth speculating that Canova stopped treating the surfaces of his sculptures not for the reason that he gives but because of the long term unpredictability of the materials that he was using. It seems hard to believe, when taking into account the fastidious way in which each piece of sculpture was finished, and the apparently strict requirement from his clients for white sculpture, that he was rash enough to go beyond merely experimenting with some of the materials that were at hand at that time and apply them to his finished works when the consequences of doing so were quite uncertain.

In the 1790s, and in common with his contemporaries, it seems that Canova was applying a variety of materials to the surface of his sculpture. At this time, and for different reasons, other sculptors were certainly applying water coloured with soot, tobacco, tea, coffee, stone dust and earth pigment washes; and clear and pigmented waxes to the surface of sculpture. John Bell[11] writing in the Art Journal in 1858, states that
> 'Canova used to do the same thing [apply a transparent wash] and tea, coffee,
> and rust water, and various other simple preparations, were tried by him and
> others for the same purpose'

Cavaceppi and Piranesi, for example, were anxious to distress the surfaces of replacement limbs and decorated infill fragments on the *pasticcio* pieces that were made for clients who were making the Grand Tour. Other sculptors like Thomas Banks and Joseph Nollekens were also anxious to emulate the mellow surface tones of the ancient marbles that they were asked to restore, and which retained their burial patina, by tinting their work with diluted coffee and tobacco water. In his account of Nollekens life,[12] J. T. Smith wrote about his activities in Rome in the 1760s.
> 'After he had dextrously restored them with heads and limbs, he stained them
> with tobacco water …'

and Thomas Banks' daughter Lavinia writing about her father in 1830 said
> 'He objected to the perfect whiteness of the marble in its natural state, and often
> employed a slight tint of coffee to stain it and give it a softness to the lights and
> shades'[13]

Carradori however, suggested an earthier recipe for matching modern marble to the antique by colouring it

> '...with a warm tint, composed of soot or lampblack (*'filiggine di cammino'*), very gentle and light, which you melt and boil with human urine, repeated many times...'[14]

The recipes for surface washes cited here illustrate that their usage was widespread amongst sculptors active in the last half of the eighteenth century and into the nineteenth, and most particularly with those who had worked, or trained, in Italy. Bell's article is anecdotal, but the letter from Sartori to Giordano shows that, at least during the early part of his career, Canova was not himself averse to practices of the type described, and which he may well have continued to use for far longer than he was prepared to admit. In 1808, Baron d'Uklanski[15] had noted that Canova applied a thin yellow wash to his statues to give them a colour similar to Parian marble, but in 1816 C.F. Fernow[16] wrote disapprovingly that Canova applied a yellowish stain containing soot to his sculptures once he had achieved the softest of surfaces with rasp and pumice. This was just one year before Canova assured the Earl of Cawdor that he had long since abandoned these practices but, as one of Canova's detractors. Fernow was probably not above seeking to make mischief in his publication.

During the early phase of his career in the 1790s, Canova was prepared to experiment even further and consider applying pigment, rather than just a transparent wash, to his sculpture. In 1796 he completed a statue of *Hebe* for Giacomo Albrizzi. The figure held in her hands a gilded cup and amphora, and wore a gilded bronze belt and necklace.

Although celebrated in Venice, it was obviously not universally well received because some time later, on 21 September 1800, Canova wrote to his friend Francesconi.[17]

> 'As far as more facial expression is concerned, it would have been quite easy for me to achieve, but it would surely have had to be paid for by being criticised by those who know beauty: Hebe would have been turned into a Bacchante. Were I to give Hebe just a tiny bit of rouge on the lips and cheeks, the face, which has the colour of death, would have become as they wanted. You would see this, and would make others to see it, and try to clean it with a handkerchief'

Canova was to make four versions of *Hebe* altogether. The Empress Josephine's (now in The Hermitage in St. Petersburg) was exhibited at the salon in 1808 and was criticised in an article in *Le Moniteur* because of the gilding, but also because of the golden yellow patina that had been applied to the flesh[18]. Another was made much later for Lord Cawdor (now at Chatsworth) between 1808 and 1814[19]. It was exhibited at the Royal Academy in 1816. This too had an applied golden yellow patina to the flesh areas and discretely rouged lips and cheeks, as did the fourth version which was commissioned at much the same time by the Contessa Veronica Guerini di

Forli.[20] Seeing Lord Cawdor's statue in London in 1817, the Duke of Bedford, who had recently ordered *The Three Graces* from Canova, wrote to him on 3 March.[21]

> 'We have an idea in this country that you use some preparation to colour your marble, and give a mellow tone to your sculptural works: but you will excuse me for saying that I should prefer to see the group of the Graces in the genuine lustre of the pure Carrara marble.'

Canova's reply again does not survive but he obviously managed to reassure his patron for Bedford writes again in May.[22]

> 'I am truly convinced by ocular demonstration that there is no artificial preparation used to give colour to the marble, and the only thing I do not quite like is a slight hint of vermilion on the lips of the Hebe, which, however, as you justly observe may easily be taken off with a wet sponge'

Did the Duke object only to the slightly rouged areas' and not to the discrete yellow stain or wash that apparently covered *Hebe's* flesh (if the note in Pavanello is correct)? Equally, he may not have been aware of it because Canova perhaps took little account of what his patron requested. Recent examination and cleaning of *The Three Graces* by the Victoria and Albert Museum has shown that there is a red/brown water soluble material present on the surface of the figures which does not extend to the altar behind them. If this is indeed a discretely applied wash, it implies that the Duke either did not object to the final overall effect, or, that he did not notice it. Equally, it is possible that Canova, then at the height of his career, did not feel particularly constrained by his patrons' requests. John Gibson certainly saw no obligation in this respect. In Gibson's biography, Matthews[23] writes of an encounter between the sculptor and Lord Portarlington's sister in Rome in 1857.

> 'Is it true that you have said to some persons that you will paint my brother's statue of Bacchus?' said her ladyship. 'Yes it is true' replied Gibson. 'But my brother told you not to paint his statue' she said sharply. 'He did so, but I am determined to colour it' responded Gibson.

At the same time that Canova was beginning to experiment seriously with the application of colour, in addition to a simple yellowish stain, he was developing a friendship with Quatremère de Quincey who was to have such an influence on the sculptural establishment of his day. For over thirty years this had been dominated by the theories of Johann Joachim Winckelman following the publication of his *Gesichte der Kunst des Altertums*[24] after 1763. A passage from this publication quoted by Drost[25] neatly summarises one of the essential canons of eighteenth-century Neo-Classicism.

> '...a body is all the more beautiful the whiter it is ... (*white emphasises the*) unity and simpicity ... (*through which*) all beauty becomes sublime'

Quatremère de Quincey, however, challenged this cherished belief and justified his arguments by reference to newly excavated Classical marble figures, reliefs, and architectural fragments that retained much original paint on their surfaces. Quatremère became a friend of Canova's in the 1780s, some thirty years before the publication of his seminal work *Le Jupiter Olympien*[26] in 1814. The Italian edition, dedicated to Canova was published in 1817. Also in his essay Drost points out:[27]

> 'He argued against the positions of the Neo-Classicists, who continued to insist that Greek art had been monochrome. With remarkable open-mindedness he noted that the Greeks hardly 'distinguished... between the pleasures of the eye and the pleasures of the mind', claiming that for them the 'variety and beauty of materials' was in no way a contradiction of 'essential beauty'.

Canova must have been an early sympathiser with this way of thinking. It is said that he enjoyed having not only Classical literature read to him whilst he worked, to make up for his lack of formal education as a child, but also passages from his friend Quatremère de Quincey's writings.[28] As Darby points out, his practice of washing the marble to remove its whiteness, and of tinting and gilding his statues, was directly encouraged by Quatremère and they collaborated on a project for a colossal polychrome statue of Religion in 1814 that was never realised. The ancient authors that were read to Canova will undoubtedly have included dramatists, philosophers, and poets but also the standards works on architecture, travel, and technology. Plato refers to the painting of statues in his *Republic*,[29] as does Virgil who describes a statue of Diana in his Seventh Eclogue. Pliny,[30] however, discusses the techniques used in the Roman period to paint sculpture in remarkable detail although the methods that he describes, and the precise meaning of certain technical terms that he used have fuelled debate at least since the early nineteenth century. The younger Richard Westmacott wrote in 1840:[31]

> 'It has been attempted to prove that the *circumlitio*, referred to by Pliny, has reference to this practice of colouring statues. It cannot, however, by any ingenuity be made to mean such painting or tinting with *different* colours as painter sculptors are advocating. The great probability is that it refers to a most careful perfection of surface both by giving a certain degree of finish or even polish to the marble, and probably by rubbing in a preparation – a varnish – capable of imparting a rich roundness or appearance of fatness, so to call it (the *morbidezza* of the Italians) to the execution; and enveloping the whole with a warm yellowish tone of colour, anticipating by these artificial means, the mellowing effect of age. But such a general tone cannot be considered in the category of colour, as it is now proposed to use it'

Not content with merely publishing discussion of the issues raised by both Pliny and his own contemporaries John Bell[32] initiated a programme of experimentation in which he sought to reproduce the processes described by Pliny. He reported on his findings, and more besides, in the *Art Journal* at the height of yet a further debate on the colouring of sculpture in 1858. The arguments centred on the exhibition of John

Gibson's *Tinted Venus* which had been completed in 1856. This is, however, not the place to repeat these arguments - they are exhaustively and elegantly articulated in the essays published in *The Colour of Sculpture* already cited.

Canova was thus exposed to the idea of colouring sculpture from quite an early point in his career. The technique of generally tinting a finished sculpture to distress newly carved surfaces seems to have been common practice amongst, at least, the Italian sculptors of his generation but, judging from the versions of Hebe, Canova sought to extend this restrained use of colour not only by the addition of metal fixings but also by the modest application of red pigment. This marks a tentative move away from monochromatic towards polychrome sculpture - something presumably regarded with suspicion, and even abhorrence, by his patrons. In 1819, Anne-Louis Girodet completed a painting of *Pygmalion and the Statue*. Commissioned by Count Sommariva, it was intended as an homage to Canova and the painting depicts the moment when the statue comes to life. In accordance with contemporary painting convention, she is shown with vermilion tinted cheeks. Blühm[35] points out that there is no proof that Girodet intended this as a reference to Canova's experiments but the dedication to Canova, and the remarks in the letter of 21 September 1800 to Francesconi[34], repeated below, perhaps indicate otherwise.

> 'Were I to give Hebe just a tiny bit of rouge on the lips and cheeks, the face which has the colour of death would have become as they wanted . . .'

When he wrote this letter, Canova was at the height of his career. Although universally admired and, it would seem, in a position to influence fundamentally contemporary sculptural taste, he appears be to trapped within the rigid Neo-Classical canon. Even at this stage, he was unable, and ultimately perhaps, unwilling, to move beyond this concept of *disegno*, that is, the purely linear expression of the artistic idea, that was at the very heart of the Neo-Classical movement, and into the world of polychromy that was explored a generation later by his pupil John Gibson. It is surely logical to conclude that Gibson can only have been introduced to these ideas whilst working in Canova's studio between 1817 and 1821.

The *Ideal Head* now at the Ashmolean remained in the family of the original owner, William Hamilton, to whom it was given by Canova in 1817, until 1995. This unbroken period of ownership means that it has been in a domestic environment since its arrival in England and was never on public display. Because of this, and the fact that it appears to have been little cleaned it was thought that it might well retain evidence of surface treatments applied by Canova in his studio. However, the Hamilton family have pointed out that it was customary for their mother to apply make-up to the face. Consequently, before even superficial cleaning could be undertaken by the Ashmolean, a regime of examination was instigated to determine whether any washes or pigment survive on the surface.

Routine examination under magnification (x9 upwards) and ordinary lighting has failed to indicate any surviving traces of applied pigment, or evidence of a deliberately tinted wash or stain on the exposed surfaces of the bust although the underside of the shoulders is slightly discoloured. This accords with Hugh Honour's[35] observation that all traces of artificial staining had vanished from all the Canovas that he had examined prior to writing his article in 1972. The fact that these have not been observed does not necessarily mean that they were not once present. Even routine dusting will dislodge an unbound layer of pigment, or finely ground stone dust, from the smooth surface of a statue, and washing it will almost certainly remove all traces. Stains are somewhat more persistent but, as the cleaning tests on *The Three Graces* revealed, they remain fugitive and therefore easily removed inadvertently. In most public collections, sculpture on open display has been cleaned many times. Most regimes previously used for cleaning white marble were designed to render the surface as white as possible and would remove any wash, or even stain, that was applied to the surface. Pigmented waxes are somewhat more difficult to remove but the traditional cleaning methods, which involved degreasing the sculpture before the application of poultices, will remove these with ease. Given that the systematic study of applied finishes on historic sculpture is a relatively new discipline, and the fugitive nature of the colouring materials used, it would be extremely surprising, therefore, if these original surfaces survived even cursory cleaning. Even where they do remain, as on *The Three Graces* (which is thought to have been treated with water either intentionally or accidentally when the roof at Woburn leaked) identifying the colouring agent used is not easy. Research undertaken at the Victoria and Albert Museum related to the cleaning of *The Three Graces*, on modern marble samples, has demonstrated that it is difficult, using an infra red spectrophotometer, to differentiate between stains on a marble surface produced by tea, coffee, and tobacco water after three washes. Published results of this work is forthcoming. On the underside of the right side of the Hamilton *Head*, it is evident that water has run down from the shoulder leaving a pale drip mark in the slightly brown and discoloured surface already mentioned indicating that it has been washed, or accidentally splashed, at some time. There is also an area that appears to have been wiped clean above the dedicatory inscription (see below). Similar drip and water run – off marks were observed on the legs of *The Three Graces*. Whether the brown and discoloured sur-face on the Ashmolean piece is merely the result of exposure to hearth or tobacco smoke, or is, indeed, the surviving and discoloured remnant of an applied surface stain, remains inconclusive at present. The cleaning of any marble surface that is stained brown is fraught with difficulty if there is even a remote possibility that the sculpture as a whole was ever discretely patinated because over time it becomes increasingly difficult to differentiate betweeen applied and incidental staining.

There is no residual evidence of previous cleaning by washing but this is probably because it was well rinsed at the time rather than because it was never washed or wiped over. There is also a total absence of any localised brown staining that can be associated with the corrosion of iron impurities in the marble, or as a consequence of the application of iron contaminated water. Similarly, discolouration caused by bacterial growth on organic surface residues and contamination of the marble due to handling, or the application of soft soap or oils is not present either. In fact, apart from two small areas of damage on the curls on the crown of the head where they tumble from the headband, and a blemish on the neck, the surface is pristine.

Microscopic examination of the surface in raking light shows the localised differences in surface texture that were applied by Canova. The face, front of the neck, bridge of the nose, and headband have an extremely smooth and reflective surface making it translucent. The sides and back of the neck, and the shoulders, are smooth but have a lightly scratched surface caused by the use of a coarser abrasive powder. The scratches run more or less vertically and, on the shoulders and lower neck/chest are quite obvious, due to the presence of ingrained surface dirt. The sides of the nose also have this less highly finished surface, although without such deep scratch marks, presumably to enhance the subtle modelling of the centre of the face as light falls upon it. The hair has a deliberately tooled matt surface. The curls of the hair were made by deep drilling and some material is lodged in these holes. Powder residues found in similar locations on *The Three Graces* are thought to be finely divided pumice perhaps left by Canova's '*lustratori*'.

Under ultra violet light, the surface of the Ashmolean *Ideal Head* can be seen to be divided into two distinct areas. Everything, apart from the hair, exhibits a consistent purple/dark grey brown fluorescence. (The small area of damage on the tip of the curls produces a clearer purple fluorescence characteristic of a more recently exposed surface). The hair fluoresces a pale grey. This differential fluorescence is most likely due to the surface morphology of the marble, but it is tempting to speculate that it could possibly be linked to a residual and discrete surface treatment.

The dedicatory inscription on the back of the socle is filled, in the Classical tradition, with red pigment which is not present on the Wellington Head [Cat. No.2]. The identification of the pigment, which appears black in ultra violet light, is in train. It has 'bled' to a limited extent onto the surfaces surrounding the incised lettering, particularly above the inscription, indicating that this area has, at the very least, been wiped over with a damp cloth. More importantly, however, the bright red pigment has largely discoloured to a blackish brown hue. This is typical of both true vermilion or cinnabar (red mercuric sulphide), and red lead, or minium (red tetroxide of lead). Under normal circumstances vermilion is a permanent pigment but, when it is exposed to direct sunlight, and particularly when it is used with tempera or watercolour mediums, it darkens. Red lead, however, is notorious for turning black or brown when exposed to hydrogen sulphide, nitric and acetic acids and, like vermilion, it will discolour in conditions where there is sunlight and high humidity.[36] Both

56

these pigments were known to the ancients but the 'minium' referred to by Pliny is, in fact, true vermilion. He calls red lead 'secondarium minium' to differentiate between the two. It would be intriguing to know for certain whether the "vermilion" referred to by the Duke of Bedford[37] in his letter to Canova regarding the red tints on the lips and cheeks of Hebe was, in fact, true vermilion, minium, or red iron oxide. Whilst vermilion and minium are very similar in hue, red iron oxide is quite different so the assumption must be that he was not referring to this.

Unfortunately, other parallels in Canova' work – and most particularly in the few documented occasions where he used red pigment on the faces of his statues – all appear to have been 'wiped away with a sponge'. Curiously enough, the Hamilton family recall that they occasionally applied make-up to their *Ideal Head* but, in common with Canova's own applications of vermilion to the faces of *Hebe*, no traces of this latterday, and unconscious, homage to the sculptor's technique remain. It may, however, well affect what we see on the surface today. Technological research on the Ashmolean's newly acquired *Ideal Head* is scheduled to continue and will be published elsewhere in due course.

1 For example, M. Misserini, *Della Vita di Antonio Canova*, Rome, 1824. The edition in Ashmolean Library is signed 'John Gibson, Rome' L. Cicognara: *Biografia di Antonio Canova*, Venice, 1823.

2 Moses, *The Works of Antonio Canova in sculpture and modelling*, London, 1824.

3 D'Este, *Memorie di Antonoi Canova*, Florence, 1864.

4 L. Cicognara, *op. cit.*

5 S. J. Memes, *Memoirs of Antonio Canova*, Edinburgh, 1825, p.553.

6 Memes, *op. cit*, p.558

7 Moses *op. cit*, p. xxiii

8 F. Carradori, *Istrutione elementare per gli studiosi della scultura*, Florence, 1802, Article 10.

9 G. B. Sartori & Canova to P. Giordani, 30 November, 1811, Biblioteca Braidense, Milan, AE. XV5. no.3: citied in Honour: 'Canova's Studio Practice -II; 1792-1822,' *The Burlington Magazine*, Vol CXIV, April 1972, p.219.

10 Cawdor Paper cited in Honour op. cit., p. 219 'Voglio anchi dirvi come so che costi si tiene credenza che io adopero ò una pecie di encausto sul marmo delle mie statue finite. Il che fu vero nella prima epoca dell' arte mia; ma non può essermi fatto untal delitto da moltissimi anni in quà. E ciò è tanto vero, che io v'invito e riverdere, e a far esaminare attentamente le due statue d'Ebe, e della Tersicore, alle quali non diedi alcun lavato ad eccezione di aver passato di sopra un penello tinto d'acqua di arena, la quale si può togliere, e lavare semplicimente con una spogna.'

11 John Bell, *The Art Journal*, London, 1858, p.19.

12 J.T. Smith, *Nollekens, his times*, London, 1828, Vol 1, p.11.

13 Letter from Lavinia Foster to Allan Cunningham, 12 February 1830, reproduced in *The Builder*, 3 January, 1863, p.4-5.

14 F. Carradori, *op. cit.*

15 Baron d'Uklanski *Travels in Upper Italy, Tuscany and the Ecclesiastical State . . . in the years 1807 and 1808*, London, 1816, Vol II, p.111.

[16] C. F. Fernow: *Ûber den Bildhauer Canova und Dessen Werke*, Zurich, 1806.

[17] Pavanello, *L'Opera Completa del Canova*, Milan, 1976, p.102, no 98. "In pointo a voler più espressione nel viso mi sarebbe stata cosa assai facile il dargliela, ma certamente aile spese di esser criticato da chii sa conoscere il bello; la Ebe sarebbe diventa[ta] una Baccante. Se all'Ebe provassero a dargli un tintino di rossetto sopra le labra e sopra le guancie vedrebbero che quel viso ora di color da morto diventerrebe appunto comme loro il vorrebbero; voi il verdreste pure e potreste farglielo veder anche a loro, già sa polisce col fazzoletto"

[18] Pavanello, *op. cit.*, p.102, no. 100.

[19] Pavanello, *op. cit.*, p.119, no. 215.

[20] Pavanello, *op. cit.*, p.119, no. 215.

[21] Bassano IV/88/7-8 in: Honour, *op. cit.*

[22] Bassano IV/88/7-8 in: Honour, *op. cit.*

[23] T. Matthews, *The Biography of John Gibson*, London, 1911, p.217

[24] Johann Joachim Winckelmann, *Gesichte der Kunste des Altertums*, Baden-Baden & Strasbourg, 1966.

[25] Wolfgang Drost: 'Colour, Sculpture, and Mimesis' in Blühm *The Colour of Sculpture*, Zwolle, 1997. p.62.

[26] Antoine-Chrysostome Quatremère de Quincy, *Le Jupiter Olympien, ou l'arte de la sculpture antique consideré sous un nouveau point de vue: ouvrage qui compren un essai sur le goût de la sculpture polychrome, etc*, Paris, 1814.

[27] Blühm, *op. cit*, p.62.

[28] Elizabeth Darby, 'John Gibson, Queen Victoria, and the idea of scuptural polychromy' in *Art History*, 4, 1981, No. 1, pp.39-44.

[29] Plato: *De Republica*, lib iv.

[30] Pliny: lib. xxxv. cap 2.

[31] R. Westmacott Jnr 'On Colouring Statues', *The Archaeological Journal*, Vol XII, 1840, p.40.

[32] John Bell *The Art Journal*, 1858, pp.69-70, 179, 230-232.

[33] Blühm', *op. cit.* p.22.

[34] Pavanello, *op. cit.* p.102.

[35] Honour, *op. cit.* p.219.

[36] R. Gettens and G. Stout, *Painting Materials*, London, 1966. (Dover Edition).

[37] Bassano IV/88/7-8 in Honour, *op. cit.*

The Ashmolean: a Fitting Home for Canova's *Ideal Head*

Michael Vickers

The purpose of this note is to show how very appropriate it is that Canova's *Ideal Head* has come to the Ashmolean. With its holdings that illustrate the long traditions of English interest in Greek and Roman painting and sculpture, in English patronage of Italian artists, and in English collection of Italian art, the Ashmolean is indeed a fitting home for this numinous work. A year or so ago, when I was asked what I thought about the possibility of the Ashmolean acquiring the *Ideal Head* that Canova presented to W. R. Hamilton I replied that it would be difficult to envisage a potential acquisition for the Ashmolean that was more appropriate. It had strong antique associations, was an important document of nineteenth-century taste, and above all, Canova's gift embodied the perennial artistic ties between England and Italy of which the Ashmolean itself is a prime exemplar.

It was from Italy that the bulk of the Ashmolean's collection of antique sculpture came: most of the collection of Thomas Howard, Earl of Arundel (1585-1616), who played a leading role in both art and politics in seventeenth-century England, was acquired there.[1] When he was in Rome in 1613, he was privileged to be allowed to excavate in the Forum and to take the statues he found (said by his enemies to have planted) home with him to England.[2] His uncle Lord Lumley had commissioned a series of busts of Tudor notables when in Italy in the 1560s (an early copy of a portrait of Henry VIII is in the Ashmolean).[3] Arundel was to continue and develop this tradition of patronage of contemporary artists. It is true that the four colossal statues in the antique manner he commissioned in 1614 from the *scarpellino* Egidio Moretti are not the most accomplished works of art, and betray the fact that Moretti was taken off work on Carlo Maderna's facade of St. Peter's. Two were supposedly of Roman generals, dressed in armour (Fig.7), and two of senators dressed in what were thought of at the time as togas.[4] Later, in 1636, Arundel brought to England Francois Dieussart, a Flemish sculptor who had learnt his craft in Rome with Bernini and whose work was far more proficient. Two of Francois Dieussart's portraits are in Oxford: the bust of the Earl (Fig.8) that now stands on the main staircase of the Ashmolean, and one of Rupert of the Rhine,[5] at the foot of the same staircase.

One piece of sculpture in the Arundel collection is of special relevance here (Fig.9): a Roman period head mounted on a bust that may or may not be a reworked classical fragment.[6] The head belongs to a type well known from nearly a couple of dozen ancient replicas of the head of a statue most would place in the fifth century BC;[7] the

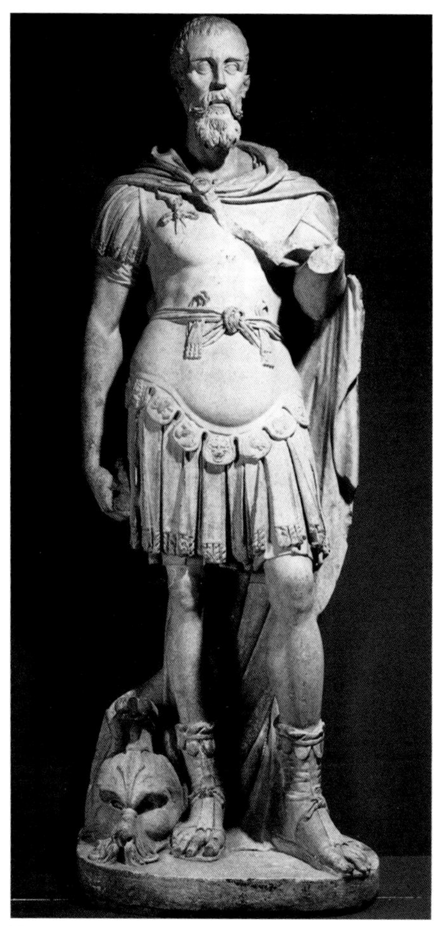

Fig. 7

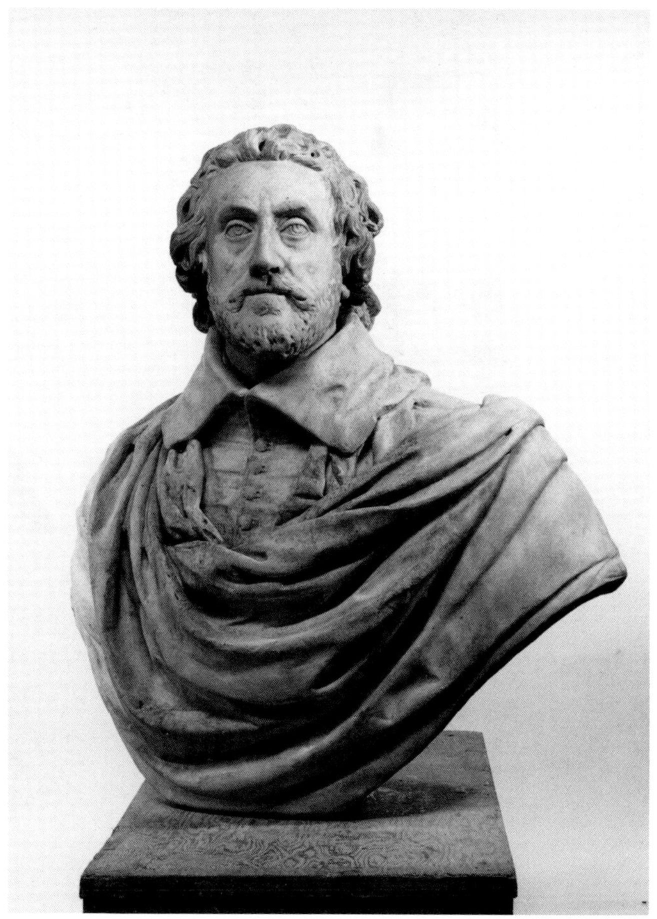

Fig. 8

existence of so many copies implies that the original statue, whichever it was, was one of considerable importance in antiquity. The idealized head, with its slightly sentimental expression and the hair bound up with a fillet, finds an obvious parallel in the head of Artemis on the East frieze of the Parthenon,[8] part of a decorative scheme of which the sculptor Phidias was the overseer. The type to which the Oxford head belongs has been plausibly identified as a reflection of Phidias' chryselephantine statue of Aphrodite Ourania at Elis.[9] If so, the flesh of the face would have been ivory, and the hair and fillet gold. The 'Oxford Bust', as this piece is known, was to have its moment of glory in the later nineteenth century when it was 'one of the gems' of the Ashmolean's collections.[10]

This was not always the case: when the painter and sculptor G. F. Watts and the archaeologist Sir Charles Newton visited Oxford to look over the Arundel Marbles in the later 1840s, with a view to 'pick[ing] out those which were of real worth for exhibition in the Ashmolean Museum', they found many of them 'neglected in a cellar'.[11]

60

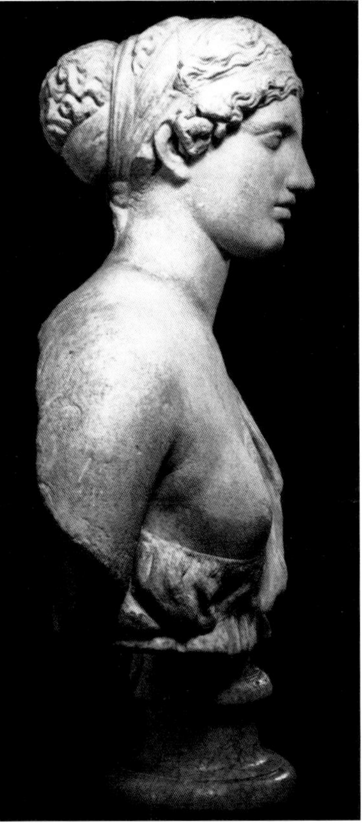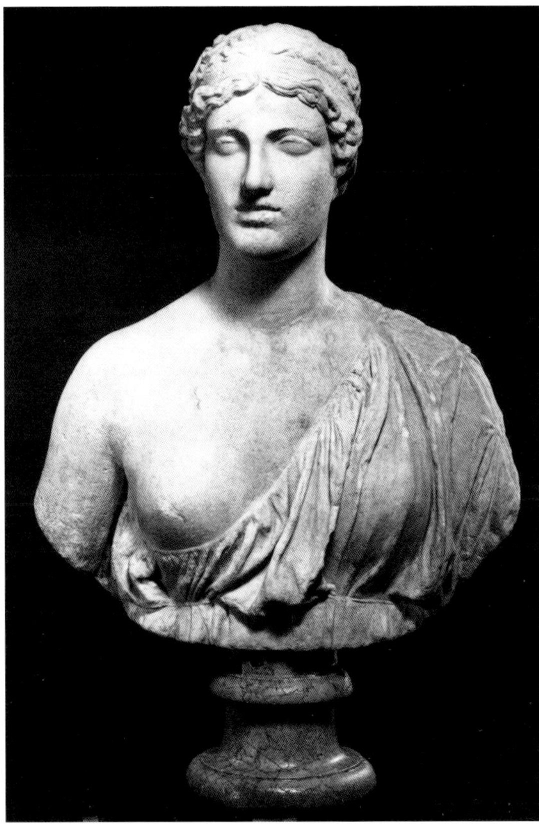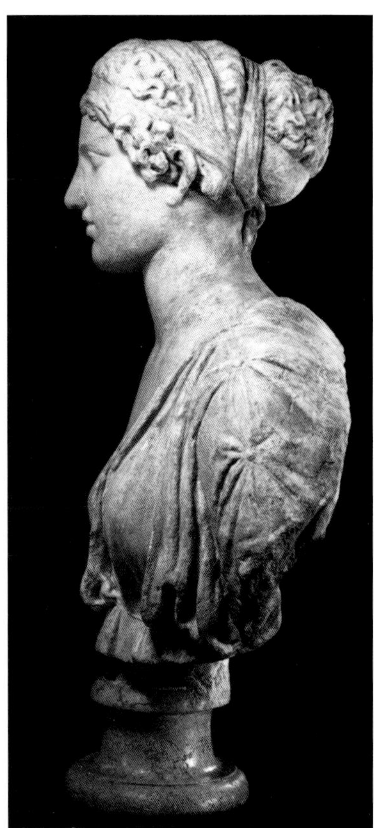

Fig. 9

Watts 'was the discoverer here of a beautiful head severed at the neck, and unhappily without the nose. The missing parts were searched for, and they were successful in finding the bust and shoulders'. Watts, who had grown up in the wake of the first wave of 'Parthenomania' which had swept England at the beginning of the century,[12] 'ranked this bust with the best art of Greece in the time of Phidias . . . casts were made from the bust and one of these always stood in his studio. The reverence in which this was held by him was so great that it inspired him to paint the transition of Galatea from marble to life [*The Wife of Pygmalion*, now at Buscot Park, Lechlade]'. Many more casts were disseminated throughout Europe and America by Watts, and the 'Oxford Bust' lies behind many High Victorian neo-classical compositions. There is no direct connection between the older Oxford head and the new one, but there is a good reason for their more than superficial similarity.

Canova was known in his day as 'the Phidias of Europe'; this was not simply a recognition of his sculptural pre-eminence, but had much to do with the fact that Canova was the foremost exponent of the neo-classical style which was consciously based on the style of the age of Phidias. Ever since the middle of the eighteenth century, the elegant simplicity of Greek art had been held up as a model for contemporary artists to emulate. Johann Joachim Winckelmann wrote in 1755 of 'noble simplicity and quiet grandeur' ('Edle Einfalt und stille Grosse');[13] he was in fact referring to the contorted and far from 'quiet' Laocoon, but the idea took root and came to be applied to Greek art of the fifth century BC. The publications of the two collections of painted pottery (or 'vases') sponsored by Sir William Hamilton had placed fresh images of Greek antiquity before a European public. The first collection, published between 1767 and 1776, was a lavish affair: four magnificent volumes full of hand-coloured illustrations.[14] The second (1791-95)[15] was more austere, but with its crisp outline drawings by the leading German illustrator Tischbein, had a pronounced effect on late eighteenth and early nineteenth century Neo-classicism. Pictures of

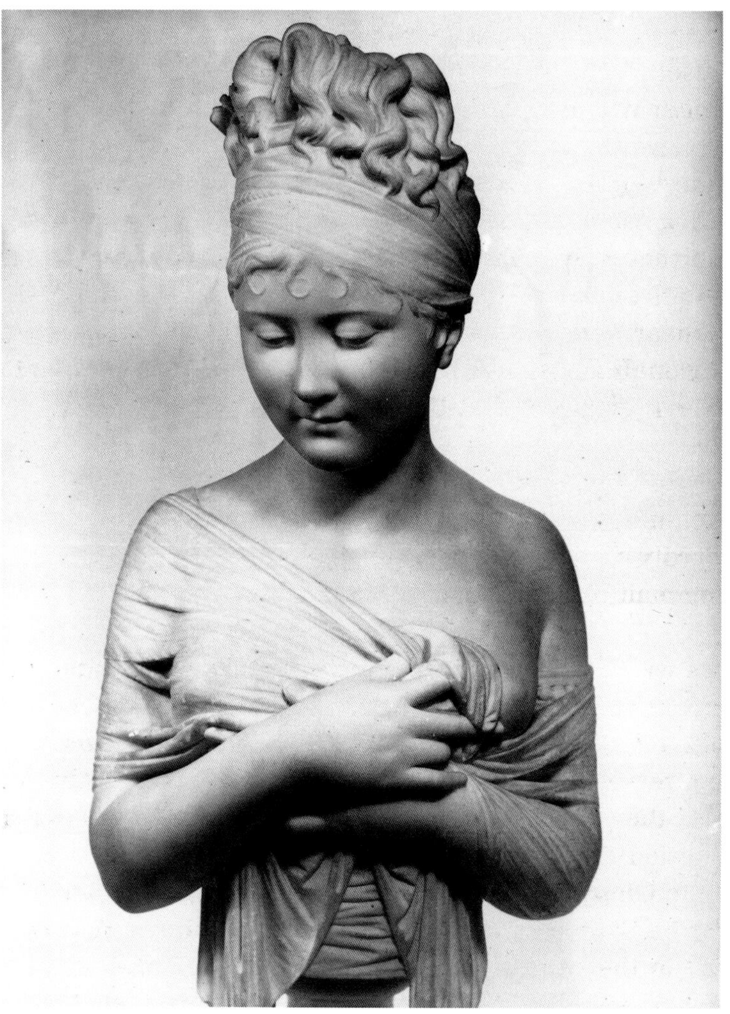

Fig. 10

62

idealised Greek maidens and matrons, with their hair frequently bound up in *sakkoi*, became the models for fashionable Parisian ladies in their chignons. Madame Récamier's coiffure, exemplified in Joseph Chinard's splendidly voluptuous portrait in the Ashmolean, (Fig.10),[16] had an interesting pedigree.

The few examples of fifth-century BC sculpture in western European collections, grave reliefs for the most part, were called into service in support of the newly fashionable style. It was with a view to 'improving the arts', to 'benefit the progress of taste' in Britain that Lord Elgin, for good or ill,[17] arranged to have large portions of the surviving sculptural decoration of the Parthenon at Athens brought to England (the principal sculptural decoration – the gold and ivory statue of Athena – had long since gone; all that was left were subsidiary ornaments). It was to Canova that Elgin offered the commission to restore the battered fragments; but a combination of Canova's reticence ('it would be a sacrilege in him or any man to presume to touch them with a chisel')[18] and Elgin's impoverishment meant that no additions were made in the manner which was still the norm. Canova's English pupil John Flaxman was of the same view. He disclosed to W. R. Hamilton that by comparison with one of the reclining figures from the Parthenon, the Apollo Belvedere (the touchstone of earlier taste) was 'a dancing master'.[19]

The Apollo Belvedere was foremost among the ancient statues seized by Bonaparte in Italy and elsewhere. The Bronze Horses from San Marco, the Laocoon and Medici Venus appear together with the Apollo in idealized representations of war booty paraded through Paris, and which were star exhibits in the Musée Napoléon, created in the Louvre palace.[20] E. P. Benson's clerihew

> It was not Napoleon
> Who founded the Ashmolean.
> He hardly had a chance,
> Living mainly in France

is familiar[21]. Less well known is the fact that the Ashmolean and Bonaparte shared (at different times) the goal of acquiring the same object. Had Bonaparte been successful in invading England, high on his list of war aims was the seizure of the Warwick Vase, a vessel which would doubtless have graced the Musée Napoléon together with his other trophies. The Warwick Vase was up for sale a few years ago, and for a brief period the Ashmolean was in serious contention for it. In the event, however, it went to Glasgow where it stands in the entrance to the Burrell Collection in Pollok Park.[22] The Warwick Vase was found in the ruins of Hadrian's Villa at Tivoli and was restored in the workshop of Giovanni Battista Piranesi. The same site and the same workshop supplied the two candelabra presented to the University of Oxford by Sir Roger Newdigate,[23] one of many Englishmen who travelled in Italy during the eighteenth century on the Grand Tour, and who had been instrumental in bringing the Arundel (by now the Pomfret) marbles to Oxford in 1755.[24] This innocent booty is now exhibited in the Ashmolean's Randolph Gallery, purpose-built to house the University's collections of Greek and Roman sculpture. The architect was C. R. Cockerell, a friend of W. R. Hamilton, and who first travelled to Greece with the latter's official sponsorship.[25]

1 D.E.L. Haynes, *The Arundel Marbles* (Oxford, 1975); D. Howarth, *Lord Arundel and his Circle* (London, 1985); Ashmolean Museum, *Thomas Howard, Earl of Arundel: Patronage and Collecting in the Seventeenth Century.* Oxford, 1985); D. Jaffé with D. Allen, D.W. Carr, A. Faber Kolb, and E. Kleeman, 'The Earl and Countess of Arundel: Renaissance Collectors', *Apollo* 144 (August, 1996) pp.3-35.

2 J. Dallaway, *Anecdotes of the Arts in England,* London, 1800, p.256.

3 M. Vickers, 'The changing face of Henry VIII', *Country Life*, April 24, 1980, pp.1248-1249; idem, 'The medal of Robert Dudley, Earl of Leicester in the Bibliothèque Nationale', *Numismatic Chronicle,* 1981 117-119, pls 22-23; N. Penny, *Catalogue of European Sculpture in the Ashmolean Museum, 1540 to the Present Day,* Oxford, 1992, 3 .195, No. 599.

4 J. Hess, 'Lord Arundel in Rom und sein Auftrag an den Bildhauer Egidio Moretti', *English Miscellany* 1, 1950, 199-216; M. Vickers, 'Lord Arundel's Roman patronage: two "lost" statues by Egidio Moretti rediscovered', *Apollo* 110, 1979, pp.224-225; Penny, 1992, Nos.64-7.

5 M. Vickers, 'Rupert of the Rhine, a new portrait by Dieussart and Bernini's Charles I', *Apollo* 107, 1978, pp.161-169; Penny, 1992, Nos. 471-2.

6 A. Michaelis, *Ancient Marbles in Great Britain,* Cambridge, 1882, pp.555-6, No. 59; M. Vickers, 'Germanicus' Tomb', *The Ashmolean* 15, 1989, pp.6-8; *idem,* 'The Oxford Bust', *The Ashmolean* 20, 1991, pp.6-8.

7 N. Himmelmann-Wildschütz, 'Eine Beobachtung an der "Oxford Bust",' *Studies in Classical Art and Archaeology, A Tribute to Peter Heinrich von Blanckenhagen,* Locust Valley, N.Y., 1979, pp.99-101, pl. 29.

8 East VI 40: M. Robertson and A. Frantz, *The Parthenon Frieze,* London, 1975, pls 14-15.

9 E. Harrison, 'A Pheidian head of Aphrodite Ourania', *Hesperia* 53, 1984, pp.379-88.

10 M.S. Watts, *George Frederic Watts: The Annals of an Artist's Life* 1, London, 1912, p.238.

11 *Ibid.*

12 I. Jenkins, 'G.F. Watts' teachers': George Frederic Watts and the Elgin Marbles', *Apollo* 120 1984, pp.176-81.

13 J.J. Winckelmann, *Gedanken über die Nachahmung der griechischen Werke in der Malerei und Bildhauerkunst,* Friederichstadt, 1755, p.21; cf. W. Winckelmann, *Edle Einfalt und Stille Grösse,* Berlin, 1909, p.60.

14 P. d'Hancarville, *Collection of Etruscan, Greek and Roman Antiquities from the Cabinet of the Hon. W. Hamilton, His Britannic Majesty's Envoy Extraordinary and Plenipotentiary at the Court of Naples,* Naples, 1766[1767]-76.

15 W. Hamilton, *Collection of Engravings from Ancient Vases mostly of pure Greek Workmanship discovered in sepulchres in the kingdom of the Two Sicilies, but chiefly in the neighbourhood of Naples during the course of the years MDCCLXXXIX and MDCCLXXXX now in the possession of Sir Wm Hamilton, his Britannic Maiestay's Envoy Extr.^y and Plenipotentiary at the Court of Naples, with remarks on each vase by the collector* (Naples,

1791-5).

16 Penny, 1992, No. 261; cf. M. Levey, *Art and Architecture of The Eighteenth Century*, Harmondsworth, 1972, p.172.

17 W. St. Clair, *Lord Elgin and the Marbles*, London, 1983, p.7.

18 *Ibid.* 152.

19 *Ibid.* 167.

20 I. Jenkins, 'Gods without altars: the Belvedere in Paris', *Proceedings of 'Il Convegno delle Statue nel Belvedere' in Honor of Richard Krautheimer*, Rome, October 1992 (forthcoming).

21 E.C. Bentley, *The First Clerihews*, Oxford, 1982.

22 R. Marks and B. Blench, *The Warwick Vase*, Glasgow, 1979.

23 Penny, 1992, Nos. 77 and 78.

24 R.F. Ovenell, *The Ashmolean Museum 1683-1894*, Oxford, 1986, p.144.

25 St. Clair, p.203.

The Catalogue

The Ideal Heads

Where are the forms the sculptor's soul hath seized?
In him alone. Can Nature show so fair?
Byron, *Childe Harold*, Canto IV, Stanza CXXII

The heads are first recorded in the *Notizie del Giorno* for 24 September, 1818,[1] when an English newspaper announced the arrival of three of them: 'tre teste di donne di squisito lavoro, una al duca di Wellington, altra a lord Castlereagh, ed altra all'onorevole Charles Longh'. There is, in the exclusion of William Richard Hamilton's name, an inference to be drawn that the busts were in some sense official or semi-official acknowledgement of Rome's debt of gratitude. This inference can be supported by others: Canova's first mention of his intention to make the busts in a letter to Hamilton, in which Hamilton's bust is not mentioned,[2] and in Pius VII's letter to the Duke of Wellington in which he promises some sort of tangible mark of gratitude.[3] Perhaps here Canova's position in relation to the Pope was, in matters of diplomacy at least, in some sense equivalent to that of Court Sculptor, a relationship with a traditional role like that of Bernini in the execution of the portrait bust of Charles I.

In a draft Chronological Catalogue prepared by Canova for publication in 1817,[4] they are listed simply as '*Quattro Teste*'. The list became the source for all subsequent references, right up to and including the *catalogue raisoné* of 1976.[5] As it did not identify the types, it did not prevent errors of identification, which occurred from the outset, and identification was not helped by the fact that two of the heads disappeared from sight and have only re-emerged in the past twenty-five years. The first British account of Canova's work was published with engraved plates by Henry Moses in 1824 with a text after the Countess Albrizzi. Individual types such as the *Calliope* or *Sappho* appear, but there is no mention of *Ideal Heads* or the gifts and their recipients. Later editions include a section in which 'Ideal Female Heads No.1, No.2 and No.3' are recorded as given to Wellington, Castlereagh and "Sir Wm. Hamilton", no doubt the source of future confusion, while Charles Long's is referred to in passing. No.2 is a *Sappho* type and indeed Hamilton referred to his as a *Sappho*[6], and No.3 is that given to Long. 'They are all three very beautiful, and closely resemble each other in style and expression, being distinguished only by slight peculiarities of features, and in the arrangement of the hair'.[7] At some time the bust given to Charles Long was thought to be a version of the Helen, and that given to Hamilton was thought to be the type *Polyhymnia* we now know to be Long's.[8]

As is now obvious, only two of the group could strictly be described as Ideal Heads within Canova's own canon, though all four belong to the wider group of named but idealised heads such as *Sappho* or *Beatrice* and *Laura*, inspired by Dante and Petrach. Sometimes the specificity of a portrait combined with the generality of an ideal, as in Juliette Récamier as Beatrice,[9] or a portrait such as that of *Eleonora d'Este* itself became the prototype for an ideal.[10] In other words there was a fluidity of ideas in which Canova expressed his images of feminine beauty. He himself acknowledged this when he referred to a portrait of 'S. M. Maria Luigia ora Granduchessa di Parma ... è stata da me cambiata nel volto con una faccia ideale'.[11] It is indeed likely that being, in effect, Court Sculptor to the Buonaparte dynasty directly influenced the development of Canova's notions of female beauty. He was expected to create icons in the Roman imperial manner, in which the portrait was subsumed into a personification. That the cheerful features of Maria Luisa Hapsburg, Empress of France, should develop into the scarcely recognisable *Concorde*, or the tough-looking Elisa Baciocchi Bonaparte into the pure idealisation of *Polyhymnia* is part of the essentially evolutionary nature of Canova's work.

Passavant observed when recording the four ideal female heads by Canova at Chatsworth that they all had 'that peculiar sweetness which characterizes his compositions' and were 'remarkable for a beauty and delicacy of finish, which seems to triumph over the inflexibility of the material'.[12]

1 No.38; B.E-98/5684
2 Canova to WRH, 7 June 1816; Private Collection.
3 See below, Cat. No.2
4 Honour (1994), pp.359-419
5 G. Pavanello, *L'opera completa del Canova*, Milan, 1976, Hereafter Pavanello, 1976
6 WRH to Canova, 25 Jan 1819; B. 1-78/1529.
7 Moses (1887 edn), plates LXXVIII to LXXX.
8 Pavanello, Nos. 288 and 286
9 *Antonio Canova*, Venice, Correr Museum, 1992, Cat. No. 146. Hereafter cited as *Canova*, Venice, 1992.
10 *Ibid*, Cat. No. 148
11 7 June 1816; B.1-78/1512
12 Passavant, Vol.II, p.22

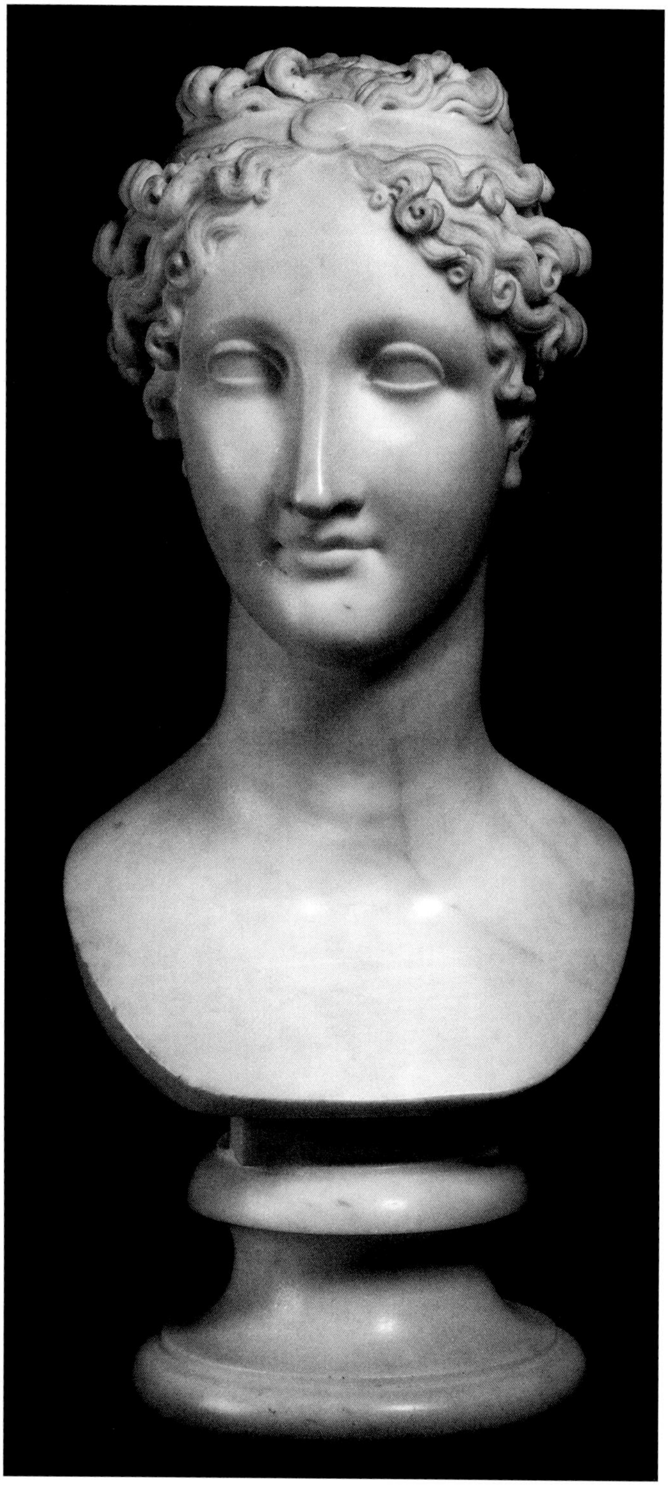

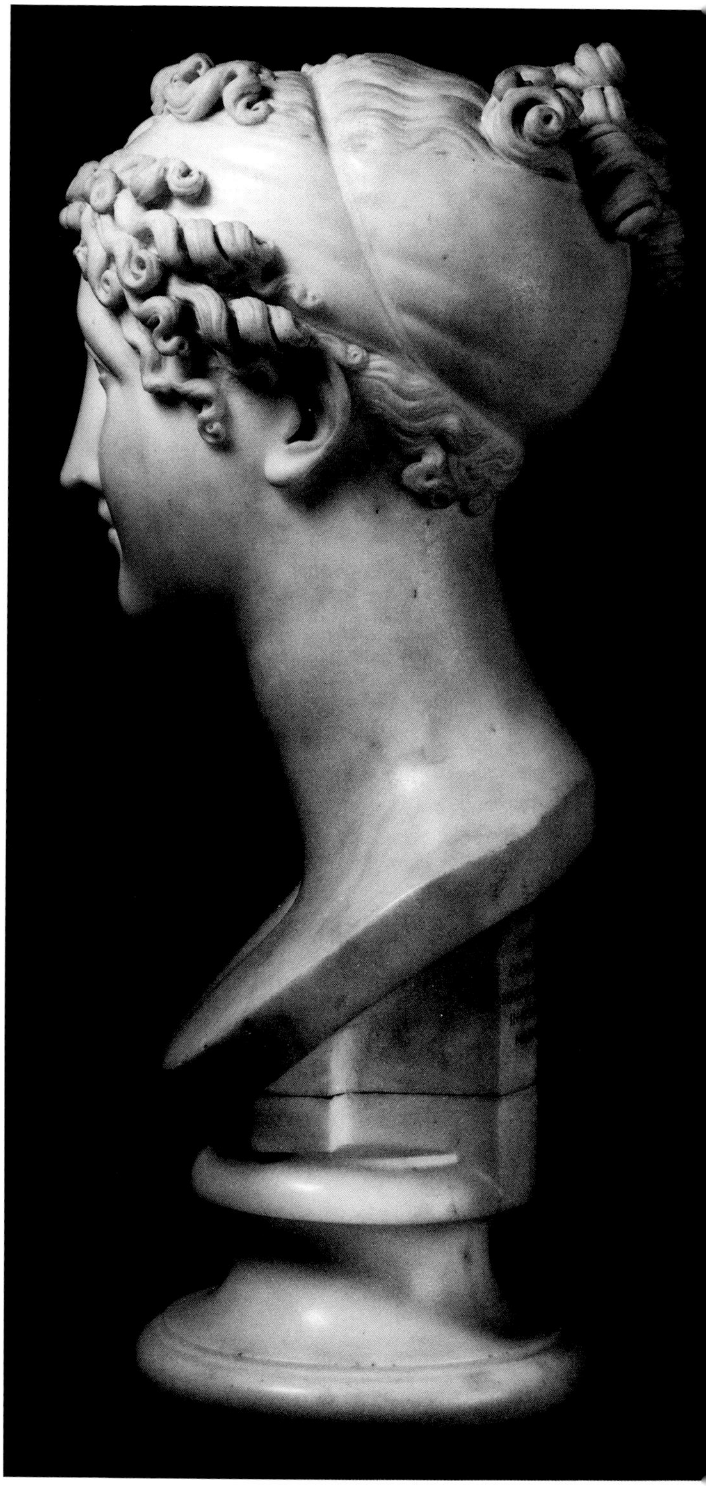

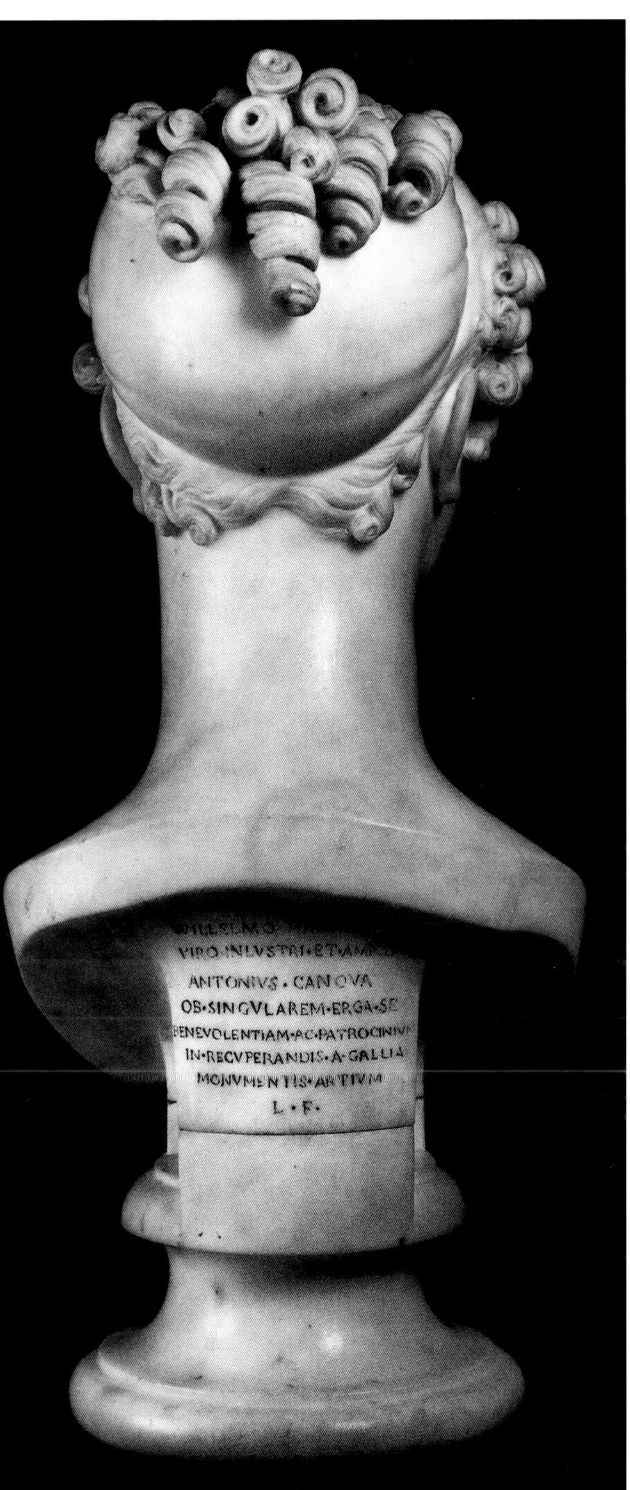

VILLELMO
VIRO INLVSTRI · ET AMICO
ANTONIVS · CANOVA
OB · SINGVLAREM · ERGA · SE
BENEVOLENTIAM · AC · PATROCINIVM
IN · RECVPERANDIS · A · GALLIA
MONVMENTIS · ARTIVM
L · F ·

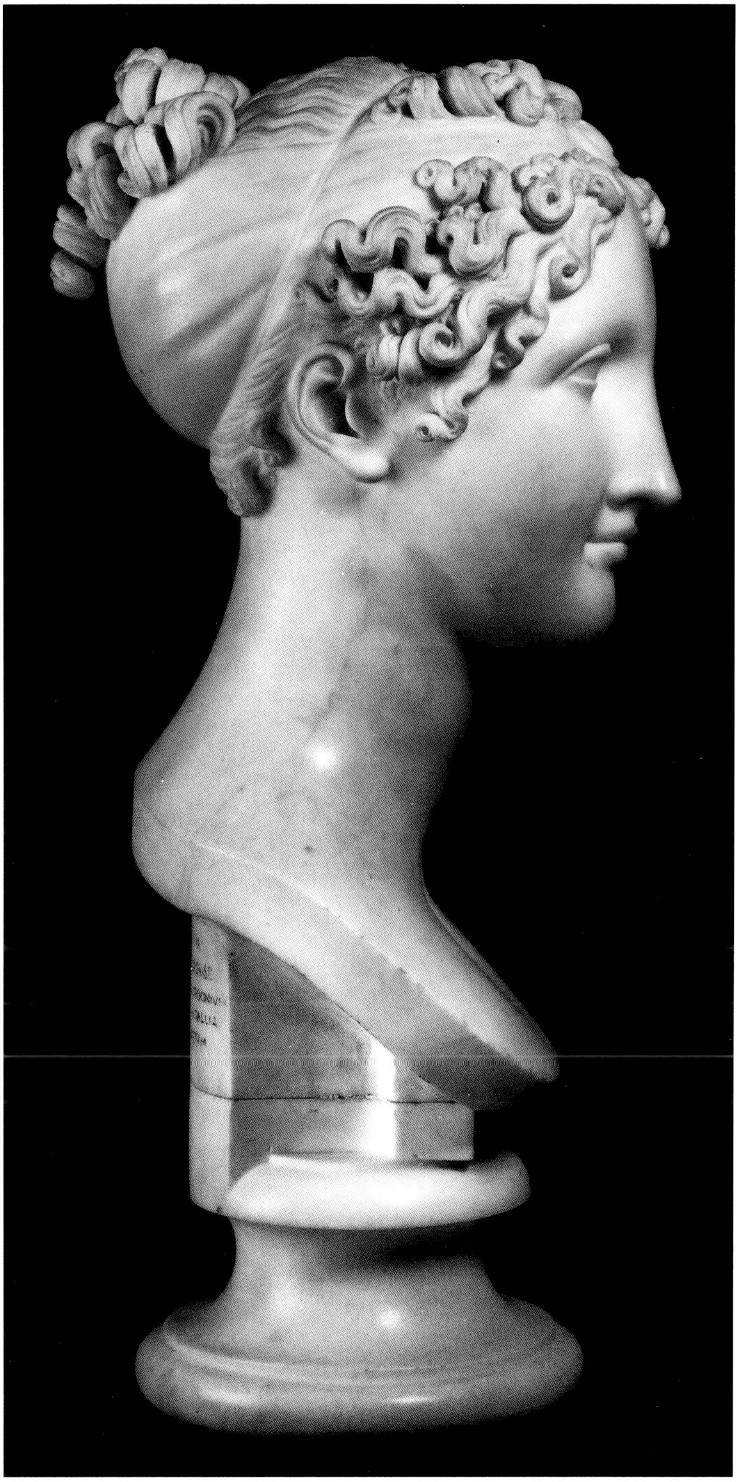

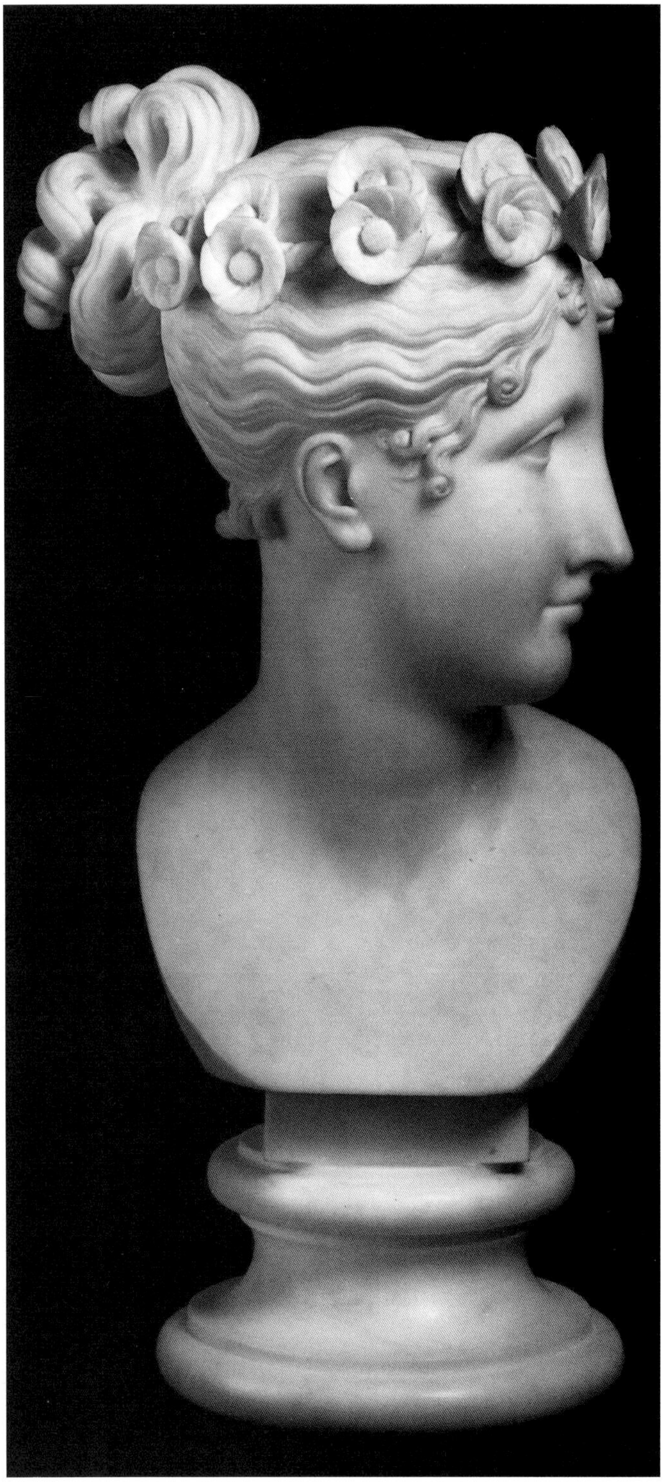

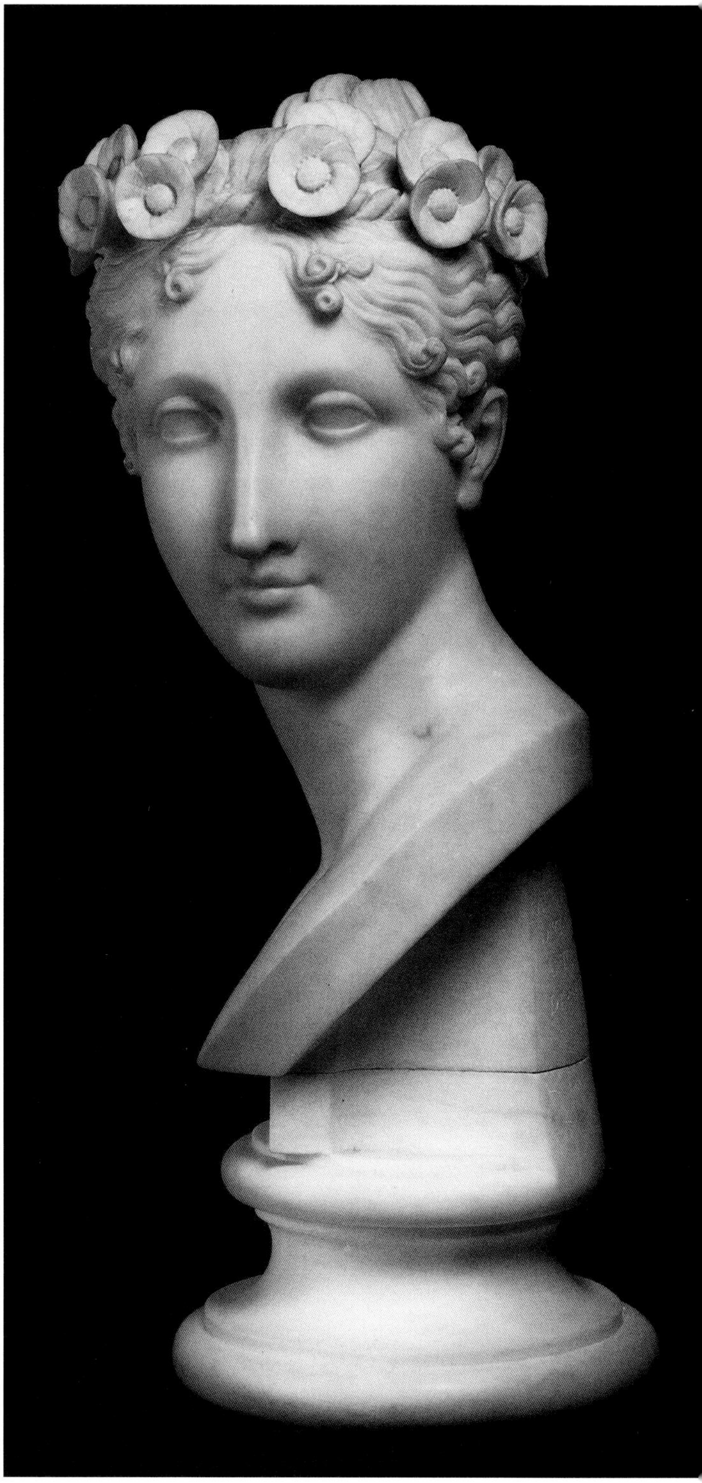

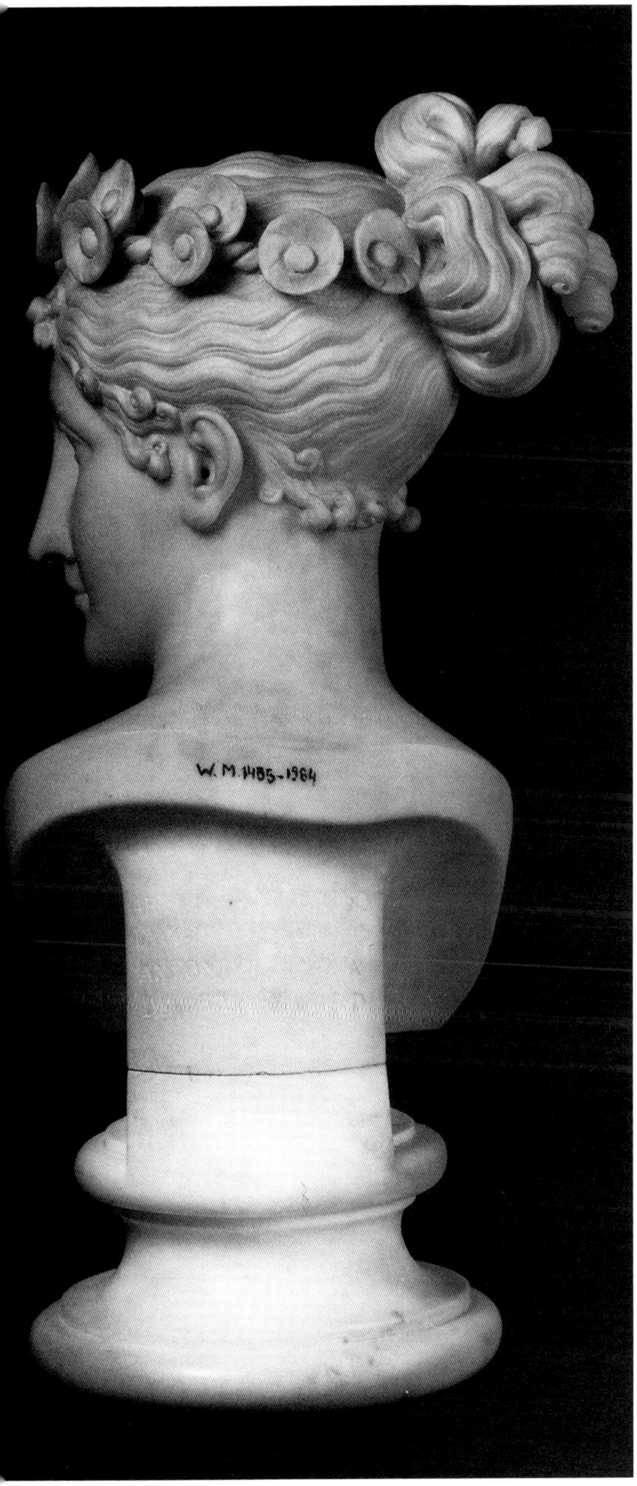

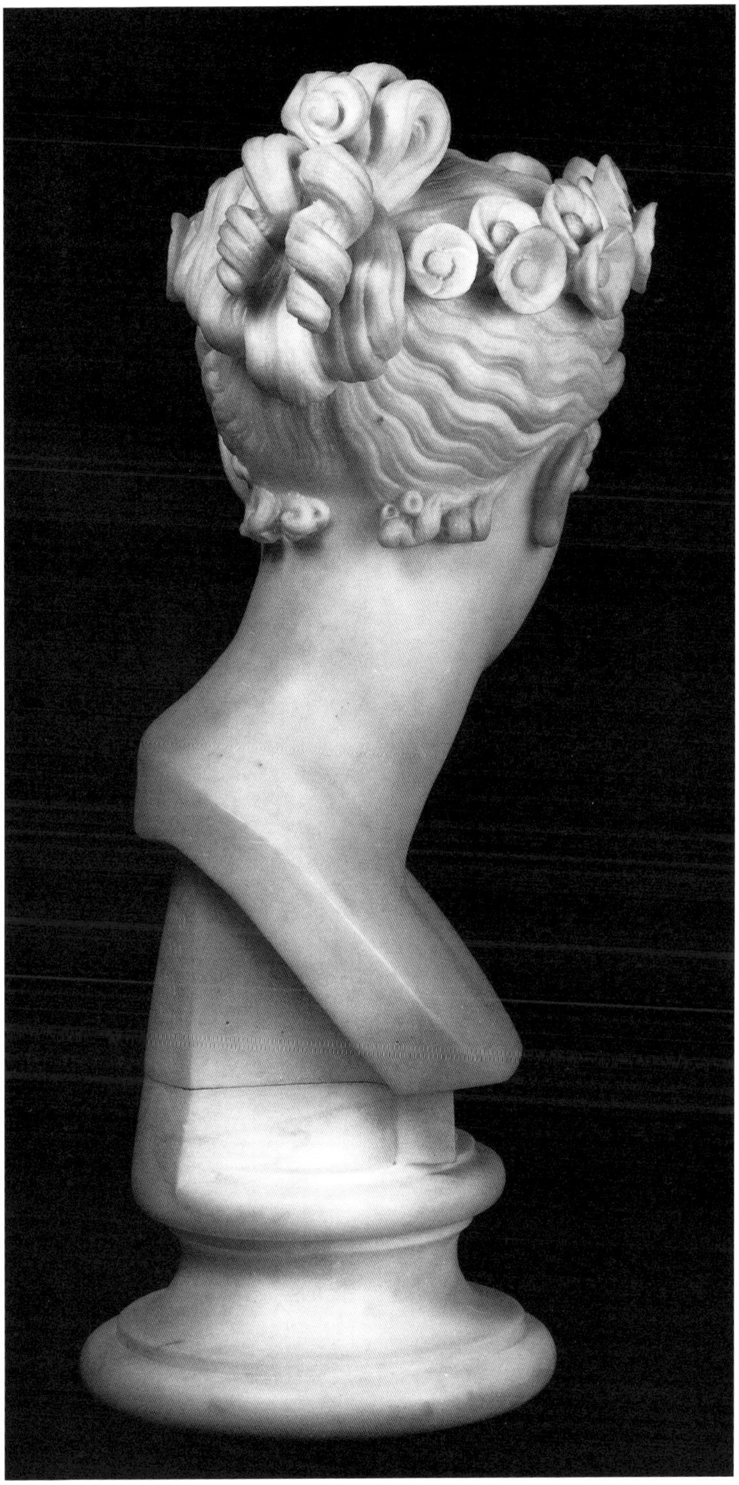

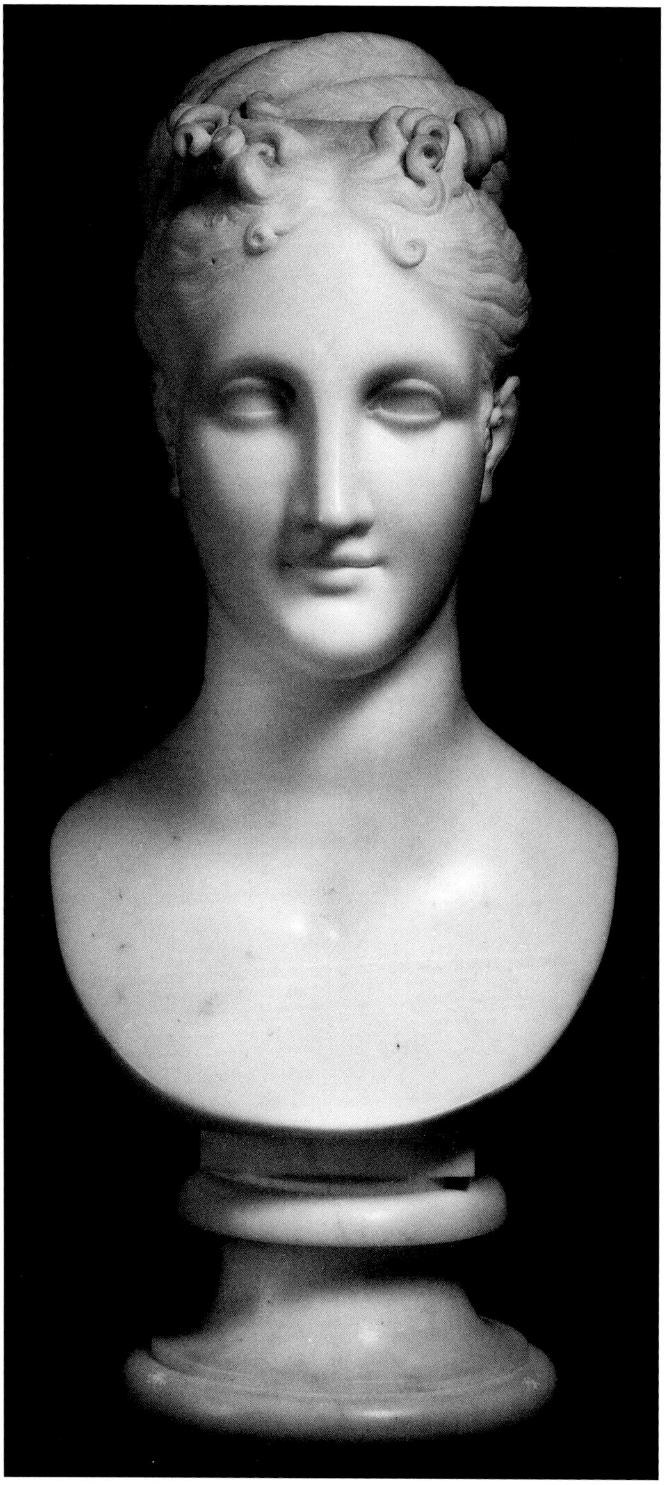

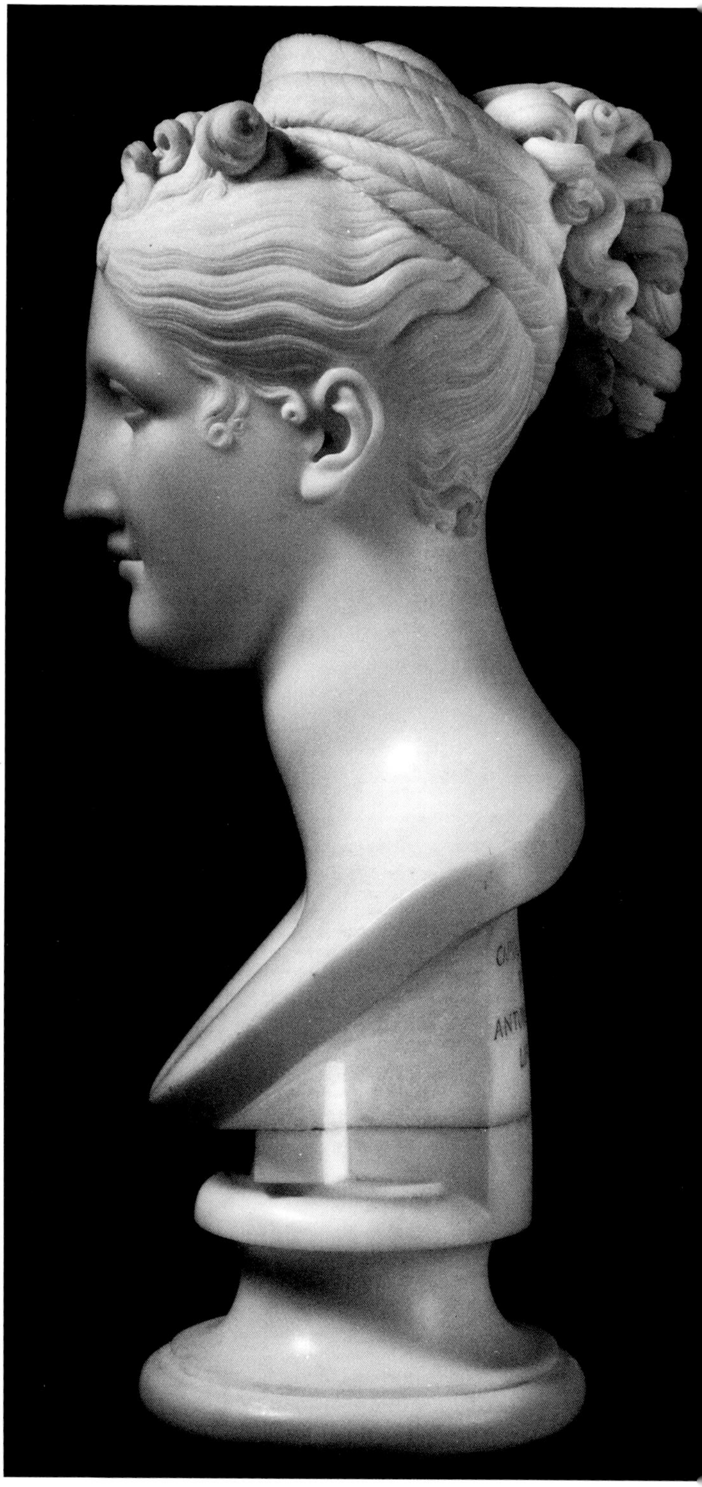

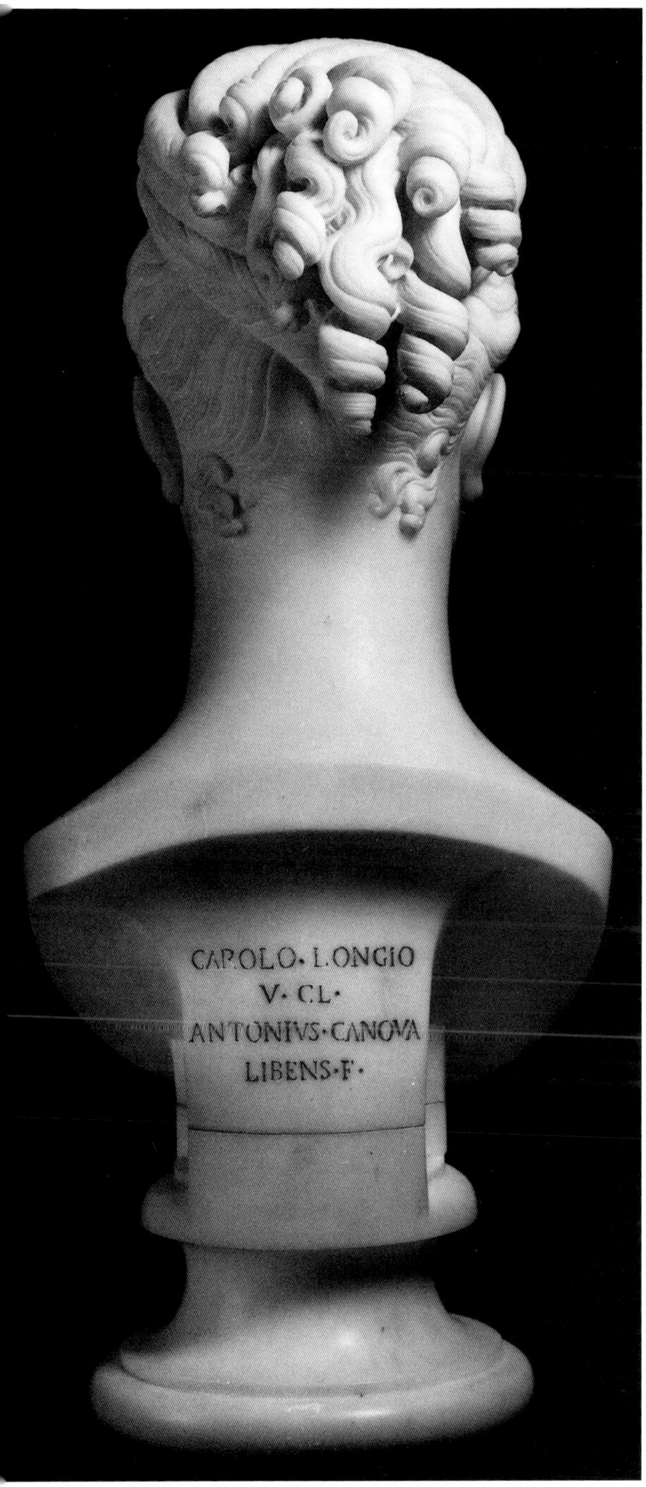

CAROLO·LONGIO
V·CL·
ANTONIVS·CANOVA
LIBENS·F·

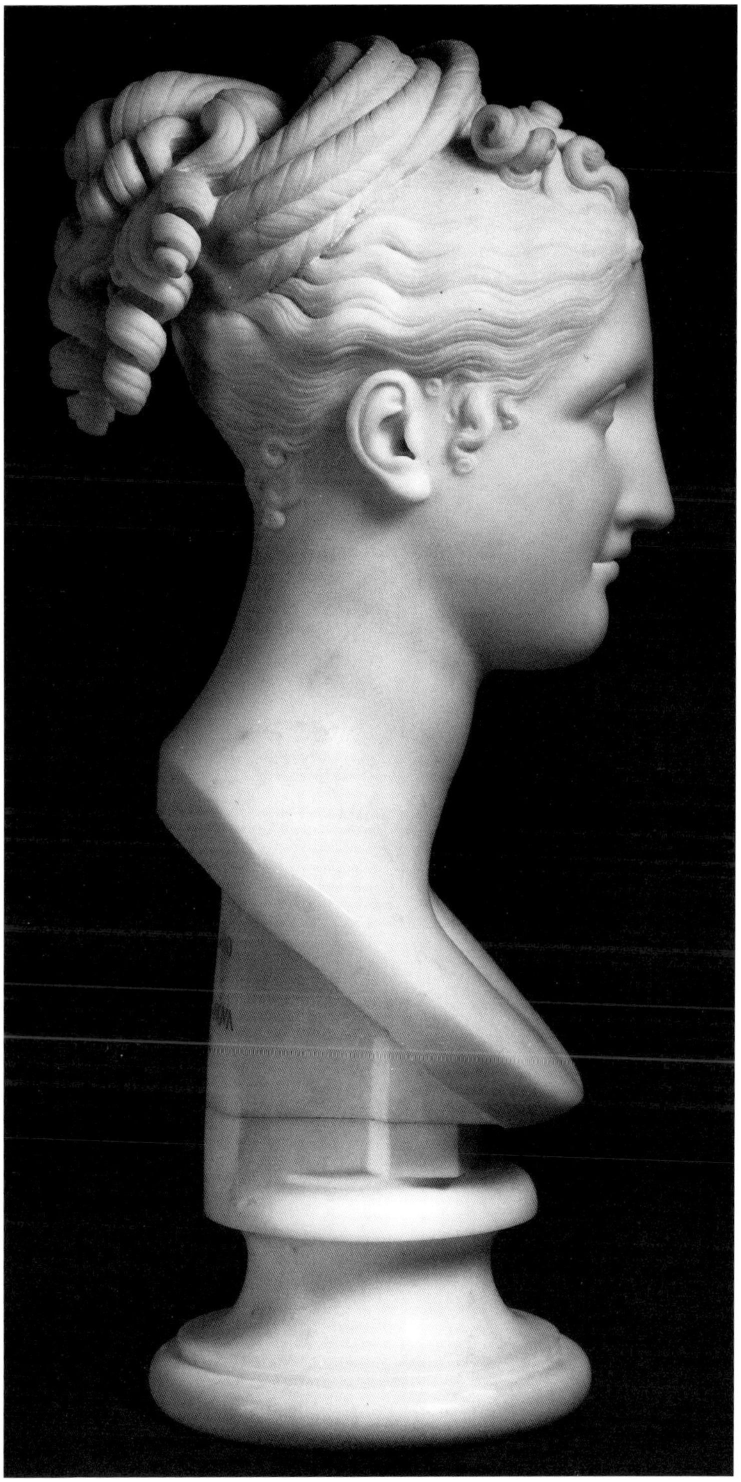

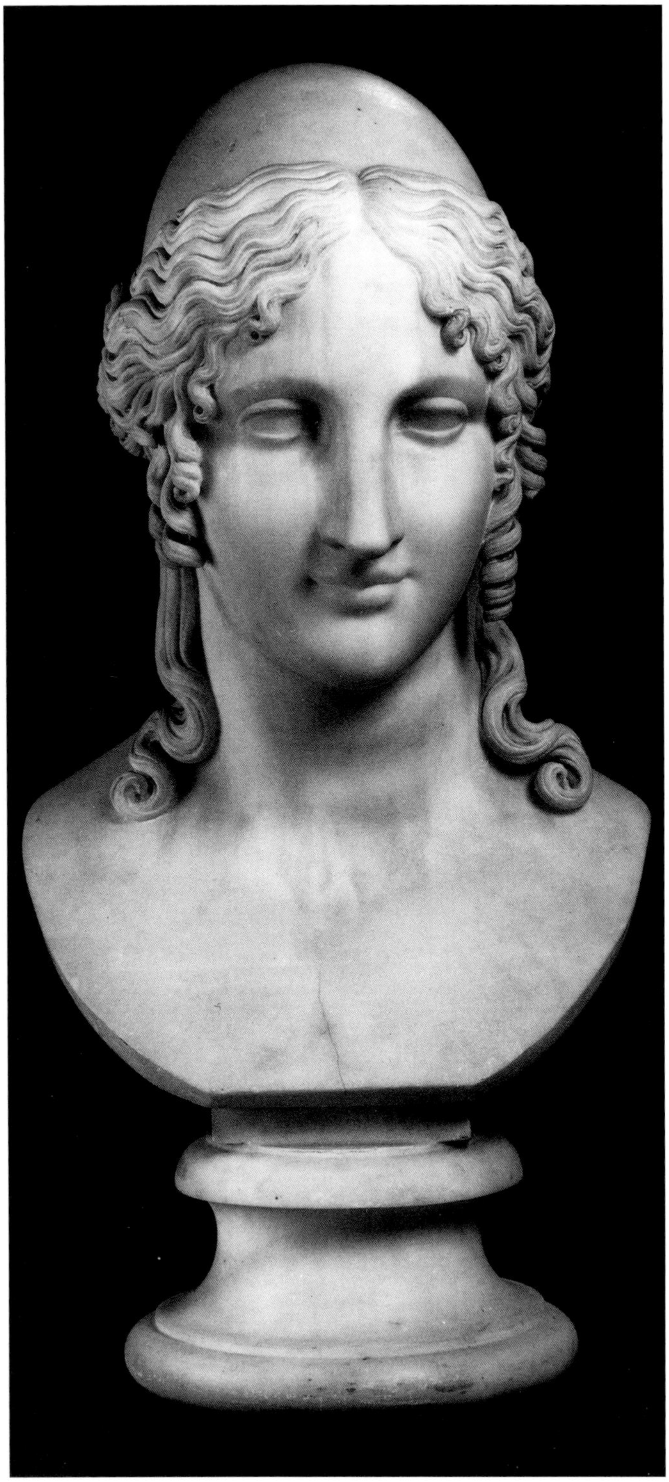

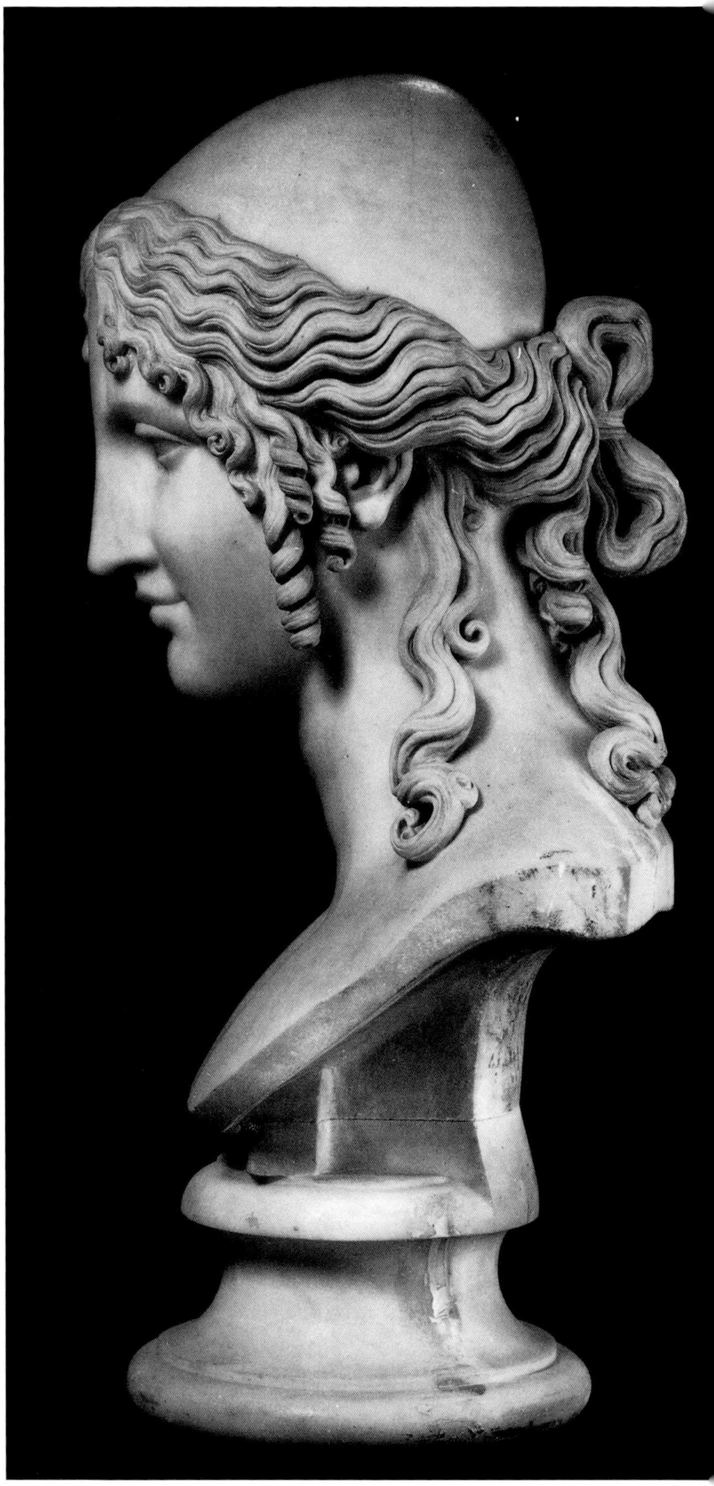

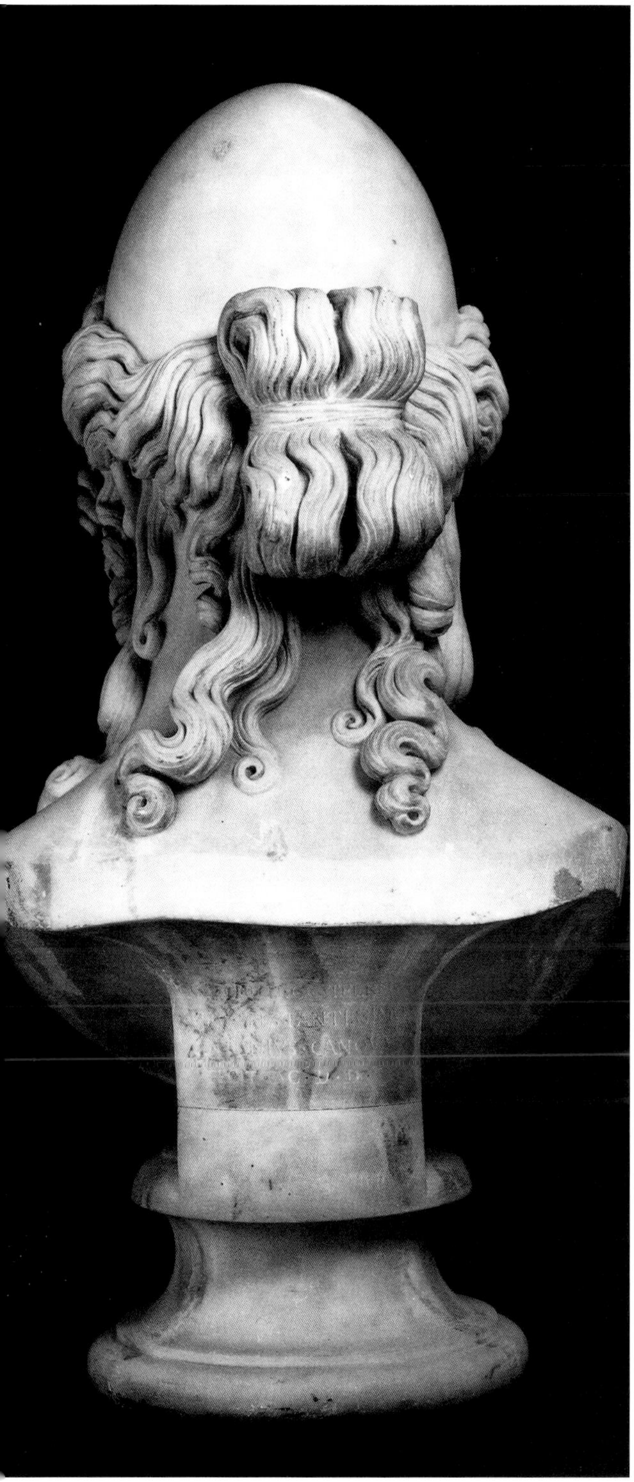

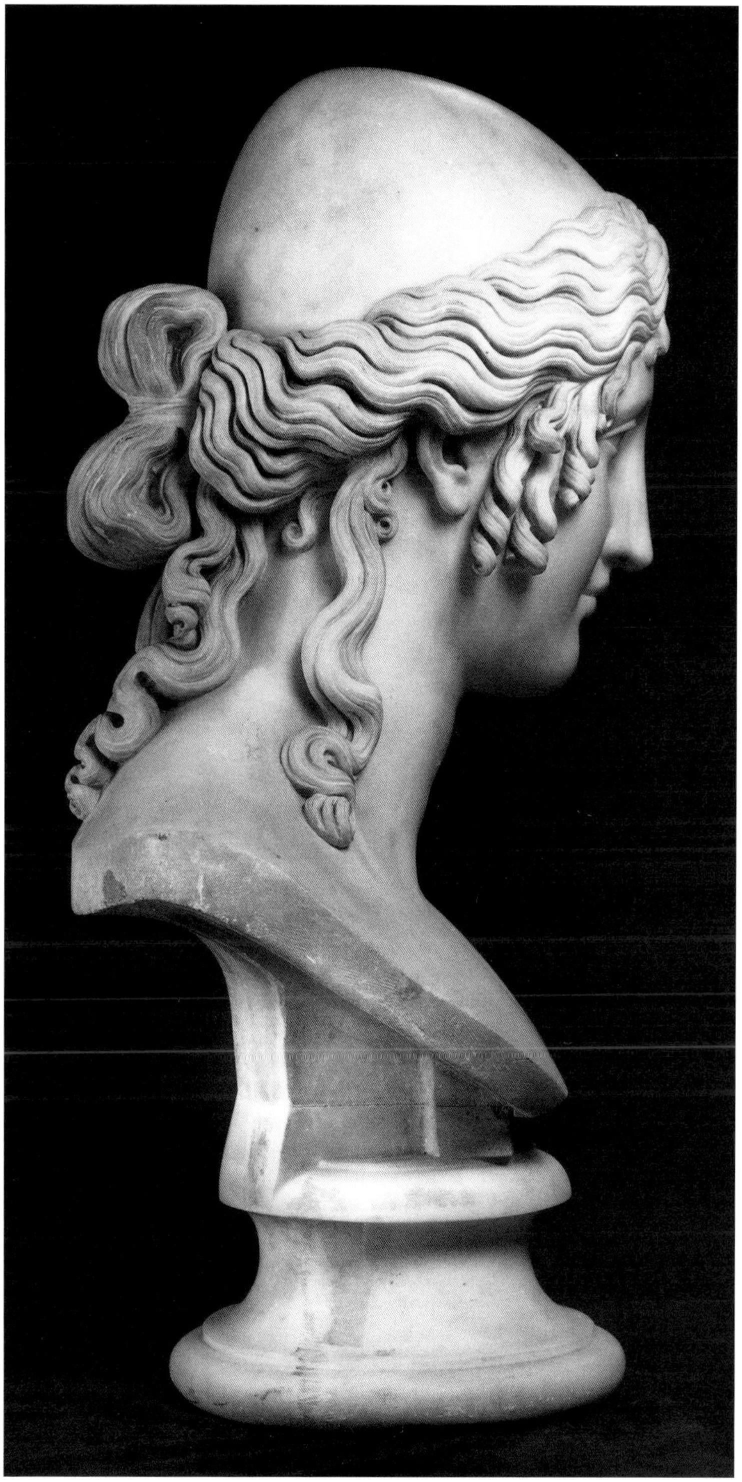

1

Antonio Canova 1757-1822

Ideal Head 1816

Marble, 54 cm.
Inscribed: WILLELMO. HAMILTONIO / VIRO. INLVSTRI. ET. AMICO /ANTONIVS.
CANOVA / OB. SINGVLAREM. ERGA. SE / BENEVOLENTIAM. AC. PATROCINIVM /
IN. RECVPERANDIS. A. GALLIA / MONVMENTIS. ARTIVM / L. F.

Provenance: 1816, presented by the sculptor to William Richard Hamilton; thence by
descent; sold Sotheby's, 7 December 1995, Lot 97; purchased Reiner Ziet, August,
1995. Literature: L. Cicognara, *Biografia di Antonio Canova*, Venice, 1823, p.66; H.
Moses, *The Works of Antonio Canova in Sculpture and Modelling*, London, 1824,
mentioned in the text of the reprint of 1887 (unpaginated); Q. De Quincy, *Canova et
ses Ouvrages ou Mémoires Historiques sur la Vie et le Travaux de ce Célèbre Artiste*,
Paris, 1834, p. 291; A. d'Este, *Memorie di Antonio Canova*, Florence, 1864, p.245;
G.Pavanello, *L'opera completa del Canova*, Milan, 1976, No. 286; H. Honour, (Ed.),
Edizione Nazionale delle Opere di Antonio Canova, Vol.i, *Scritti*, Rome, 1994, p. 406;
H. Honour, 'An Ideal Head by Canova', *Sotheby's Preview*, December, 1995, pp. 14-15;
The Burlington Magazine Vol. cxxxix, May 1997, Cover Illustration and p.363; Nat-
ional Art Collections Fund *Review* 1996, illus., and p.144.

Ashmolean Museum, 1996.395

The *Head* disappeared beyond what might be described as the art historical horizon,
until, as a result of the Council of Europe exhibition *The Age of Neo-Classicism*
(London, 1972), Hugh Honour was approached by direct descendants of William
Richard Hamilton. After its incorrect identification by Moses and others in the 1820s,
the only known record of the *Head's* subsequent history is in a photograph (Fig.11) of
the reception at Anmer Hall, Sandringham, Norfolk, for the marriage of Sir Walter
Chaytor of Croft Hall, Darlington and Miss Alexandra Hervey.[1] Queen Alexandra, the
Princess of Wales, the future Queen Mary and other members of the Royal Family
were present.[2] Anmer Hall was lent for the wedding breakfast by William Hamilton's
grandson Rear-Admiral Sir Frederick Hamilton. Seated on the floor to the left in the
photograph are his daughters, Miss Alexandra Hamilton and to the right Miss Jean
Hamilton, grandmother and great-aunt respectively of the last owners of the *Ideal Head*.
   Michael Vickers discusses source types elsewhere in the catalogue. Another possible
source may have been the bound head of *Hygiea*,[3] the full length statue of whom was

mentioned in Canova's notes on his visit to Thomas Hope's collection,[4] and which was thought by contemporaries to be by Phidias. Canova first used the motif of the hair bound in a *sakkoi* in the relief known as *Teaching the Ignorant* in 1795[5] and again in the funerary monument to Giovanni Volpato of 1804 to 1807 whose source was undoubtedly an antique *stele*.[6] The first ideal head of this type, described variously as Clio, the Muse of History, and Calliope, the Muse of Epic Poetry, now in the Musée Fabre, Montpellier, was made in 1811 and given by Canova to Luise Stolberg. Its source is thought to be one of the *Tiburtine Muses* excavated at Tivoli in 1774, acquired by Visconti for the Museo Pio-Clementino, which had been reproduced in biscuit by Volpato.[7] The gesso, with points, survives at Possagno, (Fig.12).[8] The type appears, apparently in clay, in the portrait of Canova by the Danish painter Rudolph Surlandt (1781-1862) of about 1810, suggesting that the head was modelled in the previous year.[9] A second version known as Calliope, was made in 1812 for Giovanni Rosini.[10] However, the Hamilton head differs from these prototypes in one important detail: it is set at quite a different angle to look right not left, more like the head of Maria Luisa, Empress of France (subsequently Grand Duchess of Parma), or of Elisa Baciocchi Bonaparte.[11] Countess Albrizzi described the Calliope type as 'full of soul and of thought; she seems to be meditating intently on some lofty ideas, and we almost fear to disturb the workings of her mind, which seem ready to burst in eloquent language from her lips . . . Her hair is arranged with a scrupulous care; it is

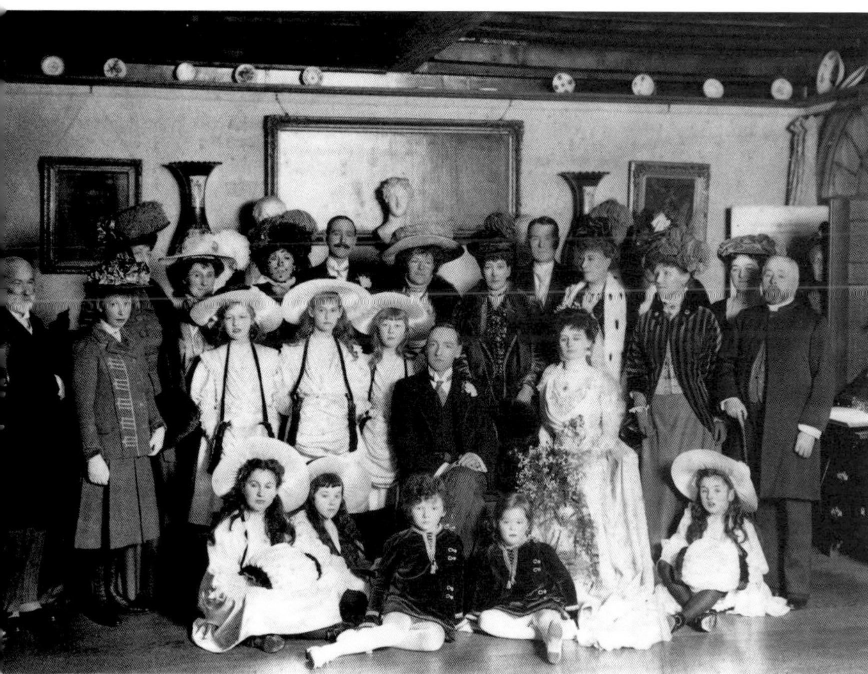

Fig. 11

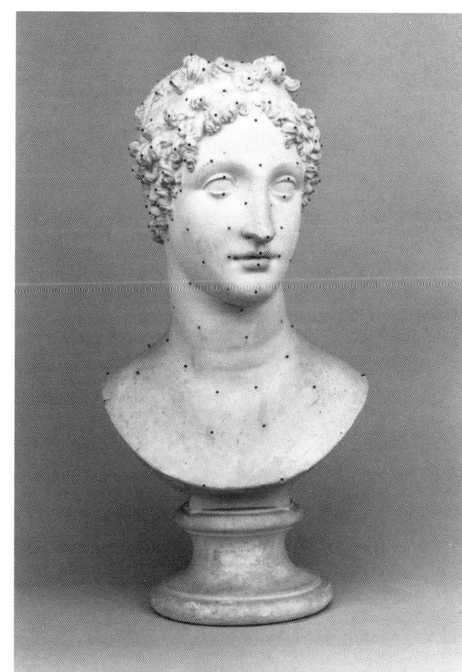

Fig. 12

parted in the front so as to reveal her high and beautiful forehead, and falling back, elegantly shades her temples and cheeks with its closely curled ringlets.'[12]

As has emerged, Canova's *Ideal Head* for Hamilton was a highly personal present, and if there was anything of a semi-official character about the others it was clearly excluded in the case of Canova and Hamilton. Canova wrote to Hamilton on 27th May 1817, the first time he mentioned that there was one for him, about 'i busti ideali di marmo, e quell'ancora distinato da me a voi, per segno della mia affezione e riconoscenza, di cui non potrò nè saprò darvi mai prove bastanti.'[13]

1   Private Collection.
2   *The Times*, 8 January 1909.
3   Watkin, pp.33-34, 48 and pl.4
4   Honour (1994), p.390.
5   Pavanello, No.92 and *Canova*, Venice (1992), Cat. No.112
6   Basilica of the SS Apostoli; Pavanello, No.179. Canova used it again for reliefs on the Traversa and Tadini monuments in 1817 and 1818-20; Pavanello, Nos.292 and 315.
7   *Canova*, Venice (1992), Cat. No.145.
8   Inv. No. S.74; Gipsoteca, Possagno.
9   Copenhagen, Thorvaldsens Museum; *Canova*, (Venice), 1992, Cat. No.8; *Antonio Canova. Tegninger Fra Museet I Bassano*, Copenhagen Thorvaldesens Museum, 1969, Cat. No.112.
10 Florence, Galleria d'Arte Moderna, Pitti Palace; *Canova*, Venice (1992), Cat. No.147; Pavanello, No.237.
11 Pavanello, Nos.225 and 267.
12 Moses, vol 2, p. 277.
13 Private Collection.

2

Antonio Canova 1757-1822

Head of a Dancer 1816

Marble, 53 cm
Inscribed: ARTVRO WELLESLEYO / DVCI WELLINGTONIO / ANTONIVS CANOVA /
DE ARTE SVA DDD.

Provenance: 1816, presented by the sculptor to the 1st Duke of Wellington; thence by
descent to the 7th Duke of Wellington; gift to the nation under the terms of the
Wellington Museum Act, 1947.
Literature: L. Cicognara, *Biografia di Antonio Canova*, Venice, 1823, p.66; H. Moses,
The Works of Antonio Canova in Sculpture and Modelling, London, 1824, mentioned
in the text of the reprint of 1887 (unpaginated); *Quarterly Review*, Vol xcii, No.184,
1853, p.465; A.d'Este, *Memorie della Vita di Antonio Canova*, Florence, 1864, p.245; E.
Wellington, *A Descriptive & Historical Catalogue of the Collection of Pictures and
Sculpture at Apsley House, London*, London, 1901, Vol ii, No.37, p.459; G. Pavanello,
L'opera completa del Canova, Milan, 1976, No.285; H. Honour (Ed.), *Edizione
Nazionale delle Opere di Antonio Canova*, Vol i *Scritti*, Rome, 1994, p.406; *The Three
Graces - Antonio Canova*, exh.cat., National Galleries of Scotland, 1995, Fig.12 S.
Jervis, M. Tomlin (Revised J.Voak), *Apsley House: Wellington Museum*, London, 1996,
p.11.
Exhibited: *The Age of Neo-Classicism*, London, Royal Academy of Arts, 1972, Cat. No.
323

Lent by the Wellington Museum, Apsley House (A branch of the Victoria and Albert
Museum).

Among the four *Ideal Heads* this one is unique. There appear to be no other versions
and there are no gessos or plasters. It is in fact the head of Canova's *Dancer with her
hands on her hips*, also known as the Muse of Dance, Nymph of the Dance and Erato,
Muse of Erotic Dance. This had been commissioned by Josephine Beauharnais,
Napoleon's repudiated wife, in about 1802 and completed in 1811-12. Exhibited at the
Paris Salon of 1812, it became in 1815, the property of the Emperor Alexander i of
Russia.[1] A second version of the *Dancer* was completed in the last year of Canova's
life, for the English patron and collector Sir Simon Houghton Clarke, friend of
Charles Long and a passing acquaintance of William Richard Hamilton.[2] There just
may be in the choice of subject an allusion to the Duke of Wellington's failure to

acquire the group of Canovas, which included the original *Dancer* from Malmaison. The miniaturist Robertson, who had been asked for his opinion of the paintings on behalf of the Duke, clearly thought that at £2,500 a bargain had been lost. Canova must surely have preferred, in the circumstances, his work in English hands rather than in those of the uncooperative Russians.[3] However the English took every precaution not to be seen to be profiting from those circumstances.

It recalls the Capitoline Flora with her chaplet of flowers, which was among the statues ceded to France under the Treaty of Tolentino in 1796.[4] On the death of the Duke in 1853, the house was thrown open to the public. The reviewer for the *Quarterly Review* remarked that the *Head*, then apparently in the Picture Gallery or Saloon, was thought by some to be Pauline Bonaparte, and commented that Canova had 'moved heaven and earth to bring about this great act of justice … never was the sword better thrown into the scale, than when the eternal city, the home of art, thus recovered by it her heir-looms – the Apollo and the Transfiguration'.[5] It was described as a *Sappho* in Evelyn, Duchess of Wellington's Catalogue of 1901, when it was in the Yellow Drawing Room. It must have been moved again soon after as it appears in the Inner Hall among other busts, on a table, in a photograph of about 1900.[6]

The Duchess quotes from the official letter to Wellington from Pius VII acknowledging the part the Duke played in the restitution of works of art to Rome in which there is implied the intention to prove Papal gratitude. There is however no correspondence from the Duke of Wellington among the Canova Archive at Bassano that might record the reception of the *Head*.

---

1 Hermitage Museum Inventory, no.18.; *Canova all'Ermitage, le sculture del museo di San Pietroburgo*, exh. cat., Rome, 1991, pp.116-119; Pavanello, no.172; *Canova*, Venice, (1992) Cat. No.134.

2 National Gallery of Canada, Ottawa; Pavanello, no.311.

3 Robertson, pp.270-1.

4 Haskell and Penny (1981) nos.40 and 41.

5 *Quarterly Review*, Vol. XCII, p.465.

6 Reproduced S. Jervis, M. Tomlin, (revised J. Voak): *Apsley House Wellington Museum*, Reprinted 1996.

3

Antonio Canova 1757-1822

Ideal Head 1816

Marble, 56.3 cm
Inscribed: CAROLO. LONGIO / V. CL. / ANTONIVS. CANOVA / LIBENS. F.

Provenance: 1816, presented by the sculptor to Sir Charles Long, later 1st Baron Farnborough; 1981, purchased on the New York art market.
Literature: L. Cicognara, *Biografia di Antonio Canova*, Venice, 1823, p.66; H. Moses, *The Works of Antonio Canova in Sculpture and Modelling*, London, 1824, Reprinted 1887, pl. LXXX; A.d'Este, *Memorie della Vita di Antonio Canova*, Florence, 1864, p.245; G.Pavanello, *L'opera completa del Canova*, Milan, 1976, No.288; E. Pilsbury, et. al., *In Pursuit of Quality, The Kimbell Art Museum*, Fort Worth, New York, 1987, pp.264-7; H. Honour, Ed., *Edizione Nazionale delle Opere di Antonio Canova*, Vol. I, *Scritti*, Rome, 1994, p.406.

Lent by the Kimbell Art Museum, Fort Worth, Texas.

There is no illustration accompanying the entry in Pavanello's *catalogue raisonné* of 1976, and the assumption made is that the head presented to Long was another *Helen*. In fact the type probably has its origin in *Head of the Seated Muse Polymnia*[1] which, commisioned in 1809 by Elisa Baciocchi Bonaparte, Granduchess of Tuscany, began life as *Concorde*. It was not completed at the time of Napoleon's fall and was eventually presented by Canova to Francis I of Austria on his marriage in 1817.[2] The type was used again by Canova in his portrait of *Caroline Murat Bonaparte* in 1813, of which only the gesso survives at Possagno.[3] It is just possible that Charles Long's *Ideal Head* is indeed that of Caroline Murat, recycled for a new political order and a new group of patrons, though the ringlets appear less abundant than in the engraving *Carolina Annunziata Regina di Napoli* by Pietro Fontana. This shows the Queen in profile looking to the right.[4] Another *Ideal Head* of this type was commissioned by the Marchesa Groslier as a present for Quatremère de Quincy, in the summer of 1816. Called *La Riconoscenza*, Canova himself said it was based on his portrait bust of Maria Luisa, Empress of France, commissioned by Napoleon in 1810.[5] It was engraved by Bernardino Consorti in the autumn of 1817.[6]

The source may be an antique portrait of Sabina or Faustina and a drawing exists of female heads similarly coiffed.[7] That the abundance of ringlets was a concession to contemporary fashion, and was recognised as such by contemporaries ('all the softness and luxuriant elegance of the Parisian headdress')[8] suggests a portrait source.

Why Charles Long was included among the four is not clear. He remains something of an *eminence grise* throughout. He never appears in the documentary evidence by name, though he may be the "ministro" referred to on a number of occasions. It is not clear whether he was in Paris at all in the autumn of 1815, but he was certainly there the following year settling financial business to do with the army of occupation. He was undoubtedly hospitable to Canova when the latter was in London[9] and later to Canova's old friend Leopoldo Cicognara, whom he had to stay several times.[10] Canova probably had sound reasons for including him. He, after all, held the purse strings and was the Prince Regent's confidant and adviser on all matters of taste and patronage. When some years later payment for the *Nymph* had been delayed, Canova asked Hamilton to intervene discreetly as 'io non vorrei muovere alcuna sillaba . . . e volendo seguitare a diportarmi colla stessa delicatezza e disinteresse che osservai finora.'[11]

Of all the responses to Canova's presents that of Charles Long was undoubtedly the most enthusiastic and fulsome. He wrote from the Army Pay Office, Whitehall, on October 6, 1818:

> Caro Signore
>
> Je n' attenderai plus long tems de vous remercier pour le Cade[au] que vous avez eu la bonté de m'envoyer – elle est tout a fait gracieuse et elegante – tous les Connoisseurs, (et beaucoup l'ont vu) l'admire extremement, et la trouvent parmi les plus jolies de vos ouvrages. Je ne sais pas comment vous < erasure > faire assez mes remerciments, pour avoir destiné cette ouvrage pour ^{moi}– mais je vous prie bien de croire qu'il n'y a personne qui sait mieux l' apprecier... [12]

Long's delight was reiterated soon after in a letter of October 23rd 1818, the main business of which was to inform Canova that the Prince Regent had immediately agreed to the exhibition of the *Nymph* at either the Royal Academy or the British Institution. Its arrival was eagerly awaited. One of the Metopes from the Parthenon belonging to M. Choiseul Gouffier was to be sold and while they were ambitious to own the fourteenth it was to stay in the Musée de Paris, and Westmacott was carrying out the Prince Regent's orders to make the Plasters from the Elgin Collection, in which the Duchess of Devonshire had an interest. He concluded:

> Il me n'est pas possible < sans > de ^{vous ecrive sans} vous repetir mille fois mes obligations que je vous dois pour la belle Maitresse que vous m'aviez envoyé, j'en suis absolument amoureux – c'est vraiment d'une beauté et d'une Elegance parfait[?] Touts les Connoisseurs <erasure> l'estime comme la tête la plus gracieuse qu'ils ont vu de vos mains – Encore mille graces et croyez que je suis toujours ami beaucoup d'estime.[13]

He later sent a snuffbox, courtesy of a Mr Bourke, though he says it is a miserable recompense 'pour la charment Tête que vous avez eu la Bonté de me donner.'[14]

Some weeks later he writes again, via Miss Berry, saying that Mr Bourke has been detained on business but he sends the snuffbox courtesy of Mr Carr, a friend, repeating the unworthiness of the object, but adding 'je sais combien je suis votre debiteur.'[15]

1 Polyhymnia was Muse of the Sublime Hymn. The coiffure is very clearly the same in the engraving *Polinnia* by G. B. Balestra of the left hand view: *Canova e l'incisione*, exh. cat., Rome and Bassano, 1994, LXIV.
2 Pavanello, no.268
3 Pavanello, no.248
4 *Canova e l'incisione*, LXV
5 Pavenello, no.283
6 *Canova e l'incisione*, LXXVI
7 Inscribed *Sabina and Faustina Mag*, Bassano Inv. No. F.7.24.1712; Illustrated in Bassi, (1959), p.260.
8 Moses (1824), p.281.
9 *Farington's Diaries*, 21 Nov 1815.
10 Long to Canova, 15 Sept 1819, B. 4-XCVI-5/1166.
11 Canova to WRH 29 Oct 1819; Private Collection.
12 B.4-XCII-22/1183
13 B.4-XCVI-3/1164
14 July 23 [1819]; B.4-XCII-13/1176
15 Sept 15 1819; B.4-XCVI-5/1166

4

Antonio Canova 1757-1822

Helen 1816

Marble, 63.5 cm
Inscribed: VICECOMITI CASTELREGHIO / VIRO PRESTANTISSIMO / ANTONIVS CANOVA / FECIT AC D.D.

Provenance: 1816, presented by the sculptor to Robert Stewart, Viscount Castlereagh, later 2nd Marquess of Londonderry; thence by descent.
Literature: L. Cicognara, *Biografia di Antonio Canova*, Venice, 1823, p.66; H. Moses, *The Works of Antonio Canova in Sculpture and Modelling*, London, 1824, mentioned in the text of the reprint of 1887 (unpaginated); A. d'Este, *Memorie della Vita di Antonio Canova*, Florence, 1864, p.245; H. Honour, 'Canova's Studio Practice-II: 1792-1822', *The Burlington Magazine*, Vol. CXIV, March, 1972, pp.214-229, Fig.18; G. Pavanello, *L'opera completa del Canova*, Milan, 1976, No.287; G. Worsley, 'Wynyard Park, County Durham-II', *Country Life* Vol. CLXXX, No.4646, 4 September, 1986, pp. 664-669, Fig.12; H. Honour, *Edizione Nazionale delle Opere di Antonio Canova*, Vol I, *Scritti*, Rome, 1994, p.406.
Exhibited: *The Age of Neo-Classicism*, London, Royal Academy of Arts, 1972, Cat. No.321.

Private Collection

One of five known versions (a sixth can now be discounted, see 3 above), this is a variation of the bust of *Helen* signed and dated 1811, given by Canova to Contessa Isabella Teotochi Albrizzi. That *Helen* was seen by Byron in Venice,[1] in the Palazzo Albrizzi, where it still is,[2] at the beginning of his exile in November or December 1816, and inspired the lines:

> In this belovèd marble view
> Above the works and thoughts of Man,
> What Nature *could* but *would not*, do,
> And Beauty and Canova *can*!
> Beyond Imagination's power,
> Beyond the Bard's defeated art,
> With Immortality her dower,
> Behold the *Helen* of the heart.
>   *On the Bust of Helen by Canova*, 1816.

A second was made for the Marchesa Groslier in 1817 or 1818, who gave it to G.B. Somariva;[3] and in 1819 the Polish Count Pach acquired a third that is in all probability the one now in the Hermitage Museum, St.Petersburg.[4] Four gessos or plaster casts survive at Possagno: two, one with and one without points, are more than life-size, and might be described as colossal;[5] while two are the size of this and three other completed marbles.[6]

On 25 January 1819 William Richard Hamilton writing to Canova to thank him for a letter delivered by the painter Harlow, and in which he introduces Charles Pullen, thanks Canova again for his own bust and continues:

> 'La testa de Elena presentata da lei a Lord Castlereagh, à ancora i suoi Ammiratori – mà noi altri in questo paese, non siamo abbastanza accrezzati ai Simboli dell' antica Mithologia, sopra le Statue, per gustare sufficientemente la bella idea della testa <u>ovata</u> – nondimeno anche noi possiamo vedere le vere bellezze della physionomia, e[?] della persona.'[7]

Thomas Lawrence wrote to Canova 'you have sent a Helen to Lord Castlereagh that even Lady Castereagh will not permit His Royal Highness [the Prince Regent] to have, and which I think is your most beautiful head, entirely justifying the old gentlemen of Priam's court in their indulgent admiration.'[8]

Helen, the subject of this *Ideal Head*, was according to legend was the daughter of Leda and Zeus in the guise of a swan. Thus Hamilton's reference to the suitability of the allusion to an egg in the forms within the bust, is, of all those presented to the four Englishmen, the most historically apposite. Her name recalls her Greekness, and she herself was symbolic of ravishment, of sequestration, of epic wars fought over aesthetic property. The *Head* is not recorded thereafter. Passavant may have seen it at Londonderry House 'in the large saloon . . . adorned with various statues and family busts in white marble', but he refers directly only to Canova's *Perseus and the Minotaur* and a *Dancing Girl* from the Fries Collection at Vienna.[9]

---

1 It was to the Countess d'Albrizzi's that Byron took Tom Moore on his first evening in Venice, 7 October 1819. W. Dowden (ed.) *The Journals of Thomas Moore*, London and Toronto, 1983, Vol.1, p.226.

2 Pavanello, no.239; *Canova*, Venice (1992), cat. no.142

3 Pavanello. no.284.

4 Inventory no.825; Pavenello, no.331; *Canova all'Ermitage: le sculture del museo de San Pietroburgo* exh. cat. Rome, 1991, pp.124-127; *Canova*, Venice, (1992), Cat. No.143.

5 Possagno Inventory S.92 - without points - currently on display in the Museo Civico, Bassano; S.221 - with points - at Possagno, not officially on display.

6 Both are in the recently restored Tower Room, one with and one without points; no inventory numbers available.

7 B.I-78/1529

8 Quoted in D. Williams, Vol 1, pp.352-3.

9 Passavant, Vol. 1, p. 178.

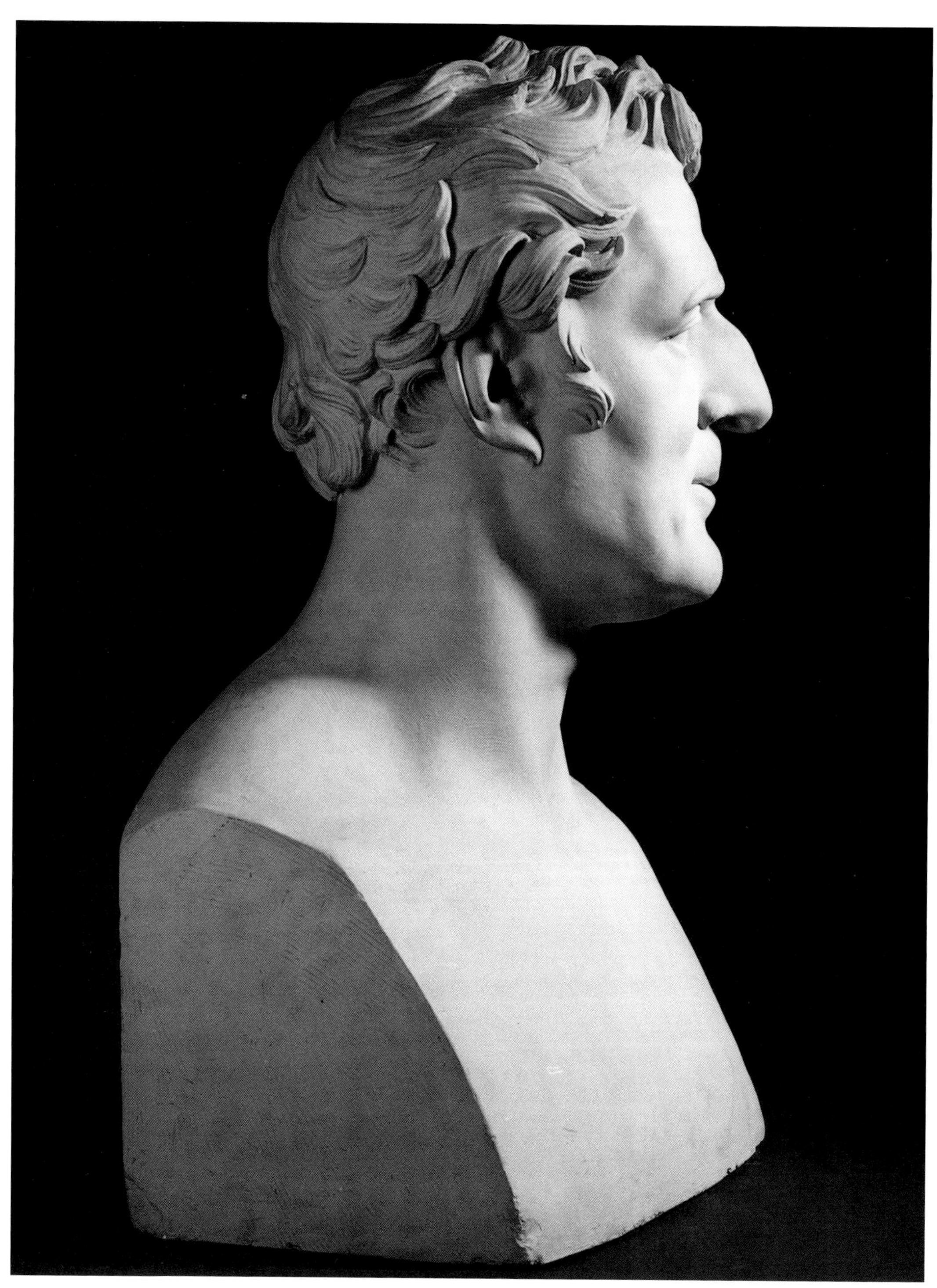

Cat. No.5

5

Sir Francis Chantrey 1781-1841

Arthur Wellesley, 1st Duke of Wellingon 1769-1852

Plaster, height 82.5 cm
Provenance: 1842, presented by the sculptor's widow to the University of Oxford.
Literature: R. Lane Poole, *Catalogue of the Portraits in the Possession of the University of Oxford*, Oxford, 1912, Vol I, No.659(147); N.Penny, *Catalogue of European Sculpture in the Ashmolean Museum, 1540 to the present day*, Oxford, 1992, Vol. III, Cat. No. 778; A Yarrington, *et al.*, 'An Edition of the Ledger of Sir Francis Chantrey R.A., at the Royal Academy, 1809-1841,' *Walpole Society*, Vol. 56, 1991-1992, fo.189b.

Ashmolean Museum, NBP778.

Described in Fisher's handwriting as 'Ditto, Colossal' this is one of two portraits of 'His Grace the Duke of Wellington' under 'Models For Busts' arranged in the Western Sculpture Gallery in the 1840s.[1] Chantrey had executed two models of the Duke of Wellington of which this was said by Mrs Lane Poole to be the earlier, modelled in 1814,[2] the year of his creation as Duke of Wellington, but laid aside until 1835.[3] The Duke of Wellington, the hero of the military successes against the French, joined the Government of Lord Liverpool in 1818, and pursued a successful if unpopular career as a politician thereafter, becoming Prime Minister in 1828. He was Chancellor of the University of Oxford, 1834-52.

In 1816 a grateful nation purchased Canova's *Colossal Figure of Napolean as Mars Pacificator* (1803-1806), and presented it to the Duke. It was despatched to Apsley House where it has been ever since. Hamilton wrote to Canova on 9th September 1816 that, purchased for '66 mila franchi . . . e liberata [erasure] sain et sauf in Londra,' it was not destined for the Museum but for the Duke, for the planned 'palazzo di nostro Scipione'[4] Canova responded in delight and proceeded to tell Hamilton exactly how it should be set up, a job that fell incidentally to John Flaxman, and begged him to ensure that it was done thus: '[fare] dipendere dalla punta della mammella destra un filo a capo di cui sia pendente una pallina di piombo, la quale deve cadere in mezzo ad una crocetta segnata sulla superficie della pianta della figura'[5]

---

[1] University Galleries Register, 1842-1935.
[2] Lane Poole, no.659.
[3] Yarrington, *Walpole Society*, Vol 56. 1991-92, 189b and 251b.
[4] B.I-78/1513.
[5] 23 September 1816; Private Collection.

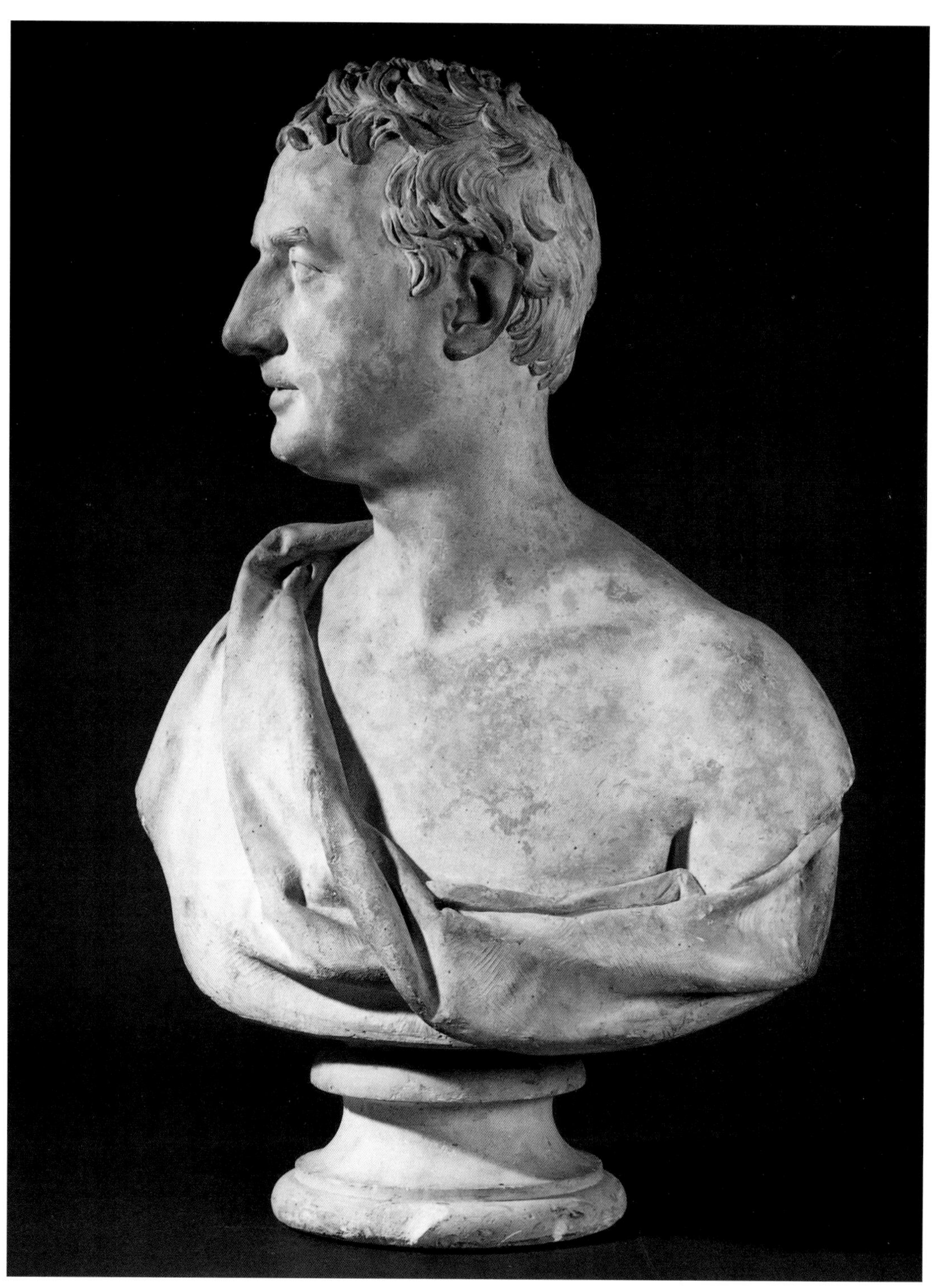

Cat. No.6

6

Sir Francis Chantrey 1781-1841

**Robert Stewart, Viscount Castlereagh,
2nd Marquess of Londonderry 1769-1822   1821**

Plaster, height including socle 75cm
Provenance: 1842, presented by the sculptor's widow to the University of Oxford.
Literature: R. Lane Poole, *Catalogue of the Portraits in the Possession of the University of Oxford*, Oxford, 1912, Vol I, No.536(24); N.Penny, *Catalogue of European Sculpture in the Ashmolean Museum, 1540 to the Present Day*, Oxford, 1992, 3 vols, Cat. No.689; A. Yarrington, *et al.*, 'An Edition of the Ledger of Sir Francis Chantrey, R.A., at the Royal Academy,1809-1841', *Walpole Society*, Vol.56, 1991-1992, fo.125b.

Ashmolean Museum, NBP689

1820 Recd. an order from Lord Viscount Castlereagh to make his Bust. price 150 guineas.

1822 To executing do do   157 10 0   Recd. payment 157 10 0
                       FC   FC[1]

The preliminary drawings were made with a *camera lucida*, (Figs 13 and 14).[2] The plaster is marked with points not much bigger than a pinhead at inch intervals, defined by circles, so that they would not be confused with pits in the plaster. It was exhibited at the Royal Academy in 1821(1132).[3] A number of versions of finished marbles exist, the Duke of Wellington ordered one in February, 1822 for the Earl of Aberdeen, in 1828 George IV ordered another and again, in 1838, the Duke ordered one for Sir Robert Peel,[4] and there are a number of replicas or studio copies.

Castlereagh, like the Duke of Wellington, was a member of the Protestant Irish Ascendancy. His entire life was devoted to politics which he combined with a military career. As Secretary for War from 1805 to 1806 and again from 1807 to 1809 he may be credited with establishing an alliance of European powers against Napoleon, paid for by the British taxpayer. From 1812 until his death ten years later he was Foreign Secretary and played a premier role in the negotiations that followed on Napoleon's fall which redrew the map of Europe.

Castlereagh's suicide in 1822 shocked the nation, and it is clear from contemporary accounts that he was probably suffering from depression brought on by overwork and the hostility aroused by his espousal of the cause of Catholic Emancipation.

Thomas Lawrence wrote a graphic account of his last hours to Canova's great friend, Elizabeth, Duchess of Devonshire, who was then residing in Rome. He described how the Marquis's pistols had been removed and how he cut his throat with a penknife 'with almost surgical Accuracy . . . Thus perished the victim of sudden [?] dispondency A Man of the Highest Courage – of the Most [even] Cheerful Temper the most undaunted Firmness. Perhaps the ablest practical Statesman in Europe – the most popular that ever yet had to calm the irritations of contending cabinets, and to make his Presence amongst them a common benefit and Pleasure.'[5] Canova wrote to Hamilton to commiserate on the death of Castlereagh on 30 August 1821, imagining how much he must have been affected by it, having worked with 'quel gran Ministro, che teneva in mano la chiave di tutti gli affari d'Europa.'[6]

[1] Yarrington, *Walpole Society*, 1991-2, 125b.
[2] Walker, *Regency Portraits*, Cat. No. 316a (13-14), pl. 765 and 766.
[3] Graves, Royal Academy Contributors.
[4] Yarrington, *Walpole Society*, 1991-2, 149b, 207a, 208b.
[5] 12 August 1822, Lawrence Correspondence, Royal Academy Archives, Law/4/47.
[6] Private Collection.

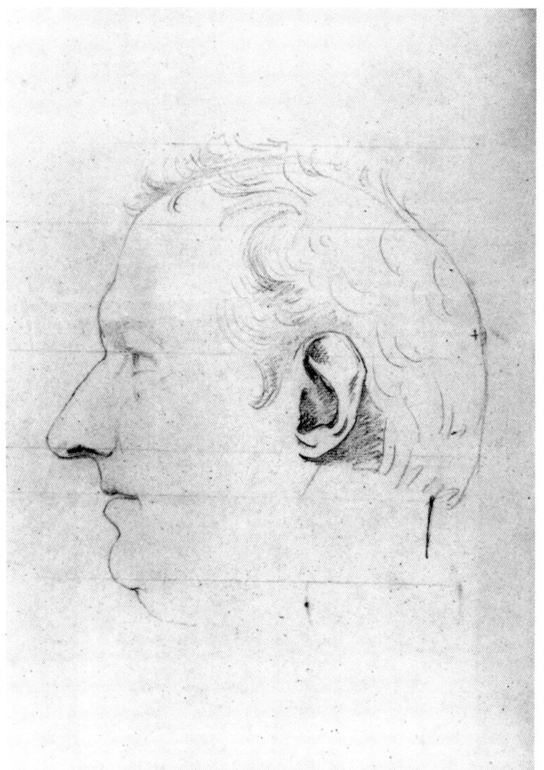

Fig. 13

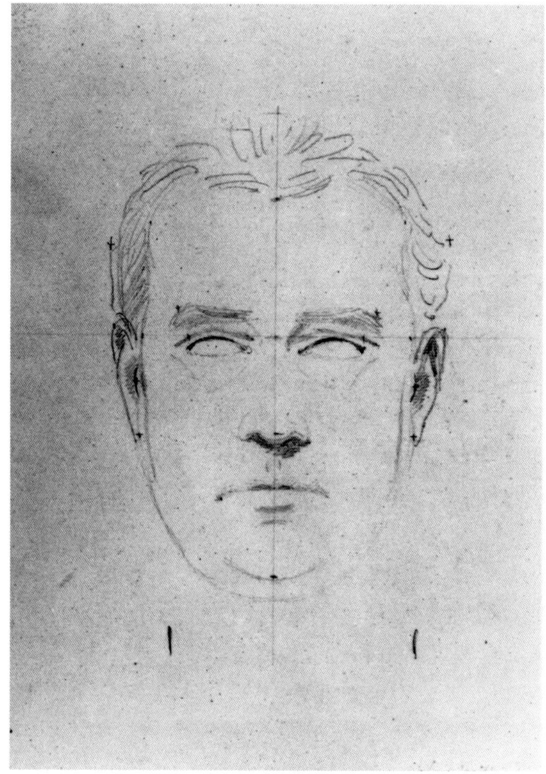

Fig. 14

7

Sir Francis Chantrey 1781-1841

Sir Charles Long, lst Baron Farnborough 1760-1838   1819 or 1820

Plaster, height including socle 76 cm
Provenance: 1842, presented by the sculptor's widow to the University of Oxford
Literature: R. Lane Poole, *Catalogue of the Portraits in the Possession of the University of Oxford,* Oxford, 1912, Vol I, No.561(49); N. Penny, *Catalogue of European Sculpture in the Ashmolean Museum, 1540 to the Present Day,* Oxford, 1992, 3 vols., Cat. No.707; A. Yarrington, *et al.,* 'An Edition of the Ledger of Sir Francis Chantrey, R.A., at the Royal Academy, 1809-1841', *Walpole Society,* Vol. 56, 1991-1992, 101b and 258a.

Ashmolean Museum, NBP707

The plaster is recorded in the 1842 register as Lord Farnborough under Models for Busts, in 'The Crypt' of Cockerell's new University Galleries.[1] The portrait had heen commissioned by Long's father-in-law, Sir Abraham Hume in 1819, who paid £120 for it. The preliminary drawings are in the National Portrait Gallery, (Figs 15 and 16).[3] The full-face, marked with guidelines and points, indicates how Chantrey rejuvenated his sitters giving them a more youthful romanticised air, reducing the thickening and broadening of middle age. The marble was exhibited at the Royal Academy in 1820 as *Sir Charles Long,*[4] and it is now in the National Portrait Gallery.[5] A replica of 1836 is in the National Gallery.[6]

In a drawing by Henry Edridge of 1805,[7] Long stands by a table on which among papers and an ink stand sits a reduced copy of the *Borghese Vase* while folios and folio volumes fill the righthand side, and a picturesque landscape recedes into the distance. The Vase, which was thought to be Greek and attributed to Phidias, was purchased by Napoleon from his brother-in-law, Prince Camillo Borghese in 1807. It was sent to Paris between 1808 and 1811 to be displayed in the Musée Napoléon, and was among the things specifically exempt from the terms which returned antiquities to Rome.[8] Long appears in a number of group portraits of the period: as an MP and Secretary to the Treasury, he sits on the Front Bench in *The House of Commons 1793-4* by K.A. Hickel,[9] *The Trial of Queen Caroline 1820* by Sir George Hayter[10] and *The Opening of London Bridge, 1831* by George Jones.[11] *Patrons and Lovers of Art,* begun *c.*1826 and completed *c.*1830 by P. C. Wonder,[12] shows Long in a group with Abraham Hume and Lord Aberdeen, and, possibly, the first Director of the National Gallery, William Seguier. The works of art in this Dutch-inspired composition include

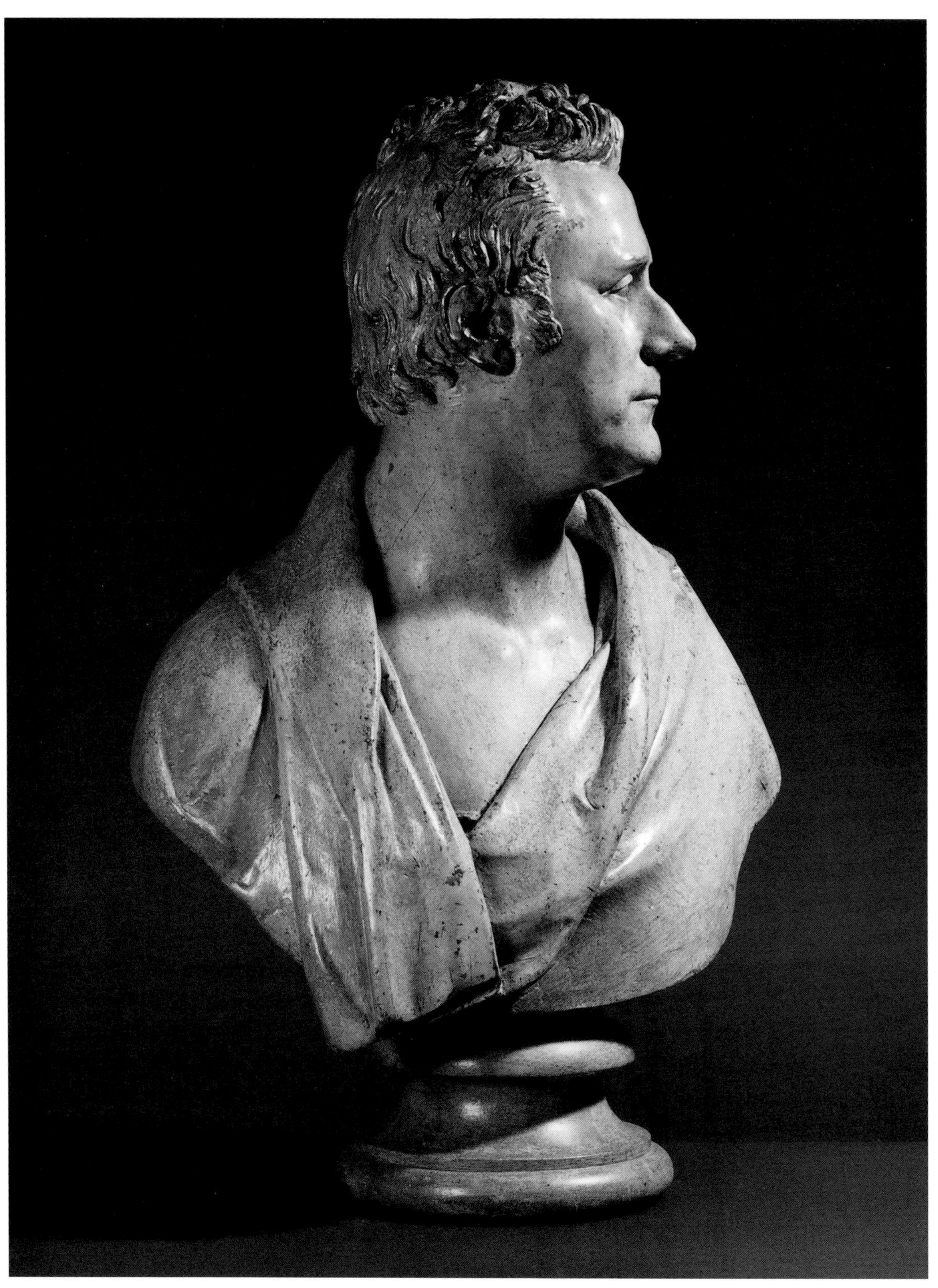

Cat. No.7

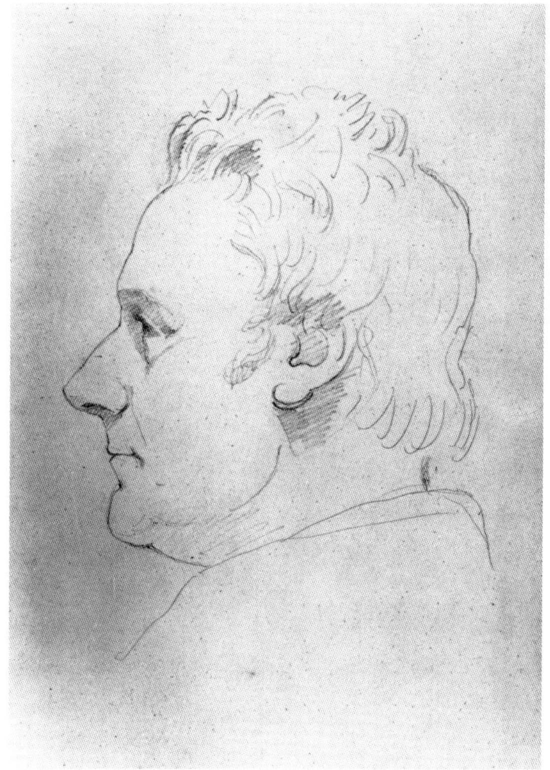 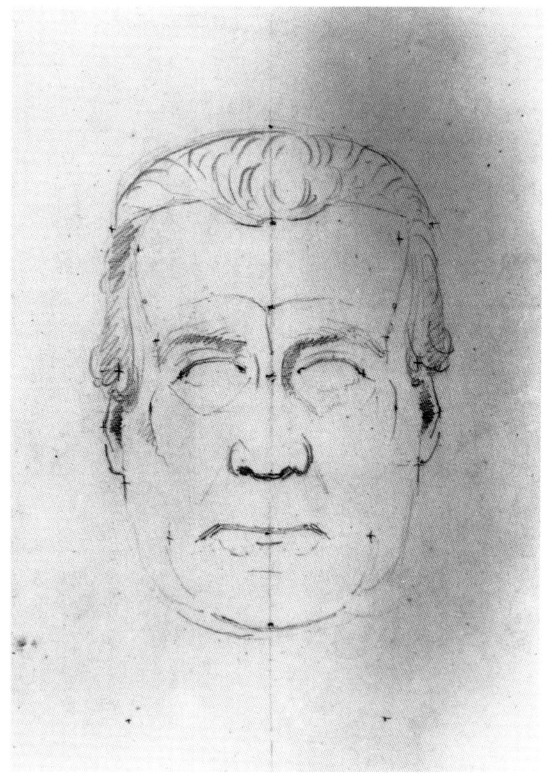

Fig. 15   Fig. 16

Canova's *Hebe* and the *Venus Italica*.

Charles Long, the son of Beeston Long of the West India merchants Drake and Long, entered Parliament in 1789 and soon achieved office under Pitt, eventually becoming Paymaster General in Lord Liverpool's government. He held this post until his retirement in 1826. Knighted in 1820, he was created Baron Farnborough in 1826. He was a Fellow of the Royal Society and President of the Committee for the Inspection of National Monuments, set up to supervise the selection of sculptors for the numerous monuments to the heroes of the Napoleonic Wars. He was a Fellow of the Society of Antiquaries, and became a Trustee of the British Museum in 1812 and was one of the original Trustees of the National Gallery. He wrote *Short Remarks and Suggestions upon Improvements now carrying on or under consideration* (1826) in which he made the case for a grand plan and building programme for London and declared 'In the person of George IV are united the discriminating judge and the liberal patron of the arts . . . may his reign form an era in the annals of taste, as it ever will in the annals of glory.'[15]

In 1793 Long married Amelia (1762-1837), one of the daughters of Sir Abraham Hume (1749-1838), collector, FRS and founder member of the Geological Society, of

Wormleybury, Herts and his wife Amelia Egerton who was sister to Francis Henry Egerton, 8th Earl of Bridgewater (1756-1829). An accomplished amateur artist in her own right, Amelia Long, who had been painted by Reynolds,[14] was a favourite pupil of Thomas Girtin (1775-1802). Her work has often been confused with that of Dr Thomas Monro (1759-1833).[15] It was perhaps through her agency that Long contributed to the care of John Robert Cozens (1752?-1797) in his insanity.[16] She was respected as a judge of art, and as a skilled horticulturist laid out the gardens at Bromley Hill Place.[17] Long and his wife died within a year of each other. Their monuments at Wormley, Herts, and Saxmundham, Suffolk are by Sir Richard Westmacott. Long rebuilt Bromley Hill Place, adding a picture gallery, and his collection was a notable one. He is recorded buying a Francesco Mola at the Orleans Collection Sale in 1799.[18] He left many of his pictures to the National Gallery. William Hamilton described the mile and a half of grounds at Bromley Hill Place as follows:

> 'A great variety of scenery and glades opened along the woods and heath, with much taste and trouble. But the Gardens are the most enjoyable possible, particularly at this season of the year. The rhododendrons in great beauty, and a melancholy mossy flat converted into a fairy like flower garden, watered by a clear trout stream.'[19]

1 University Galleries Register, 1842-1935.

2 Yarrington, *Walpole Society*, 1991-2, 101b.

3 NPG 316a (79-80); Walker, *op. cit.*, pl.420.

4 R.A. Catalogue No.1046.

5 NPG 2090; Walker *op. cit.*, No.421.

6 National Gallery 2246. Commissioned in 1833 but not paid for until 1842, the date 1836, is inscribed on the back of the bust; Chantrey Ledger 258a.

7 Walker, NPG4046, pl.419.

8 Haskell and Penny, No.81.

9 NPG 745; Walker, *op. cit.*, pl.1502-32.

10 NPG 999; Walker, *op. cit.*, pl.1525-32.

11 Sir John Soane's Museum; *Ibid.*

12 Private Collection; Illustrated in P. Funnell, 'The London Art World and its Institutions',in *London - World City 1800-1840*, exh. cat., C.Fox (ed.), p.159. Preparatory oil sketch; NPG 793; Walker, *op.cit.*, pp.616-7.

13 Quoted in J. Morley, *Regency Design 1790-1840*, London, 1993, p.151, fn.153.

14 In 1788; National Portrait Gallery Archive.

15 I. Williams, *Early English Watercolours*, p.248.

16 *Ibid.*, p.80.

17 Views of Bromley Hill Place by Buckler are in the British Library; B.L. Add MS 36367, ff. 181-92; Colvin, *Dictionary*, p.829.

18 Passavant, Vol. II, p.191.

19 WRH to Henry George Hamilton, 21 June 1837; TSS Mss, Frederick Terrick Hamilton, 1911; Private Collection.

8

Studio of Sir Thomas Lawrence

Antonio Canova

Oil on canvas: 94.8 x 74.5 cm
Frame: matt oil gilded with composition ornament 132.5 x 113 x 11 cm
Provenance: William Richard Hamilton; by descent to the present owner.

Private Collection

During Canova's visit to London, Lawrence made a drawing of him,[1] and the next day began a portrait in oils. There was a natural sympathy between them. They had met the previous month in Paris when Lawrence went to see the treasures of the Musée Napoléon before they were returned to their rightful owners. A journalist in *The Courier* reported 4 October, 'when the Venus [de' Medici] was put into the cart on Monday Sir T. Lawrence, Mr. Chantrey and Canova burst into tears.'[2]

Lawrence exhibited a portrait of Canova at the Royal Academy Exhibition, 1816. Was this the portrait he began in November? If so, it already belonged to Hamilton who wrote to Canova, 22 December, 1815, 'Il quadro di Lawrence piace assai. Ognuno mi fà complimenti sul possesso [?] d'un tal capo d'opera.'[3] Or was it the portrait said to have been commissioned by the Prince Regent and later given by him to Canova's brother, who bequeathed it to the Gipsoteca Canoviana at Possagno? What about the portrait exhibited here which has come down in Hamilton's family? Is it Lawrence? Or is it studio? Or is it Lawrence and studio? Although fine, it is surely not from the hand of Lawrence himself. The head does not have the strength of the head at Possagno. The expression is too gently sweet. The texture of the fur, velvet and linen of Canova's dress do not have the verve of the brushwork of Lawrence. There are letters in the Biblioteca Civica at Bassano del Grappa from Hamilton to Canova which perhaps explain it. They are written in such indecipherable Italian that translation is hazardous. One of November 1816[4] seems to imply that Lawrence has asked him to send his portrait of Canova out to Canova in Rome, and another, of March 1817[5] that a copy was to be made for him. Lawrence himself wrote to Canova in 1818, 'By a kind arrangement with Hamilton I am permitted to send for your disposal the Picture for which you sat to me on the morning of your departure . . . painted in one sitting'[6]

Lawrence came to Rome on the last lap of his European tour in 1819, and according to a letter in *The Collector*, 20 January 1820[7] the 'head of Canova' painted by him in London was entirely repainted in Rome. Was this the portrait that had belonged to

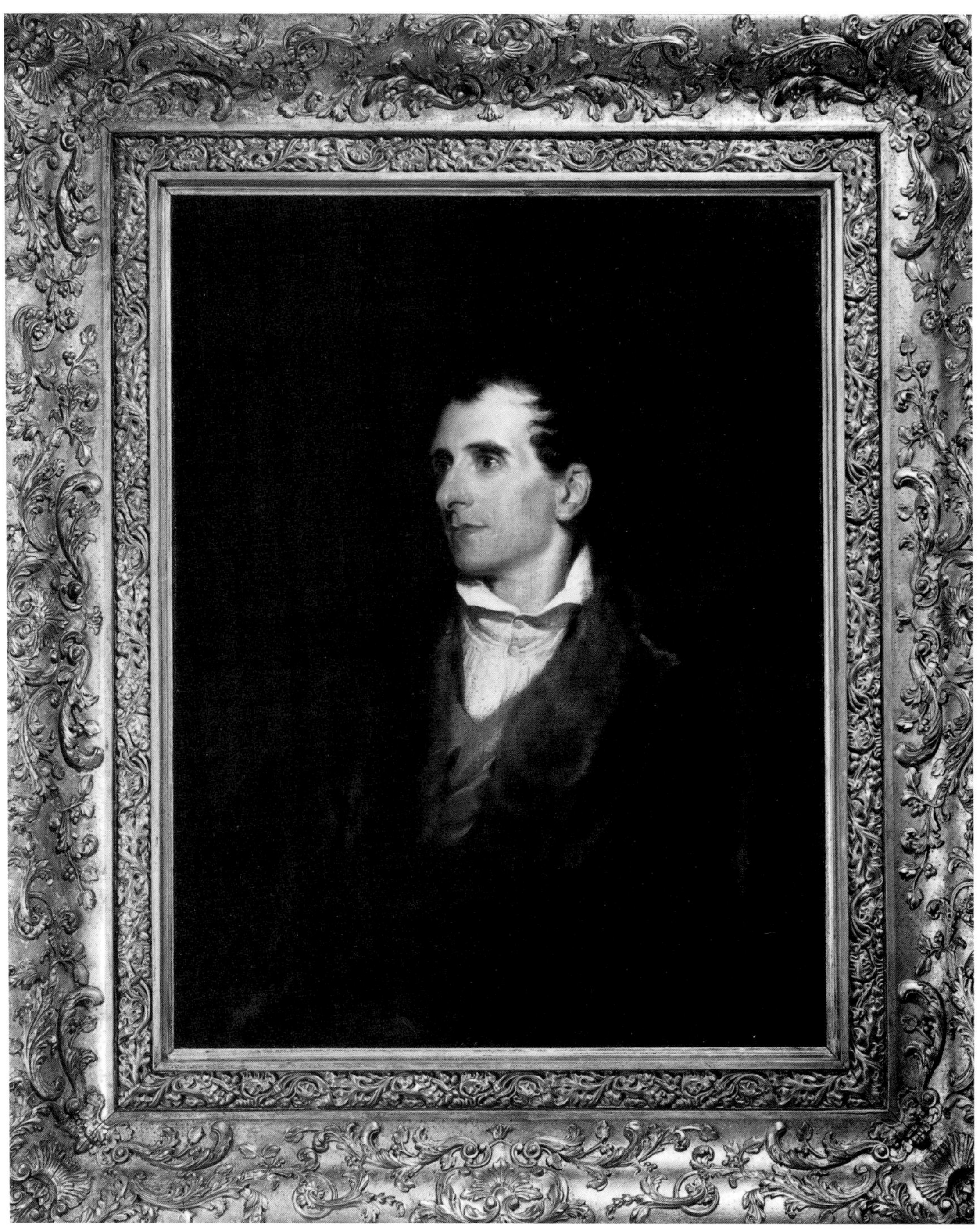

Cat. No.8

Hamilton? One might assume so. The letter goes on to say that the repainted portrait was to be a present to the Pope but no such portrait is recorded in the Vatican today and the statement was probably based on rumour. How does this all fit in with the portrait at Possagno? If the Regent did commission the 1816 portrait where was it housed before he gave it to Canova's brother? Presumably after Canova's death in 1822? It is difficult to believe that the Possagno portrait is not the R.A. 1816 portrait. But is it the Hamilton portrait somehow metamorphosed? Difficult to believe too. If it is not, where is the Hamilton portrait? Out of this muddle of speculation what can one safely say? Only that the Possagno portrait is indubitably a fine and autograph Lawrence and that the portrait in this exhibition is fine studio, no doubt the copy mentioned in the letter of March 1817. The design of both is the same.

There are about twenty versions and copies of the Possagno portrait recorded. The demand for them reasserts the universal esteem in which Canova was held. Both Lawrence and the Prince Regent, now George IV, contributed handsomely to the monument to Canova carved by his pupils in S. Maria Gloriosa dei Frari, Venice.

Lawrence always took an intense interest in the framing of his paintings and it is interesting that the ornament of the frame here is so clearly French in origin and that it is oil gilt, Lawrence's preferred finish. It is of a type made by George Morant and Sons, 'House Decorators, Carvers, Gilders, and Picture Frame Makers to his Majesty' of 88 New Bond Street who supplied Thomas Lawrence with a number of patterns and widths of moulding.[8]

[1] *Sir Thomas Lawrence*, National Portrait Gallery, London, 1979, Cat. No.78.
[2] D.M. Quynn. 'The Art Confiscations of the Napoleonic Wars' in *American History Review*, L, April, 1943.
[3] B. I-78/1507.
[4] W.R. Hamilton to Canova, 8 November, 1816; B.I-78/1516.
[5] W.R. Hamilton to Canova, 3 March, 1817; B.I-78/1520.
[6] Lawrence Correspondence Royal Academy, LAW 3/228.
[7] D. Williams, Vol. II, p.228.
[8] *George Morant (1770-1846)*, Arnold Wiggins and Co., leaflet, n.d. [1996].

9

Luigi Rados (1773-1840) after Roberto Focosi

Antonio Canova

Stipple with etching, image 34.4 x 29.3 cm
With the engraved inscription: *Roberto Focosi disegno *** Luigi Rados incise / ANTONIO CANOVA / Nato nel 1757 in Possagno da umili ed onesti genitori. Avviato ancor giovanetto nell'arte paterna dello scarpellino spiegò in poi / il suo genio creatore, fissando colle sue opere immortali l'epoca del risorgimento della scultura. Frà tanti suoi lavori si pregiano particolar= / mente le statue di Giunone, Clio, Venere, Psiche, i Pugilatori ecc. Fu pure Archeologo, Architetto e Pittore, e l'eccelso Tempio in sua patria / coi quadri da lui dipintivi, sono monumenti che sfideranno la durata de'secoli. Pontefici, Sovrani, ed Accademie gareggiarono nell' onorarlo. All' eccel= / lenza del suo cuore accoppiò sempre quella dell' inteletto. Dotto, umile, magnanimo e religioso compianto da tutta Europa, morì in Venezia li 13 8bre. 1822. / Dedicato all' Illustrissimo *** Signor Marchese / FEBO *** D'ADDA / Consigliere di Governo, Cavaliere *** dell'I.R. Ordine di Leopoldo, / Ciambellano attuale di S.M.I.R.A. *** L'Imperatore d'Austria ecc. ecc. ecc. / In segno di venerazione Luigi Rados D.D.D.*

Ashmolean Museum, Hope 1323

The inscription reads like an obituary and the print clearly was *in memoriam*. A number of attributes appear without any apparent rhyme or reason: the unfurled design on the left is for the ground plan of Canova's mausoleum at Possagno which he designed himself. It was paid for with some of the income which the Pope and the Roman State awarded Canova in recognition of his achievements in Paris. Some of the money went towards the foundation of a school for the children of Possagno, and to this day the Gimnasio Canova draws pupils from a distance in the Province of Bassano del Grappa. The herm must symbolise the influence of the Greek on Canova's work. Behind him on an easel is a version of the relief known as *Giving Food to the Hungry* which became incorporated in the monument to Maria Christina of Austria, in the Augustinerkirche, Vienna, while to the right are a model for one of the Pugilists, *Damoseno*, now in the Vatican, and a herm head of Pius VII. Canova himself leans on a stand on which rests a giant foot, perhaps one of those now in the garden at Possagno. [Illustrated p.viii].

10

Pietro Fontana (1762-1837) and A. Agricola after Antonio Canova

Pope Pius VII

Etching with engraving, plate 42.3 x 31.6 mm
With the engraved inscription: *A. Canova sculp. *** A. Agricola delin. *** P. Fontana
incidit – / PIVS SEPTIMUS PONTIFEX MAX. / Viro Eminentissimo Josepho Fesch
S.R.E.C. Archiep. Lugdunensi / Nat. Gall. ad Pont Max. Oratori. / Petrus
Fontana, et Josephus D'Este scalptt. Lineares – / Nomini, Eminentiaeq. ejus
dicatissimi / D.D.L.L. Merito *** Cum. Privil. Pont.*

Literature: Rome and Bassano del Grappa, 1993, *Canova e l'incisione*, Cat. No. XLI

Ashmolean Museum, Hope 7145

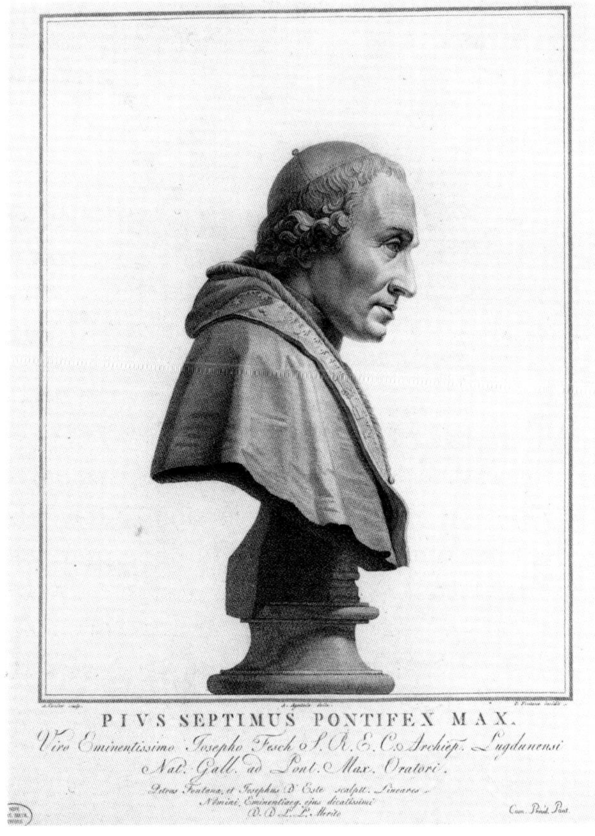

Cat. No.10

Luigi Barnaba Chiaramonti (1742-1823), was elected Pontiff at the Venice Conclave of 1800, and in 1801 signed a concordat with France re-establishing the Church in France. He crowned Napoleon Emperor at Paris in 1804 when he negotiated a *modus vivendi* for the Papal States. However in 1809 Napoleon declared an end to the temporal power of the Papacy, Pius was arrested and exiled, only to return on Napoleon's abdication in 1814. Canova's portrait bust of Pope Pius VII was begun in 1803 and was sent to Paris the following year for Napoleon's coronation as Emperor, through the agency of Cardinal Fesch. Canova received an emolument of 6,000 *franchi*.[1] It is now in the Musée d'Histoire, Versailles. A version of 1807 presented by Canova to Pius VII is in the Protomoteca Capitolina, Rome.

Canova received a formal letter of acknowledgement from Pius VII, dated 26 October,[2] while still in Paris:

> Dilecte, Fili, Salutem, et Apostolicam Benedictionem = Non potevamo ricevere notizia più lieta di quella della decretata restituione dei Monumenti antichi, dei Codici, ed altri oggetti preziosi. Conoscendo Noi quanta parte ha avuto in questo felice successo il di Lei merito personale, non possiamo astenerci dal farlene i Nostri più vivi ringraziamenti, e dal manifestarlene la Nostra particolar gratitudine. Roma, che tanto Le deve per la gloria del di Lei Scalpello, Le sarà debitrice ancora di sì fortunata ricupera, e il di Lei nome, che ha già tanta celebrità per le rare produzioni, che onorano il Nostro Socolo, acquisterà ancor quella di avere ricondotto nella Sede delle belle Arti i Monumenti li più preziosi. Nel congratularcene con Noi stessi, che possediamo un Uomo colmo di tanti meriti, l'assiuriamo della Nostra speciale stima, e benevolenza, in pegno della quale Le diamo di tutto Cuore la Paterna Apostolia Benedizione.
>
> Datum ex Arce Pandulphi die 26. Octobris 1815 Pontificatus Nostri Anno XVI.
>
> [Signed] Pius PP. VII.

---

[1] Pavanello. no.156.
[2] B. E-57/5643.

11

Charles Baugniet (1814-1886)

William Richard Hamilton 1779-1859

Lithograph, image 45.4 x 34.7 cm
With the lithographed inscription: *Baugniet 1850 / London;* and the engraved inscription:
PUBLISHED BY HERING & REMINGTON, 137, REGENT ST. / WILLIAM RICHARD HAMILTON ESQRE. F.R.S. / SECRETARY TO THE SOCIETY OF DILETTANTI / PROOF / M.N. HANHART, LITH. PRINTERS.

Ashmolean Museum, Hope 3329

Hamilton holds a cameo with what appears to be the helmeted head of Athena, perhaps by Pistrucci. An engraving by R. J. Lane after an earlier portrait of Hamilton by Thomas Phillips R.A. (1770-1845), was also published by Hanhart (Fig.17) (Private Collection). In 1911 the Society of Dilettanti gained permission for a copy to be made by Dorofield Hardy from the original in the collection of Hamilton's grandson, Lord Belhaven and Stenton.[1] Hamilton appears in a group portrait of the Society of Antiquaries by Daniel Maclise which appeared in *Fraser's Magazine* in 1832.

William Richard Hamilton was the eldest son of Anthony Hamilton (1739-1812) descendant of the Hamiltons of Wishaw in Lanarkshire, and a collateral of the Lords Belhaven.[2] Anthony Hamilton was the son of a Lincoln's Inn lawyer and married Anne, daughter of Richard Terrick, Bishop of London. He was Archdeacon of Colchester, vicar of St. Martin's-in-the-Fields, and finally rector of Hadham in Hertfordshire, where he died in 1812. There is a monument to him in the parish church at Much Hadham by John Charles Rossi R.A. (1762-1839), who had won the Academy Travelling Studentship in 1785 and spent three years in Rome.

Hamilton was educated at Harrow and appears to have matriculated at both Oxford and Cambridge but did not complete at either, due to ill health that dogged him through a long life. He became attaché and private secretary to Thomas Bruce, 7rd Earl of Elgin in 1799, at the age of 22, when Elgin was appointed ambassador to the Ottoman Court at Constantinople. His sponsor wrote of him: 'He has much good sense, and a great activity of mind; he is industrious and in the highest degree anxious to render himself useful. His manners are pleasing and his principles perfectly good so you may use him at once as your companion, your confidant, and your fag.'[3]

He was entrusted with diplomatic missions of importance in the eastern Mediterranean, and was in Egypt as the French withdrew after the Battle of Alexandria. The

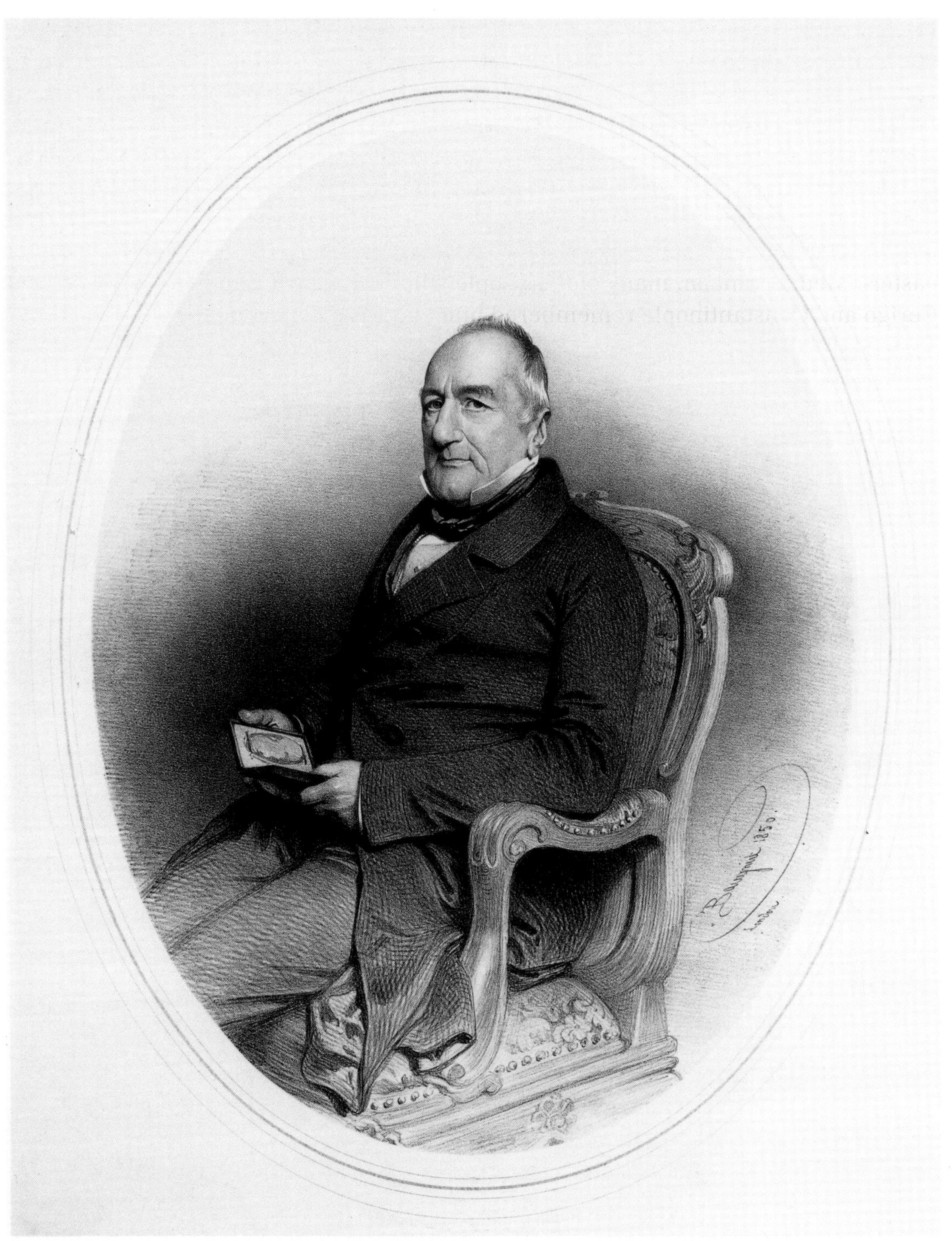

Cat. No.11

French had, contrary to the terms of the treaty which he had negotiated,[4] removed the trilingual stone now known as the Rosetta Stone (Cat. No.12). Hamilton took the opportunity, while in Egypt, to travel, and wrote a description of the expedition in *Aegyptiaca* published in 1809 (Cat. No.14). He was in Rome in 1799 and again in 1803 on Lord Elgin's behalf, on business associated with the Elgin Marbles.[5] He assisted in the removal and transport of the frieze and metopes from the Parthenon, and wrote a spirited defence of this action which was published anonymously in 1811 (Cat. No.13). Twenty years later when his son Henry was on a British ship policing the eastern Mediterranean, many of the people who had known Hamilton at Alexandria, Cerigo and Constantinople remembered him and were kind and attentive to his son.[6]

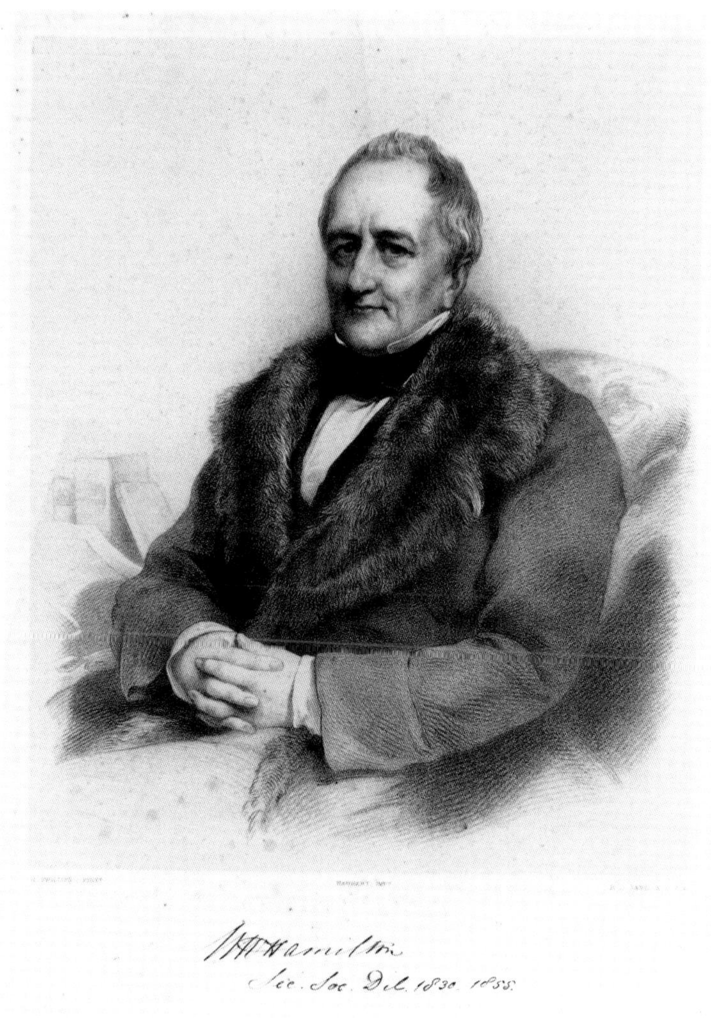

Fig. 17

He married Juliana, daughter of John Udny in 1804. There are two Udny monuments in Chichester Cathedral, one to Sarah Udny (1811), by John Flaxman and the other, to Ernest Udny (1808), by Henry Westmacott. Of his seven children the eldest, William John, became a distinguished geologist, the fifth, Frederick William, became a General and was knighted. Henry George, born in 1808, entered the Navy as a 1st Class Volunteer in 1822, but retired early for want of promotion due to peace time and a change of government. It was in his family that the *Ideal Head* remained.

Hamilton became Under-Secretary of State for Foreign Affairs in 1809, a post he held until 1822, and in this capacity he attended the Peace Conference at Paris which oversaw the restitution of the works of art requisitioned by Napoleon's armies. Letters from WRH to his wife were 'chiefly occupied with the scandal of the day and the proceedings for the recovery of the pictures'[7]

When he was appointed as His Majesty's Minister to the Court of Naples, a post he held for not quite three years (twenty years after Sir William Hamilton, with whom he has often been confused, had been recalled to London after the French invasion of Italy), Hamilton renewed his friendship with Canova. He was clearly a good committee man for in 1817 he was nominated to the Committee for the unrolling of the Herculaneum papyri for the Prince Regent as Castlereagh's representative.[8]

The stand he took on the Elgin Marbles (Cat. No.13) meant that Hamilton was, on two occasions, refused membership of the Society of Dilettanti which had initially opposed the purchase of the Elgin Marbles. He was elected in 1811 and went on to succeed Sir Thomas Lawrence, and became its longest serving Secretary, from 1830 to 1859. As Secretary he received the letters of William Gell from Naples which led to the Society publishing Gell's *Topography of Rome.*[9]

A Fellow of the Royal Society and a Trustee of the British Museum from 1838 to 1858, he was a founder of the Royal Geographical Society of which he later became President, an active member of the Royal Institution and the Royal Society of Literature, being balloted for Vice President in 1845.[10] Hamilton was also involved in the foundation of the Institute of British Architects. The skills he had used in drafting papers for Castlereagh, Wellington and Canova in 1815 he redeployed in composing the loyal addresses of the various societies of which he was a member on the accession of Queen Victoria in 1837.[11]

Among his other publications were translations of the plays of Aristophanes in 1835 and 1836 and, more polemically and characteristically, *On the propriety of adopting the Greek style of architecture in preference to the Gothic, in the construction of the new Houses of Parliament* (1836), dedicated to Queen Victoria, and, revealing a wider perspective, a *Vindication of the treaty of 1783 respecting the North Eastern Boundary of the United States*, in 1842.

Hamilton had, from about 1815, a country house, Stanley Grove (Fig.18), in Chelsea between the King's Road and Fulham Road, which had been built at the end of the

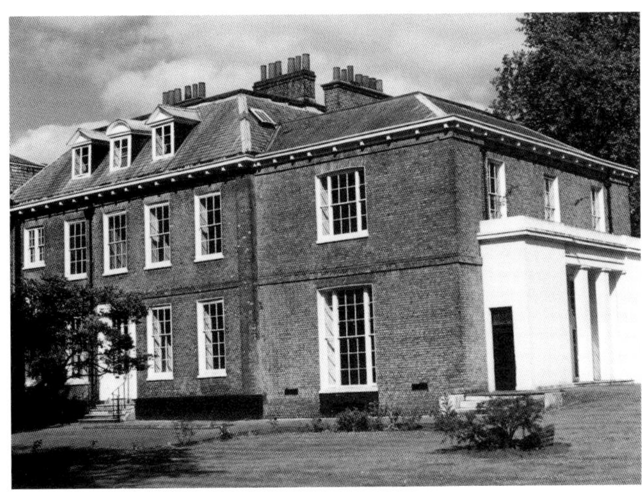

Fig. 18

seventeenth century. To this he added a library in which he displayed casts from the Parthenon frieze and metopes, the rosso antico obelisks that were a present from Pope Pius VI and, it may be presumed, his *Ideal Head* by Canova and the portrait of Canova by Lawrence (Cat. Nos. 1 and 8). Hamilton sent a design of the chimneypiece wall to Canova in 1817 (Fig.4).[12] He sold the house and grounds to the National Society in 1840 and a training school, St Mark's College, was built.[13] This later became part of King's College, London, and at the time of writing it is empty and for sale.

Hamilton, as Baugniet's portrait suggests, remained alert and interested throughout a long life. A letter of thanks he wrote to the naturalist Sir Richard Owen (1804-1892), presents an engaging image of two men, one of them the author, aged nearly 80, absorbed in discussing the 'remains of an Ichthyosaur' in the pavement while the Oxford Street crowd swirled round them.'

1 Harcourt-Smith, p.85
2 *DNB* is incorrect in stating that there was a collateral relation to Sir William Hamilton (1730-1803), who was himself a grandson of the Duke of Hamilton.
3 Col. Anstruther to Lord Elgin, 19 March 1799; Clay, p.1.
4 *Annual Register*, 1859, pp.430-31.
5 *Memorandum* (1815 ed.), pp.4 and 39.
6 Letters from Henry George Hamilton from HMS Cambrian, 1822-23, TSS, Frederick Terrick Hamilton, 4 June 1911; Private Collection.
7 WRH to HGH, TSS *cit.*, p.93.
8 Derry, p.642.
9 Clay, p.2.
10 Balloting List, Royal Society of Literature, 24 April 1845; Dawson Turner Papers, Trinity College, Cambridge.
11 WRH to HGH 16 July 1837; TSS *cit.*, p.60.
12 B.I-78/1539.
13 L. Gomme (ed.), *Survey of London, The Parish of Chelsea* (Part II), vol. IV; London, 1913, p.43-44, pls. 45-51; also N. Pevsner, *The Buildings of England - London 3: North West;* London, 1991.
14 WRH to Richard Owen, 2 Dec 1856; Richard Owen Papers, Natural History Museum Library, 237.

Cat. No.12

12

Cast of the Rosetta Stone

Inscribed face only, plaster of Paris with surface wash; 96 x 76 x *c.* 1.5cm. Ashmolean Museum, Department of Antiquities

The original: fragmentary stela of black basalt inscribed in Egyptian (hieroglyphic and demotic texts) and Greek; 114 x 72 x 28 cm. British Museum EA 24

With the British landing at Abuqir Bay on 8 March 1801, the French occupation of Egypt, which had opened with their arrival in Alexandria in July 1798, began to draw to a close. Bonaparte's grand oriental enterprise had brought with it an army of scholars as well as soldiers, and the fate of the Scientific Commission and the materials it had assembled was bound up with the progressive surrender of the French forces to the Anglo-Turkish invaders; the French commander-in-chief, General Jacques Abdallah Menou, held out in Alexandria until the end of August. Under Article xvi of the treaty of capitulation to which he finally acceded, the British demanded the surrender of the scientific collections formed by the French, and also the antiquities gathered together in Alexandria awaiting shipment to France. In September 1801, William Hamilton arrived from Constantinople to join in the negotiations for these, a task which he discharged in the company of Edward D. Clarke, the traveller and mineralogist who was making his third visit to Egypt in the wake of the victorious British forces.

The most celebrated item amongst those antiquities was the 'trilinguar Tablet' or Rosetta Stone, which took its name from the village 44 miles east along the coast from Alexandria, where the French had apparently found it while improving the defences in 1799.[1] A fragment of a large stela commemorating the honours bestowed on Ptolemy v Epiphanes by the priests of Egypt on 27 March 196 BC, it is inscribed with an identical text in Egyptian and Greek – thus bi- not trilingual, but using the two Egyptian scripts current in the Ptolemaic period, formal hieroglyphs followed by the demotic of everyday use (mistaken for Syriac by the first observers). Since the Greek text could be read, the stone's potential for aiding the decipherment of the hieroglyphic script, and thus the dead language of ancient Egypt – a problem which had vexed Western scholars since the Renaissance – had been immediately recognized (by the engineer in charge at Rosetta, Lt. François-Xavier Bouchard, it is said). The British were anxious that this linguistic prize, which had retreated from Cairo to Alexandria with the members of the *Institut d'Égypte*, should be theirs.[2]

Of almost equal interest to Hamilton and Clarke was the great stone sarcophagus of Nectanebo II (British Museum EA 10) which was reputed by Arabic sources to be the resting place of Alexander the Great; this had been removed by the French from the mosque on the site of the church of St Athanasius, where it had been serving as a water cistern, and it was now lying in the hold of the hospital ship *La Cause*, at anchor in the inner harbour of Alexandria, where it was inspected by both Clarke and Hamilton.[3] Along with the other antiquities gathered ready for shipment at the harbour, and shown to the English party by a French officer, it was in due course surrendered to the British.[4]

It seems that Clarke, armed with a passport to enter Alexandria and a chalk tracing of the Rosetta Stone (made by a member of the *Institut*) to aid identification, had made a preliminary visit to Menou on 11 September to request permission to copy the inscriptions on the stone and open negotiations on the surrender of the antiquities, but the business had not gone well.[5] The matter was referred back to the British commander, Gen. J. H. Hutchinson, and on Saturday 12 September, he set out again, this time with Hamilton, for another difficult parley with the irascible General Menou, who apparently viewed the stone as his personal property. Hamilton's brief account of the affair noted Menou's 'reluctance' to yield up his treasure,[6] but his companion, with less diplomatic restraint, recalled

> We remained near the outside of the tent; and soon heard the French General's voice, elevated as usual, and in strong terms of indignation remonstrating against the injustice of the demands made upon him. The words *'Jamais on n'a pillé le monde!'* diverted us highly, as coming from a leader of plunder and devastation ...[7]

Despite this blustering reaction, Menou did, however, acquiesce to the surrender of the stone, which was lying concealed under mats in a warehouse with the rest of his baggage, and its transfer from the French to the British – in the persons of Hamilton, Clarke and a Mr Cripps – took place in an Alexandrian street. The officer charged with its delivery 'recommended its speedy conveyance to some place of safety, as he could not be answerable for the conduct of the French soldiers, if it were suffered to remain exposed to their indignation ...'[8] The loss to the French was indeed great, but after the abrasive encounter with Menou, Hamilton and Clarke went on to a congenial meeting with members of the *Institut d'Égypte*, which demonstrated that the *savants*, at any rate, bore their adverse fortunes with civilized grace.

His task accomplished, Hamilton set off in October on the journey to Upper Egypt which bore fruit in his published *Aegyptiaca*. The Rosetta Stone, together with the other antiquities, left for England, where, following its arrival in February 1802, it was deposited at the Society of Antiquaries. On 29 April, the Society's Council resolved that a sulphur cast of the inscriptions on the stone be taken by 'Mr Papera if he can execute the same . . . otherwise by Mr Pasci', and invitations were to be extended to 'Mr Wilkins, Professor White and Dr Chandler' to inspect and copy the stone if they wished.[9] In July the Antiquaries resolved to have plaster casts prepared from the stone by Mr Papera and despatched, together with a letter from the Secretary, to the Universities of Oxford, Cambridge, Edinburgh, and Dublin; the receipt of letters acknowledging the casts, and also engravings of the inscriptions which the Society had sent out, were minuted in December,[10] and in June 1803 the stone itself was transferred to the British Museum.

The relationship of the cast on display to that received by Oxford University in 1802 is unclear, since no records of the Antiquaries' gift have so far been traced in Oxford. This is, however, likely to be the cast recorded in the Ashmolean Museum by the Revd Greville Chester in 1881,[11] and as its form – a flat rendering of the inscribed surface only, not a replica of the entire Rosetta Stone – corresponds to that of the other early casts,[12] it seems that it may indeed be the original 1802 example received from the Society of Antiquaries. Despite their efforts to stimulate attempts on the decipherment of hieroglyphs, the Antiquaries waited in vain for the revelation to come from a British source, and two decades were to pass before Jean François Champollion announced in his *Lettre à M. Dacier, relative à l'alphabet des hiéroglyphes phonétiques, employés par les Égyptiens ...* (1822) the first stages in the decipherment. It was his boyhood curiosity on hearing about the Rosetta Stone from J. B. J. Fourier, erstwhile secretary of the French Institute in Cairo, which had set him upon the path which led, via the ideas proffered by scholars of many nations, to the ultimate success which the discovery of the stone in 1799 had seemed to promise.[13]

1 C. Andrews, *The Rosetta Stone,* London, 1981, gives a concise account of the pertinent facts.
2 The news of the discovery appeared in September in the *Courier de l'Égypte* 37 (29 fructidor, An VII), and copies of the text immediately went into circulation: C. C. Gillispie and M. Dewachter, *Monuments of Egypt. The Napoleonic Edition'* Princeton, 1987, pp.21-22.
3 E.D. Clarke, *Travels in Various Countries of Europe Asia and Africa,* 11.2: *Greece Egypt and the Holy Land,* London, 1914, p.247; W. Hamilton, *Remarks on Several Parts of Turkey,* I: *Aegyptiaca,* London, 1809, p.403. The two visits appear to have been made separately; Clarke's much more detailed account dates his to 10 September.
4 The colourful story of its situation in the hospital ship was erroneously transferred to the Rosetta Stone in the account given of Hamilton in *DNB* VII, p.1119, followed by E.R. Dawson and E. P. Uphill, *Who Was Who in Egyptology,* 3rd rev. edn. by M. L. Bierbrier, London' 1995, p.188.
5 Clarke, *Travels,* pp.270-1.
6 *Aegyptiaca,* p.403.
7 Clarke, *Travels,* p.273.
8 Clarke, *Travels,* p. 274
9 Council minute book of the Society of Antiquaries, 29 April 1802. I am most grateful to my colleague Arthur MacGregor, Director of the Society of Antiquaries, for providing this and the information cited below, and also many helpful suggestions. Joseph White was Laudian Professor of Arabic at Oxford, and 'Dr Chandler' is perhaps the author of *Marmora Oxoniensia,* Richard Chandler; Mr Wilkins is perhaps to be identified as the

orientalist and Sanskrit specialist, Charles Wilkins. The preparation of such a large sulphur cast as the inscriptions would require is perhaps unusual, but was undoubtedly intended to yield the clearest possible impression; the French had employed the same casting medium while the stone was in Cairo; Gillispie and Dewachter, *Monuments of Egypt*, p.22.

10   Society of Antiquaries minute books, 8 July and 3 December 1802. It seems that at both Oxford and Cambridge, the University received a cast, the Professor of Greek an engraving. Cf. M. Raper, *Archaeologia* 16 (1812), p.208; the stone's brief residence with the Antiquaries is noted by Joan Evans, *A History of the Society of Antiquaries*, Oxford, 1956, pp.199-200.

11   *Catalogue of the Egyptian Antiquities in the Ashmolean Museum, Oxford*, Oxford, 1881, p.87 no.1425.

12   Inspection of the original surface of the back of the cast is unfortunately prevented by the modern fibreglass mount into which it has been set. I am grateful to Dr Lawrence Keppie for bringing to my notice the similar cast registered in the Hunterian Museum in 1812: although the University of Glasgow was not one of the original recipients of the Antiquaries' donation, it seems that there was a subsequent wider distribution of casts after the stone had entered the collections of the British Museum – whither the French were also constrained to go for a cast from which to complete the illustrations for the *Description de l'Égypte*, Gillispie and Dewachter, *Monuments of Egypt*, p.22.

13   Among the many accounts of the decipherment of hieroglyphs, Erik Iversen places Champollion's work within the widest context; *The Myth of Egypt and its Hieroglyphs in European Tradition*, Copenhagen, 1961, pp.137-45.

13

Relief section from the frieze of the Parthenon, Athens

Plaster in two parts, 107 x 216cm overall
Ashmolean Museum, Cast Gallery

Hamilton had become private secretary to Thomas Bruce, seventh Earl of Elgin on his appointment as British Ambassador to the Ottoman Court at Constantinople, in 1799. He was on board the *Mentor*, the ship carrying the Elgin Marbles, when it sank in a matter of minutes, in a storm off the port of Cerigo (modern day Kithira) on the island of Kithira off the southern Pelopennese, in 1803. Lives were saved only by men jumping from the bowsprit onto the rocks. Hamilton spent several months supervising the diving for the marbles, having, by his own account, procured 'some very expert divers from the islands of Syme and Calymno, near Rhodes, who were able with immense labour and perseverance, to extricate a few of the cases from the hold of the ship, while she lay in twelve fathoms water.' The rest may have been recovered later, after the storms of two winters had broken the ship up.

This description, given in the third person, appears in the anonymous *Memorandum on the subject of the Earl of Elgin's pursuits in Greece*, first published in 1811, of which Hamilton sent a copy to Canova in March, 1816, (Fig.19).[1] From the outset

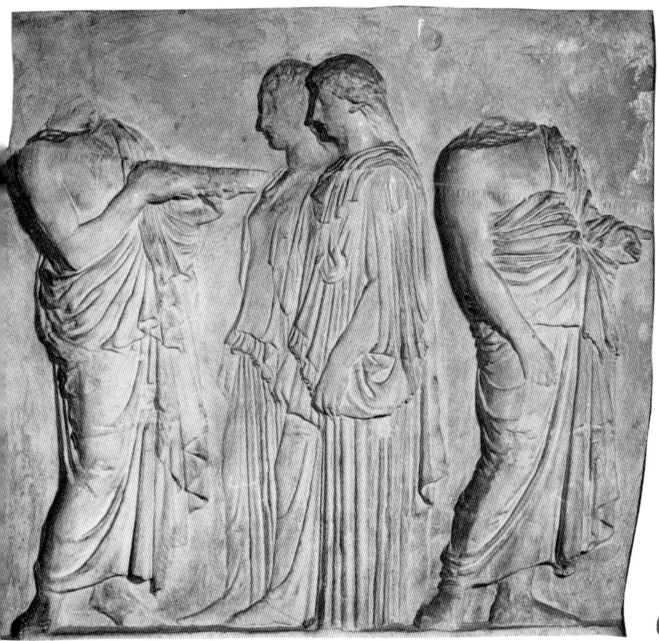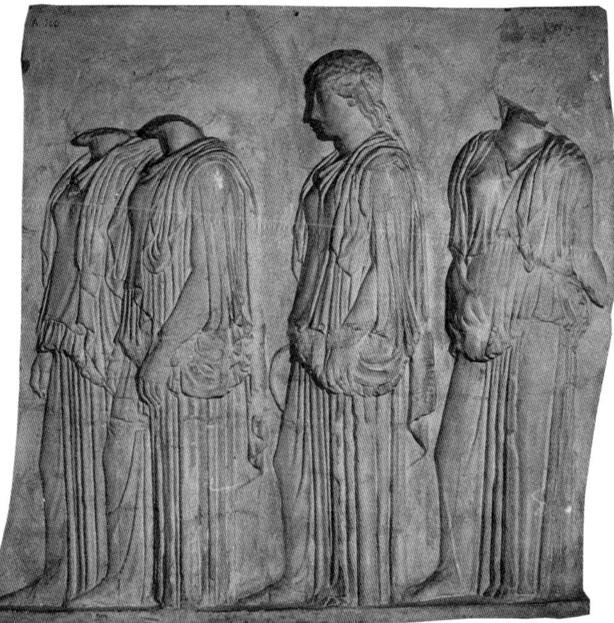

Cat.No.13

there had been an educative purpose to the operation, as Hamilton explained how Lord Elgin's original intention had been to take a party of artists and architects, modellers or cast makers, to 'rescue from oblivion, with the utmost accurate detail, whatever specimens of architecture and sculpture in Greece had still escaped the ravages of time, and the barbarism of conquerors.' Hamilton himself went to Rome in 1799 to engage 'two of the most eminent *formatori* to make the *madreformi* for the casts'. Six artists worked on the project for two years, and measured drawings, plans and moulds were brought back to London. It was the depredation that the sculpture was exposed to, of which Hamilton provides a colourful, and no doubt justificatory, account that persuaded Elgin to take more radical action, with the added fact that a team of French artists, who had been engaged in the removal of works from the Parthenon before the Revolution were waiting for the diplomatic opportunity to renew their activities.[2] Permissions were granted, undoubtedly on the strength of the English success against the French in Egypt, and houses of Turkish occupation bought and demolished.

On Elgin's return through Europe in 1803, he had planned to have the sculpture restored in Rome, but Canova's advice was decisive, for he said it would be sacrilege to presume to touch with a chisel work by the ablest artists the world had ever seen, and which had never been retouched.[3] Hamilton's account makes it quite clear that Canova saw the marbles in Rome in 1803-4, when they were brought to him for restoration.

Thus it was that two hundred cases containing fifteen metopes representing the Battle of the Lapiths and Centaurs, and four sections of the frieze of the Temple of Athena Nike, and fifty-six additional pieces of sculpture from the pediment and elsewhere, a caryatid from the Erechtheum, a hundred or so inscriptions and much else besides, found their way to London, and were displayed in an annexe to the Earl's house in Park Lane, as 'Elgin's Museum'.[4] They became the subject of a long running international debate on their merits and those of the accepted Antique canon, most of which had formed the star attractions in the Musée Napoléon.[5] In England two camps developed. One was led by Richard Payne Knight collector, benefactor of the British Museum and arbiter of taste, who guided the Society of Antiquaries and the Dilettanti Society in considering them at best workshop copies after Phidias. The other centred on the Royal Academy under its President, the painter Benjamin West, where the opinion was that these marbles were masterpieces by Phidias himself.[6] In 1810 or 11 Elgin found himself constrained to sell them, perhaps he had always intended to do so, but the debate became more personal. It was at this point that Hamilton published his account. In 15 February 1815 Lord Elgin presented a petition to the House of Commons and a Select Committee was set up under the chairmanship of Henry Bankes M.P., to consider the purchase of the marbles for the nation. It took evidence from Dr Hunt, chaplain to Elgin's embassy,

Hamilton, Lord Aberdeen in his capacity as President of the Society of Antiquaries, Charles Long, Payne Knight, Sir Thomas Lawrence, John Flaxman as Professor of Sculpture at the Royal Academy, Nollekens, Chantrey, Rossi and Westmacott and others. All were asked to compare the Greek marbles with the Apollo Belvedere and other Roman pieces, which many of them had seen that summer in Paris. The committee referred obliquely to 'a Sculptor, eminent throughout Europe', and annexed Canova's views to the official report. We know Canova saw the marbles on a number of occasions during his visit to London, and everyone reported his enthusiasm for them. Thomas Phillips R.A. reported to Dawson Turner 'I hear from Flaxman that he is highly delighted indeed with Lord Elgin's marbles & regards us as very rich in sculpture'. Hamilton reissued his *Memorandum*, reinforced with a number of appendices of opinions and letters in support of the worth of the marbles, including those of A. L. Millin, Curator of Medals in the Louvre and Professor of History and Antiquities, and E. Q. Visconti Curator of Antiquities at the Louvre under Denon, who, but for Napoleon's fall, might have bought them from Lord Elgin for the Louvre.

On March 26, Hamilton wrote to Canova to tell him among other things that the Government had agreed to buy the marbles for £35,000.[10] Canova had clearly asked for a cast of the so called *Hercules*, and in June asked for one of the river god, *Ilissus* in its stead,[11] and in the event got them both. In October Hamilton wrote with the news that the marbles currently in a temporary building were to have "una Galleria finita".[12]

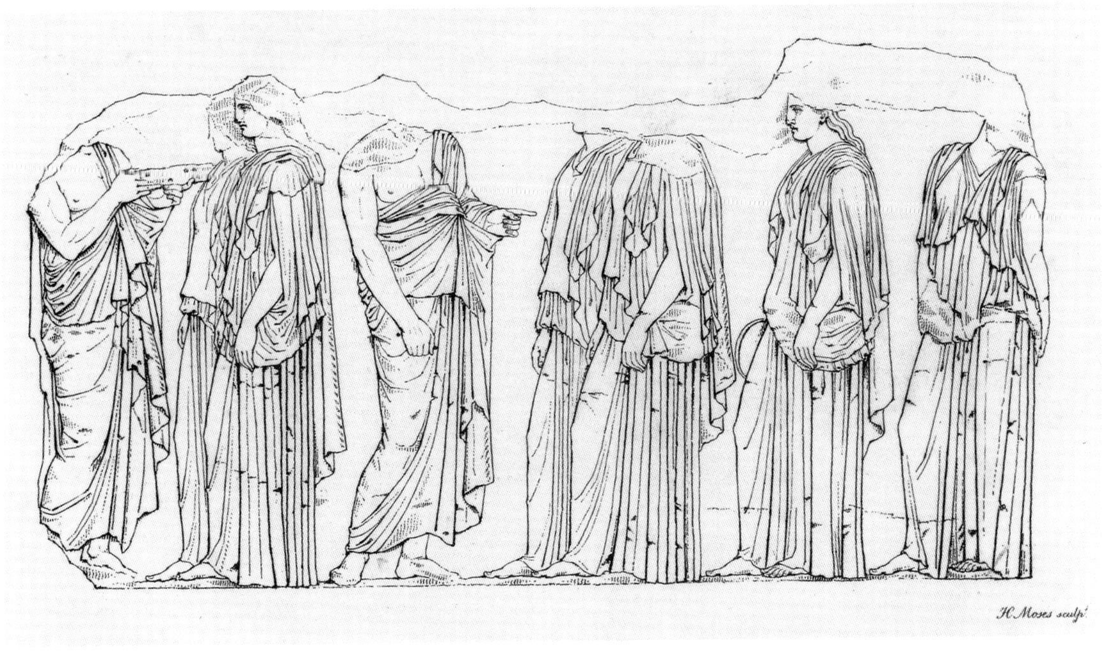

Fig.19

Elgin appears not to have met Canova when the latter was in England or earlier when himself in Rome in 1803, for Hamilton wrote a letter of introduction for the Earl and his family when they visited Rome again in 1819, describing him as "al quale dobbiamo tutti la conservazione di tanti miracoli dell'antica Grecia".[13]

Models for a commemorative medal were designed by Benedetto Pistrucci (1784-1855), who had been Hamilton's protegé from his arrival in England in 1815. Made between 1817 and 1820, it included many of the main relief sculptures but, like so much of Pistrucci's work it was never completed.[14]

[1] 26 March, 1816; B.1-78/1506bis. Canova acknowledged its arrival in a letter dated 7 June 1816; Private Collection.The second edition of 1815 included three engravings by Henry Moses. A German translation of the *Memorandum* was published in Leipzig and Altenburg in 1817.

[2] *Ibid.*, pp.1-10.

[3] *Ibid.*, pp.39-40.

[4] From 1807 to 1811 and thereafter at Burlington House, Piccadilly.

[5] M.Pavan, 'The Horses of San Marco in the neo-classical and romantic epochs', *The Horses of San Marco, Venice*, exh.cat.(Trans J. & V. Wilton-Ely), Royal Academy, London, 1979, pp.111-115.

[6] Hamilton published a letter of West's to Elgin, dated 6 February 1809, in which West described how he had combined parts of individual reliefs into compositions for classical subject paintings, and argued the educative benefits for the arts of the marbles; *Memorandum*, Appendix A, pp.47-53.

[7] An acerbic but full account of the Committee's proceedings is to be found in Williams, Vol 1, pp.393-409.

[8] 'Report from the Select Committee of the House of Commons on the Earl of Elgin's Collection of Sculptured Marbles, &c.', *Gentleman's Magazine*, Vol.86, No.1, April and May 1816, pp.324-8, and 405-8.

[9] 10 November 1815; Dawson Turner Papers, Trinity College, Cambridge.

[10] B.I-78/1506bis.

[11] Canova to WRH, 7 June 1816; Private Collection.

[12] WRH to Canova, 18 October 1816; B.I-78/1514.

[13] WRH to Canova, 2 October 1819 B.I-78/1535.

[14] I.Jenkins, 'Athens rising near the pole': London, Athens and the Idea of Freedom', *London World City 1800-1840*, exh.cat. (ed. C. Fox), Essen, 1992. ill. p.149.

14

William Richard Hamilton

Remarks on several parts of Turkey
Part I Aegyptiaca, or some Account of the Antient and Modern State of Egypt,
as obtained in the years 1801, 1802

Accompanied with etchings, from the original drawings taken on the spot by the late
Charles Hayes
Printed for T. Payne London 1809
Two Volumes: Preface and Text, 30 x 48 cm
Bookplate: Coltermann.

Ashmolean Library, Griffith Collection.

Hamilton had travelled to Upper Egypt from Alexandria with Captain Leake and
Captain Hayes in October 1801. Leake had subsequently lost all his papers and
fifteen rolls of *papiri*, when the ship *Mentor* sank in the Bay of Cerigo, and Hayes, for
whom the book was in some sense a memorial, had since died. They were to survey
the country and Hamilton, besides, to give an account of its political state, for which,
under General Hutchinson the British had been accused by both the Turks and the
Mamlukes of duplicity. Hamilton provided an anthropological account of the way of
life on the Nile, commented on the architecture and inscriptions, and recorded
plants and customs. He provided a transcript and a translation of the Greek copy of
the decree recorded on the trilingual stone found at Rosetta.
    The volume of plates of lithographs by Samuel John Neele, Theodore Abraicco
and John Powell includes two plates by the latter showing the harbour at Alexandria.
Plate xvi the *Eastern Harbour & Pharos of Alexandria from the Site of the old Palace*
(plate size 47.1 x 75.5 cm) published on 1st January 1810, and Plate xvii a view of the
Old Port of Alexandria from the West Angle of the old City, both show ships of the line
and must convey something of the scene as the French attempted to remove the
Rosetta Stone. Hamilton never carried out his plan to record other parts of Turkey.
    Hamilton owned a Rameses ii which he set under a hawthorn tree by the Fulham
gate of Stanley Grove.[1]

1 Letters from WRH to HGH 1837-8; TSS *cit.*, p.46.

15

Letters from Canova to William Richard Hamilton

Private Collection

The surviving correspondence conducted in Italian between Canova and William Richard Hamilton amounts to some seventy letters. Fifty or so of those to Canova from Hamilton, the first dated 5 December 1815 the day of Canova's departure from London,[1] are in the Museo Civico de Bassano. Nineteen of those from the sculptor to Hamilton begin in April 1816 and continue until August 1822, and are in a private collection in England. Many begin in the form of an introduction to a visitor to Rome or conversely of an acquaintance returning to London from Rome, this being the surest method of delivery, though even this was hazardous.

They are evidence of a genuine and profound friendship which encompassed business, views on the state of the world and the arts, their mutual healths and that of their families and friends. The affection and esteem is clear throughout, it shines through the accepted expressions of a more formal age, sometimes on Canova's part with a surprising fierceness, and it extended to members of their two families, to Hamilton's two sisters and to the Abate Sartori Canova. In a letter of 7 June 1816 after an apparent silence on Hamilton's side, Canova wrote: 'La sera del dì 4 decorso mi ha consolato infinitamente. Ella non deve punto aver meraviglia, se il Suo lungo silenzio mi pose in qualche afflizione. Bisognava che io l'amassì ben poco per tollerare senza dolor sommo la mancanza delle sue lettere, e dell'assicurazione della Sua preziosa amicizia. Ella però me ne dà nuove testimonianze e coll' espressioni gentilissime della presente, e coll' accennarmi d'avermene scritto dell'altre per sugione di qualche suo amico, il quale veniva in Italia, e che io non viddi ancora',[2] Canova devoted a whole paragraph to his concern for one of Hamilton's boys who had had a misadventure, for 'poichè mi sono creato già un debito sacro di reputar mie propie tutte le Sue fortune'.

Hamilton continued to help Canova in various ways, sorting out some legal matter for Antonio's son, Alessandro d'Este,[3] and ensured that Canova was paid for the Prince Regent's *Nymph*.[4]

On Hamilton's side there are repeated hopes – an almost Chekovian refrain – of a return to Italy, but work kept him in Downing Street, until the spring of 1821[5], when they arrived *en famille* in Rome from Naples, 'questo Paradiso', to stay with Canova.[6]

---

[1] WRH to Canova, 5 December 1815; B.V-496/3493. Hamilton sent a small packet to C. R. Cockerell with Canova.

2 Private Collection.

3 Canova to WRH, 4 June 1818, and 17 December 1819; Private Collection.

4 Canova to WRH, 29 October 1819, and 25 January[?], and 24 February 1820; Private Collection.

5 WRH to Canova 2 April, 11[?] May, and 7 June 1821; B.I-78/1543-1545.

6 WRH to Canova, 7 June 1821; B.I-78/1545; and Canova to WRH, 14 May 1815; Private Collection.

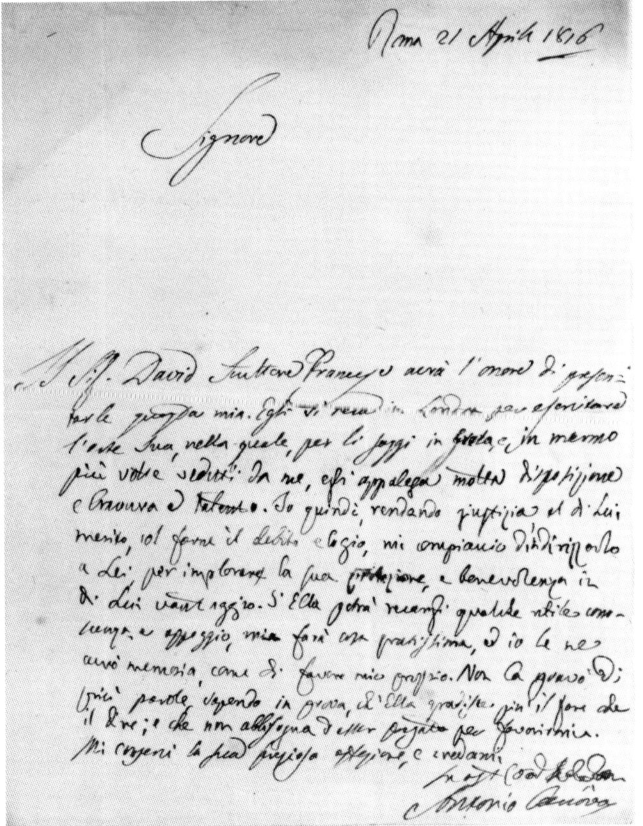

Cat. No.15

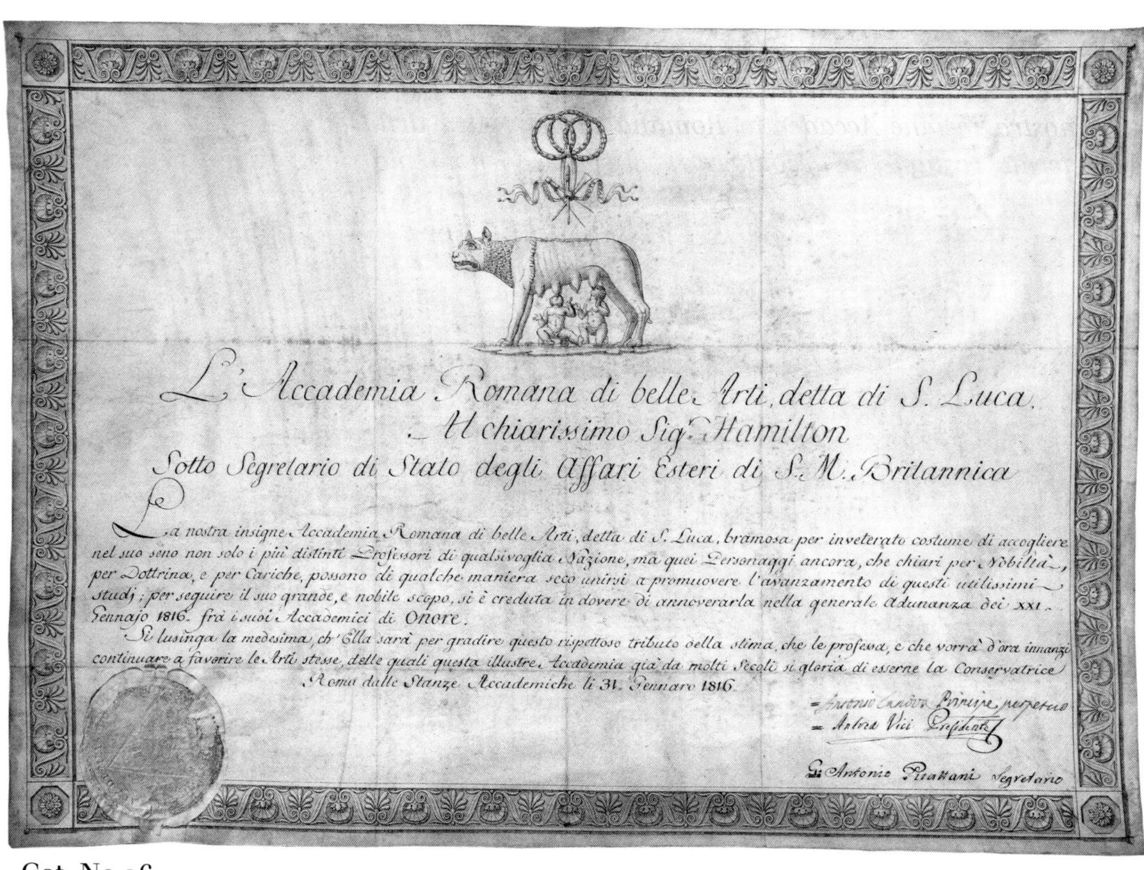

Cat. No.16

16

Certificate of the Accademia di San Luca

Pen and ink on vellum, 32.1 x 45.2 cm

Inscribed: *L'Accademia Romana di belle Arti, detta di S. Luca, / Al Chiarissimo Sig[r]
Hamilton / Sotto Segretario di Stato degli Affari Esteri di S.M. Britannica.*
*La nostra insigne Accademia Romana di belle Arti, detta di S. Luca, bramosa per
inveterato costume di accogliere / nel suo seno non solo i più distinti Professori di
qualsivoglia Nazione, ma quei Personaggi ancora, che chiari per Nobilità, / per
Dottrina, e per Cariche, possono di qualche maniera seco unirsi a promuovere l'a-
vanzamento di questi utilissimi / studj; per seguire il suo grande, e nobile scopo, si è
creduta in dovere di annoverarla nella generale Adunanza dei XXI / Gennajo 1816, fra
i suoi Accademici di Onore.*

*Si lusinga la medesima, ch'Ella sarà per gradire questo rispettoso tributo della
stima, che le professa, e che vorrà d'ora innanzi / continuare a favorire le Arti stesse,
delle quali questa illustre Accademia già da molti Secoli si gloria di esserne la
Conservatrice Roma dalle Stanze Accademiche li 31. Gennaro 1816.*
[Signed]   Antonio Canova Principe perpetuo
Andrea Vici Presidente
G: Antonio Puattani Segretario

Private Collection

In a letter of 8 April 1816, Hamilton wrote to Canova thanking him for the news
'extra- officialmente, il distinto onore, hò ricevuto dalla famosa Academia di San
Luca'[1] and By 4th May he had an official letter from the President and Vice President
of the Academy, dated 23rd January, informing him of his election to 'quella illustre
Società' and begging Canova, 'caro mio amico', to accept his gratitude for this
demonstration of their friendship.[2]

On 4 July Canova wrote to say the envelope with the certificates, one for Hamilton
and one for Benjamin West, President of the Royal Academy, was in the box with the
Titians, one for Hamilton and one for Dr Granville, and some engravings.[3]

---

[1] B. I-78/1508.
[2] WRH to Canova, 4 May 1816; B.I-78/1509.
[3] Private Collection.

Canova's Visiting Card

Etching, 4.8 x 7.7 cm
Lettered: A. CANOVA
In an envelope inscribed by Mary Somerville: *Canova's Visiting Cards*
Bodleian Library, Oxford (Somerville papers, Dep c.370 Box 20 MSC-2).

The Principal and Fellows, Somerville College

There is no evidence that Canova met William and Mary Somerville in London in 1815, though it is entirely possible, as Canova met so many of their mutual acquaintance. William Somerville had been in Paris earlier in the year.[1] When the Somervilles went to Rome two years later, they called on Canova on their second day,[2] and again a week later.[3]

1 Patterson, p.20.
2 Mary Somerville to Jane Pringle, 26 December 1817; Somerville Papers: Dep.C.357/MSFP-4.
3 Somerville Papers: Dep.C.355/MSAU-1.

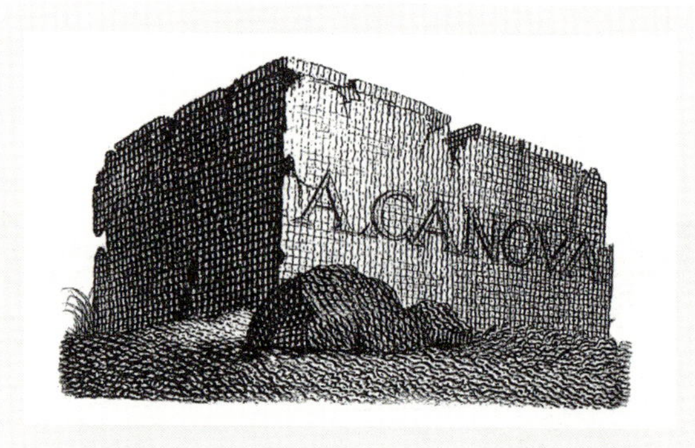

Cat. No.17

Romain Jeuffroy 1749-1826

Napoleon 1 / Venus de Medici

Bronze, 4.9 cm
Obverse: Bare head of Napoleon to right.
Signed: JEUFFROY FECIT.
Inscribed and dated: DENON DIR.G.D. MUSÉE D'ARTE. 1803
Reverse: Venus de' Medici with a dolphin.
Inscribed: AUX ARTS LA VICTOIRE L'AN IV DU CONSULAT DE BONAPARTE.
Provenance: 1833, Ashmolean Ms. Cat. 1098.
Literature: Bramsen 280.
Exhibited: Oxford, Ashmolean Museum, *The Most Beautiful Statues*, 1981, Cat. No.76

Ashmolean Museum, Heberden Coin Room.

This medal was presented to Napoleon on a visit to the Musée Centrale des Arts by Vivant Denon, the Museum's Director. The remarkable and versatile Baron Dominique Vivant Denon (1747-1825), had proved himself a survivor (not unlike Talleyrand himself) in a long and varied life as a diplomat, artist, archaelogist, collector and writer under Louis xv, Louis xvi and the Revolutionary Council. He accompanied Napoleon on the ill-fated Egyptian expedition. He had since 1802 been in effect the creator of the Musée Napoléon.[1] He became Director of the Monnaie des Médailles and was responsible for a semi-official Medallic History of Napoleon in imitation of that conceived for Louis xiv to record contemporary events.[2]

[1] Bazin, pp.176-80.
[2] Jones, p.100.

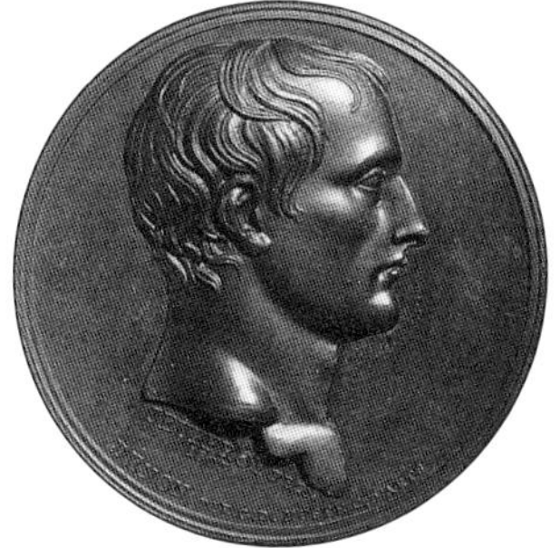
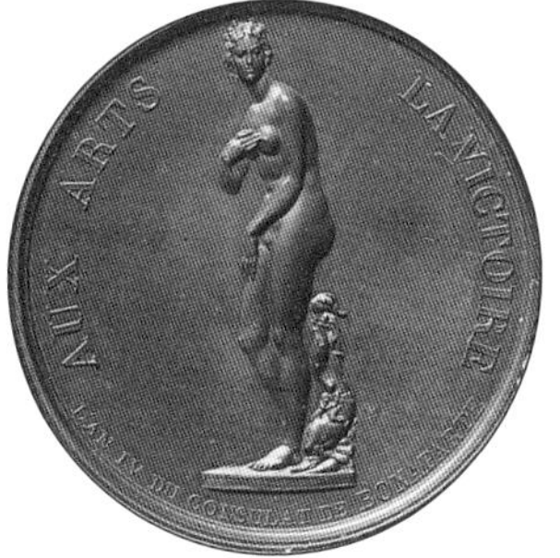

Bertrand Andrieu 1761-1822

Musée de Louvre / Salle de l'Apollon 1804

Bronze, 3.45 cm
Obverse: Laureated head of Napoleon to right.
Reverse: Salle de l'apollon
Inscribed in exergue: MUSEE NAPOLEON. ANDRIEU F. DENON D.
Provenance: 1879, presented by Sir Walter Calverley Trevelyan (Ash. Mus. 1879.441)
Literature: Bramsen 370.
Exhibited: Oxford, Ashmolean Museum, *The Most Beautiful Statues*, 1981, Cat. No.71

Ashmolean Museum, Heberden Coin Room.

Struck like Cat. No.20 to mark the dedication of the Apollo and Laocoon Rooms in
the Louvre, Napoleon's head appears in profile over the doorway. They can be dated
exactly to 31st December 1804.[1]

[1] Edwards, no.6, p.16, pl. V.

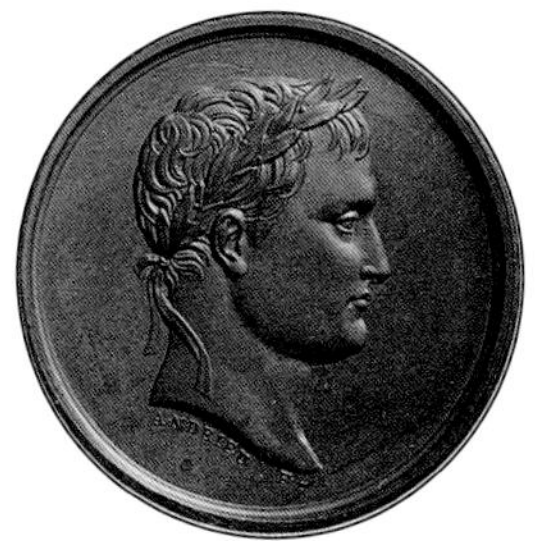 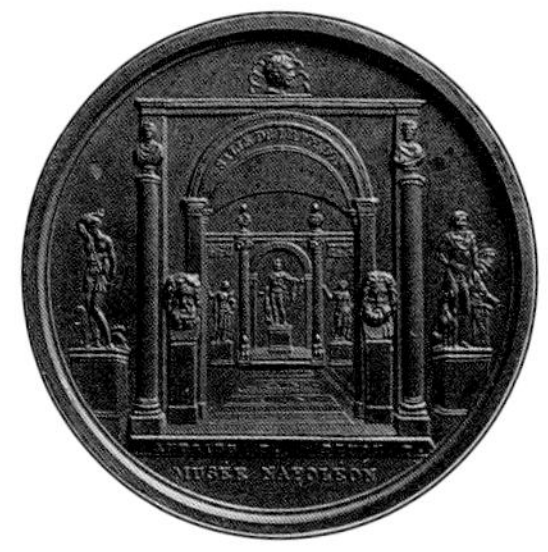

20

Bertrand Andrieu 1761-1822

Musée de Louvre / Salle de Laocoon

Bronze, 3.45 cm
Obverse: Laureated head of Napoleon to right.
Reverse: Salle de Laocoon
Inscribed in exergue: MUSÉE NAPOLÉON / R.F. / ANDRIEU F. DENON D.
Provenance: 1879, presented by Sir Walter Calverley Trevelyan (Ash. Mus. 1879.440)
Literature: Bramsen 367; F. Haskell and N. Penny, *Taste and the Antique, The Lure of Classical Sculpture 1500-1900*, New Haven and London, 1981, fig.63.
Exhibited: Oxford, Ashmolean Museum, *The Most Beautiful Statues*, 1981, Cat. No.72

Ashmolean Museum, Heberden Coin Room.

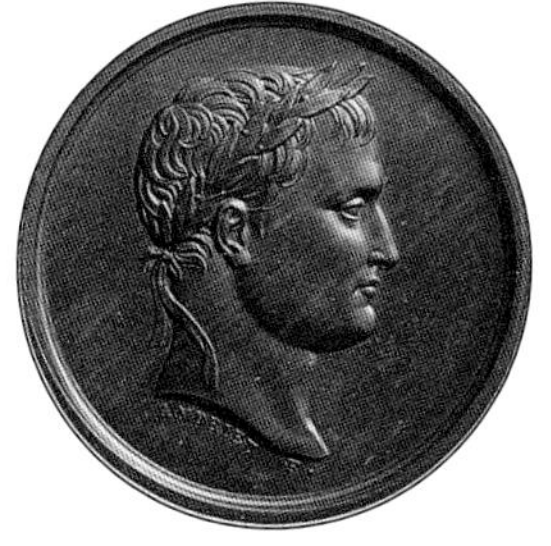
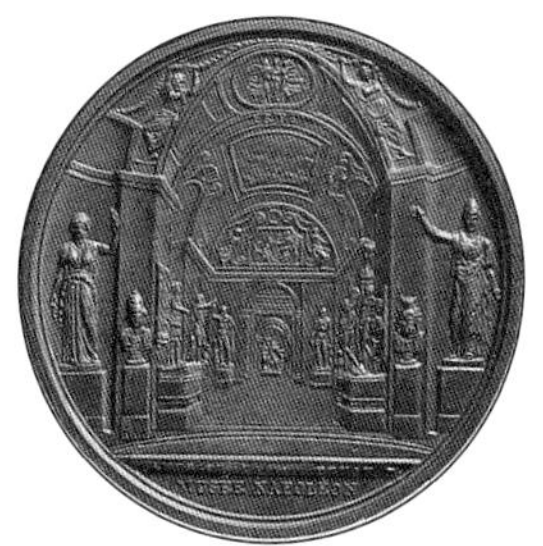

Nicholas Brenet 1773-1846

The Duke of Wellington's Entry into Paris, 7 July 1815.

Bronze, 4 cm
Obverse: Bust to the right.
Signed: Brenet.
Inscribed: ARTHUR DUKE OF WELLINGTON / MUDIE D.
Reverse: Colonade of the Louvre.
Inscribed in exergue: THE ENGLISH ARMY / ENTERS PARIS / THE VII OF JULY / MDCCCXV.
Provenance: Christ Church Collection.

Ashmolean Museum, Heberden Coin Room.

From Mudie's National series No.36. James Mudie set out to create a British rival to Denon's Imperial Medallic History, dedicated to George IV. A number of French medallists, Brenet among them, came to London to work on the National Series.

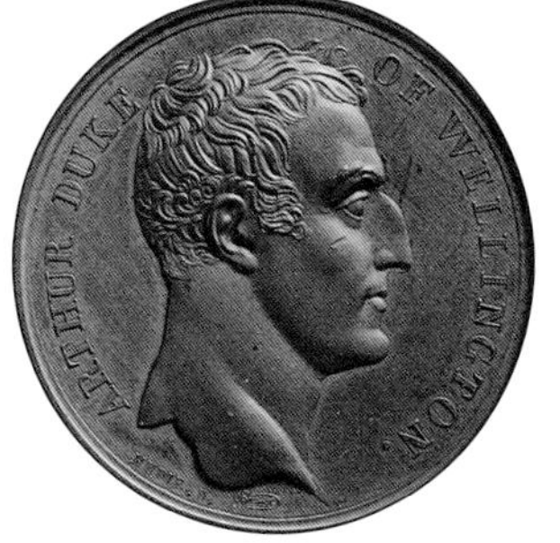
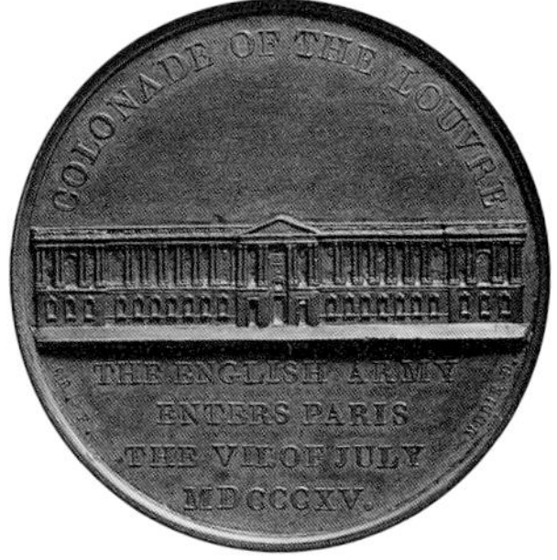

George Mills *c.*1792-1824

The Prince Regent England gives peace to the world.

Bronze, 4 cm
Obverse: Laureated bust facing left.
Inscribed: GEORGE PRINCE REGENT MDCCXVI J. MUDIE D. G. MILLS F.
Reverse: Britannia seated with olive branch, receives the world from Victory.
Inscribed in exergue: ENGLAND GIVES PEACE TO THE WORLD 1814 DUBOIS F.
MUDIE D.
Provenance: Christ Church Collection.

Ashmolean Museum, Heberden Coin Room.

From Mudie's National series No.28. issued in 1820.[1]

[1] Brown, vol 1, no.776.

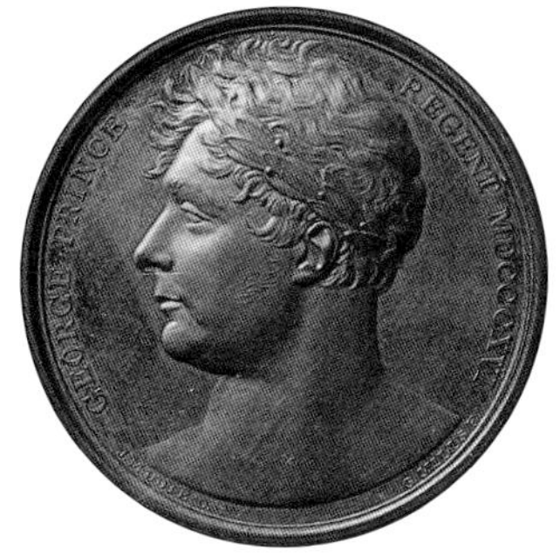
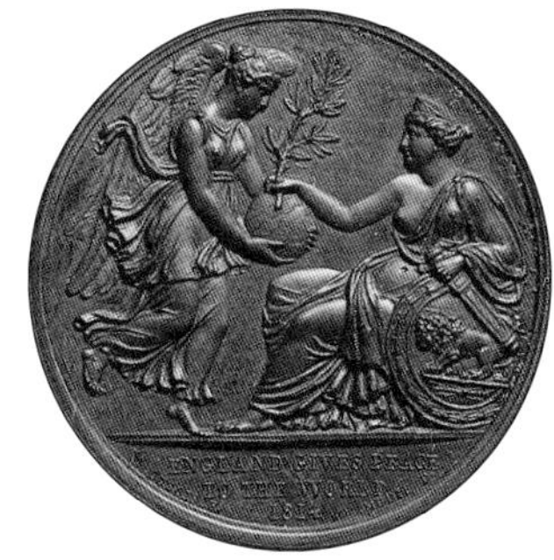

Bibliography

C. Andrews, *The Rosetta Stone*, London, 1981

E. Basi, *La Gipsoteca di Possagno: Sculture e Dipinti di Antonio Canova*, Venice, 1957

E. Bassi, *I Disegni di Antonio Canova*, Museo Civico di Bassano, 1959

G. Bazin, *The Museum Age*, Brussels, 1967

L. Bramsen, *Médailler Napoléon le Grand ou description des médailles, clichés, repousses et médailles-décorations relatives aux affaires de la France pendant le Consulat et l'Empire*, Paris and Copenhagen, 1904

L. Brown, *A Catalogue of British Historical Medals, 1760-1960*, London, 1980

E. Clay, (ed.), *Sir William Gell in Italy, Letters to the Society of Dilettanti, 1831-1835*, London, 1976, Vol I

C. Castellaneta, *L'opera completa di Hayez*, Milan, 1971

L. Cicognara, *Biografia di Antonio Canova*, Venice, 1823

H. Colvin, *A Biographical Dictionary of British Architects 1600-1840*, 3rd Edition, New Haven and London, 1995

W. Derry, (ed.), *The Journals and Letters of Fanny Burney (Madame D'Arblay)* Vol. x, Oxford, 1982

A. d'Este, *Memorie della Vita di Antonio Canova*, Florence, 1864

E. Edwards, *The Napoleon Medals, A complete series of the Medals struck in France, Italy, Great Britain and Germany from the commencement of the Empire in 1804 to the Restoration in 1815*, London, 1837

J. Farington, *The Diary of Joseph Farington RA 1793-1821*, (ed. K. Garlick, A. Macintyre & K. Cave), Yale, 1978-84, Vol. XIII, January 1814 - December 1815

K. Garlick, *Sir Thomas Lawrence*, London, 1954

K. Garlick, *Sir Thomas Lawrence*, Oxford, 1989

K. Garlick, 'Catalogue of the Paintings, Drawings and Pastels of Sir Thomas Lawrence', *Walpole Society*, Vol. 39, 1962-1964

L. Gomme, (ed.), *Survey of London, The Parish of Chelsea*, London, 1913, Vol. IV

A. Graves, *The Royal Academy of Arts, A Complete Dictionary of Contributors and their Work from its Foundation in 1769 to 1904*, London, 1905-06

R. Gunnis, *Dictionary of British Sculptors 1660-1851*, London, nd [new edn, 1964]

G. Hamilton, *A History of the House of Hamilton*, Edinburgh, 1933

W.R. Hamilton, *Memorandum on the subject of the Earl of Elgin's Pursuits in Greece*, Edinburgh, 1811, 2nd Edition 1815

C. Harcourt-Smith and G. Macmillan: *The Society Of Dilettanti, Its Regalia and Pictures*, London, 1932

F. Haskell and N. Penny, *Taste and the Antique*, New Haven and London 1981

B.R. Haydon, *The Diary of Benjamin Robert Haydon* (ed. W.B.Pope), Harvard, 1960 Vol . 1, 1808-15

U. Hiesinger, 'Canova and the Frescoes of the Galleria Chiaramonti', *The Burlington Magazine* Vol. cxx, October 1978, pp.655-665

H. Honour, 'Canova's Studio Practice – I: The Early Years' and 'Canova's Studio Practice – II: 1792-1822', *The Burlington Magazine*, Vol. cxiv March and April 1972, pp.146-159 and 214-229

H. Honour (ed.), *Scritti* Vol 1, *Edizione Nazionale delle Opere di Antonio Canova*, Rome 1994

D. Irwin, *English Neo-Classical Taste*, London 1966
D. Irwin, *John Flaxman 1755-1826 – Sculptor, Illustrator, Designer*, London, 1979
D. and F. Irwin, *Scottish Painters at Home and Abroad: 1700-1900*, London, 1975
S. Jervis, M.Tomlin (Revised J. Voak), *Apsley House. Wellington Museum*, London, 1985;
revised 1996
M. Jones, *The Art of the Medal*, London, 1979
R. Lane Poole, *Catalogue of Portraits in the Possession of the University, Colleges, City and
County of Oxford*, Oxford, 1912-25, 3 vols.
J. S. Memes, *Memoirs of Antonio Canova*, Edinburgh, 1825
H. Moses, *The Works of Antonio Canova in Sculpture and Modelling, engraved in outline by
HM with Descriptions from the Italian of the Countess Albrizzi and a Biographical Memoir by
Count Cicognara*, London, 1824, 2 Vols. Reprinted 1887
J. Morley, *Regency Design 1790-1840*, London, 1993
A. Muñoz, *Antonio Canova: Le Opere*, Rome, 1957
J. D. Passavant, *Tour of a German Artist in England*, London, 1932; reprinted Wakefield, 1978
E. C. Patterson, *Mary Somerville and the Cultivation of Science 1815-1840*, Boston, 1983
G. Pavanello, *L'Opera completa del Canova*, Milan, 1976
N. Pevsner, *The Buildings of England, London 3: North West*, London, 1991
Q. De Quincy, *Canova et ses Ouvrages ou Mémoires Historiques sur la Vie et les Travaux
de ce Célèbre Artiste*, Paris, 1834
A. Robertson, *Letters and Papers of Andrew Robertson, A.M.*, (ed. E.Robertson), London, 1895
[Walter Scott], *Paul's Letters to his Kinsfolk*, Edinburgh, 1816
D. Stillman, 'The Gallery for Lansdowne House: International Neoclassical Architecture and
Decoration in Microcosm', *Art Bulletin*, No.52, 1970, pp.75-80
R. Walker, *Regency Portraits*, National Portrait Gallery, London, 1985, 2 Vols.
E. Wellington, *A Descriptive & Historical Catalogue of the Collection of Pictures and Sculpture
at Apsley House, London*, London, 1901
D. Williams, *The Life and Correspondence of Sir Thomas Lawrence Kt*, London, 1831, 2 vols
I. Williams, *Early English Watercolours and Some Cognate Drawings by Artists Born not
later than 1785*, Cirencester, 1970
A. Yarrington, I.D. Lieberman, A. Potts and M. Baker, 'An Edition of the Ledger of Sir Francis
Chantrey, R.A., at the Royal Academy, 1809-1841', *Walpole Society*, 56, 1991-2
D. Watkin, *Thomas Hope and the Neo-Classical Idea*, London, 1968
Margaret Whinney, *Sculpture in Britain 1530-1830*, Harmondsworth, 1964

Exhibition Catalogues

Copenhagen, Thorvaldsens Museum, 1969, *Antonio Canova: Tegninger Fra Museet I Bassano*
Edinburgh, The National Galleries of Scotland, 1995, *The Three Graces: Antonio Canova*,
(ed. H. Honour and A. Weston-Lewis)
Essen, Villa Hügel, *London-World City 1800-1840*, (ed.C.Fox), 1992
London, Royal Academy and Victoria and Albert Museum, 1972, *The Age of Neo-Classicism*
London, Royal Academy, 1979, *The Horses of San Marco, Venice*, (trans J.&V. Wilton-Ely)
London, National Portrait Gallery, 1979, *Sir Thomas Lawrence 1769-1830*, (M. Levey)
London, National Portrait Gallery, and Mappin Art Gallery Sheffield, 1981, *Sir Francis
Chantrey, 1781-1841, Sculptor of the Great*, (A. Potts)

Oxford, Ashmolean Museum, 1981, *'The Most Beautiful Statues': The Taste for Antique Sculpture 1500-1900*, compiled by F. Haskell and N. Penny
Rome, Fondazione Memmo, Palazzo Ruspoli, 1991-1992, *Canova all' Ermitage: le scultura del museo di San Pietroburgo.*
Rome, Istituto Nazionale per la Grafica and Bassano, Museo-biblioteca-Archivio, 1993-4, *Canova e l'incisione*
Venice, Museo Correr, 1992, *Canova,* (ed.G. Pavanello & G. Romanelli)

Manuscripts

Biblioteca Civica, Bassano del Grappa. Cited as Bassano [B.] followed by reference number given in A. Sorbelli, *Inventari dei manoscritti delle biblioteche d'Italia: Bassano del Grappa,* Vol. LVIII, Florence, 1934
Somerville Papers, on deposit, the Bodleian Library, Oxford
The Dawson Turner Papers, Trinity College, Cambridge
Correspondence of Sir Thomas Lawrence, The Royal Academy of Arts, London
Council Minutes, The Royal Academy of Arts, London